"Couples play out symbolic themes that can come
as 'I will be abandoned' or 'my partner should meet
bination of acceptance and commitment therapy
work, the authors describe how to detect these them ... they produce, and to change the avoidant coping strategies that rapidly turn these themes in disrupted relationships. ACT and cognitive behavioral therapists alike will feel at home inside this model, scaling their existing skills into effective couples work. A conceptual and pragmatic step forward. Highly recommended."

—**Steven C. Hayes, PhD**, codeveloper of ACT

"There are no two authors in this world better equipped to marry the disciplines of ACT and schema process work than Lev and McKay. The way in which they bring their expertise to the specific challenges facing couples is nothing short of superb. When we get right down to it, couples work is difficult, and our technologies often fail us. This book is the state of the art in contextual behavioral approaches to couples therapy, and it should be on every therapist's bookshelf, regardless of their theoretical stance."

—**Dennis Tirch, PhD**, coauthor of *The ACT Practitioner's Guide to the Science of Compassion*, and founder of The Center for Compassion Focused Therapy

"This book elegantly combines the strengths of ACT, schema therapy, and nonviolent communication in a very clear and coherent treatment approach to problems faced by couples. Reading it leaves you with the great and rare feeling of knowing what to do, and the confidence that it will really help your clients."

—**Matthieu Villatte, PhD**, coauthor of *Mastering the Clinical Conversation*

"This is the ACT textbook we needed to have! A comprehensive and ever-so-practical guide to helping couples overcome their problems and build rich, intimate relationships. I especially like the way schemas are incorporated to fast-track defusion, acceptance, and self-awareness. Packed full of tools, techniques, exercises, and transcripts of therapy sessions, this excellent resource is a must for any ACT therapist who works with couples. And as a bonus, it'll give you a lot of great ideas for improving your own relationships. If you want to help couples stop struggling and start loving, this book is for you."

—**Russ Harris**, author of *The Happiness Trap* and *ACT Made Simple*

"Lev and McKay weave together their collective expertise in schema therapy, couples therapy, and ACT to bring us this much needed ACT-for-couples therapist guide. Whether you are new to schema work or ACT, or are a seasoned veteran, this well-organized, easy-to-follow book will be a valuable addition to your therapy bookshelf. Replete with sample dialogue and experiential practices, this is a must-have for any clinician who works with couples or with individuals in relationships—so basically all of us!"

—**Jill Stoddard, PhD**, coauthor of *The Big Book of ACT Metaphors*

"This book for practitioners beautifully synthesizes two distinctive therapy traditions, schema-focused therapy (SFT) and ACT, into a powerful step-by-step approach to couples therapy. Key SFT and ACT concepts and associated intervention strategies are presented in an easy-to-read, practical style. The authors present numerous highly revealing in-session dialogues designed to demonstrate each step of their novel treatment approach. Conducting effective couples therapy is a demanding enterprise; this book will materially increase your clinical skills and help you improve the lives of couples in distress."

—**Kirk Strosahl, PhD**, cofounder of ACT, and coauthor of *Inside This Moment* and *Brief Interventions for Radical Change*

"As a compassion-focused (CFT) therapist, I was thrilled to see Avigail Lev and Matthew McKay's clear and crisply written application of ACT to couples therapy. This excellent melding of schema therapy and ACT provides a compassionate and inherently de-shaming context for working with the tricky and acutely painful ways that attachment dynamics can wreak havoc in couple relationships. In their empirically supported approach, the authors guide clinicians in identifying problematic attachment-related schemas, and then in using the technology of ACT to help couples develop mindfulness, reduce experiential avoidance, improve perspective-taking, and address the barriers to values-based action so that they can build better relationships and happier lives."

—**Russell Kolts, PhD**, professor of psychology at Eastern Washington University, and author of *CFT Made Simple* and *The Compassionate-Mind Guide to Managing Your Anger*

"This book successfully combines ACT with a schema-based approach to treating couples. The advantage of a schema formulation for therapists is that it clearly establishes a focus for treatment. It helps therapists identify schemas that underlie many conflicts, and use acceptance and emotion exposure techniques to facilitate distress tolerance. Therapists learn extremely useful strategies to help their couple clients face—rather than run away from—old unavoidable thoughts and feelings, and focus on shared values as an alternative to experiential avoidance. This well-written book uses simple, straightforward, accessible language, and does not require any prerequisite knowledge of ACT or schema therapy. With its many worksheets, exercises, and sample dialogues, this book is a great resource for any therapist who wants to help clients lead a less conflictual, richer, and more fulfilling life."

—**Georg H. Eifert, PhD**, professor emeritus of psychology at Chapman University, and coauthor of *The Mindfulness and Acceptance Workbook for Anxiety*

"This book is a valuable resource for any ACT or schema-focused therapists working with couples. This text teaches how to effectively recognize and address maladaptive patterns and interpersonal styles in couples therapy, and offers a variety of clear and applicable examples, exercises, and worksheets. The authors seamlessly weave together schema therapy and ACT for couples in a meaningful way that is accessible and enriching for clinicians both new and experienced in this work. This book is bound to be an appreciated addition to any therapist looking to deepen their ACT or schema-focused couples therapy."

—**Laura Silberstein-Tirch, PsyD**, director at The Center for Compassion Focused Therapy; adjunct assistant professor at Albert Einstein College of Medicine; president-elect of the ACBS New York City Chapter; consulting psychologist at Memorial Sloan Kettering Cancer Center; and executive director of The Compassionate Mind Foundation USA

"One of the greatest assets a couples therapist can provide to a couple in distress is a clear, accepting, honest description of the different perspectives and experiences each member of the couple brings to a conflict. On this foundation of perspective taking, couples can begin to hear each other, connect again, and eventually move forward together. Schema therapy offers great insight into the range of perspectives and experiences a person might bring to conflict—the schema formulations have withstood the tests of time, clinical practice, and clinical trials. In turn, the core processes of ACT center on relating to such experiences—in ourselves and others—in flexible and values-based ways. By melding the insights of schema therapy with the processes of ACT, Lev and McKay offer clinicians and their clients a clear, practical framework for understanding what is happening in the heat of conflict, and beginning to build bridges of understanding and acceptance. This is a wonderfully useful, readable guide that every couples therapist (or therapist who works with people in relationships) will find to be of immediate and enduring value."

—**Gareth Holman, PhD**, psychologist in private practice; lead author of *Functional Analytic Psychotherapy Made Simple*; and founding partner of OpenTeam, a consulting firm dedicated to helping business teams apply the science of psychological flexibility to communicate and collaborate more effectively towards purpose

ACCEPTANCE *and* COMMITMENT THERAPY *for Couples*

A Clinician's Guide
to Using Mindfulness,
Values & Schema Awareness
to Rebuild Relationships

AVIGAIL LEV, PsyD
MATTHEW McKAY, PhD

CONTEXT PRESS
An Imprint of New Harbinger Publications, Inc.

Distributed in Canada by Raincoast Books

Context Press
An imprint of New Harbinger Publications, Inc.
5674 Shattuck Avenue
Oakland, CA 94609
www.newharbinger.com

Cover design by Amy Shoup; Acquired by Catharine Meyers;
Edited by Marisa Solis; Indexed by James Minkin

Library of Congress Cataloging-in-Publication Data on file

19 18 17

10 9 8 7 6 5 4 3 2 1 First Printing

Contents

FOREWORD

Looking Together: Values-Based Romantic Relationships

Antoine de Saint-Exupéry once said, "Love does not consist of gazing at each other, but in looking together in the same direction." In *Acceptance and Commitment Therapy for Couples*, authors Avigail Lev and Matthew McKay uniquely combine the emotional and cognitive patterns established in childhood with a behavioral intervention designed to foster psychological flexibility in the service of well-being in a protocol intended to promote vitality and values-based living in romantic relationships. The key goal of integrating schema work into acceptance and commitment therapy (ACT) in this treatment for couples seeking counseling is not only to quickly and clearly map and conceptualize interpersonal problems encountered by couples but also to assist couples in cultivating psychological and behavioral flexibility so that they make relationship choices that are guided by personal values rather than problematic schema activation. Ultimately, individuals in partnership are guided to stronger and healthier relationships that are grounded in the present moment as well as hope for the future.

In this book, Lev and McKay explain that learning in childhood involves cognitive and emotional processes that influence behavior; but if these are problematic, the cognitive and emotional experiences themselves do not need to be restructured or eliminated to promote healthy functioning. Rather they can be encountered, acknowledged, and responded to in a manner that supports growth inside relationship. This task involves acceptance of thoughts and emotions on both an intrapersonal and interpersonal level. Helping couples to recognize the patterns of learning that are triggered in troubled interactions and bringing awareness and presence to the larger context of relationship functioning set the stage, in this integrated intervention, for taking action that leads to the very connection couples seek—belonging and love.

In *Acceptance and Commitment Therapy for Couples*, you will be taken through a journey integrating schema work and formulations into the six core processes of ACT—acceptance, defusion, present moment, self-as-context, values clarification, and committed action. You will also be guided in the application of this integration to couples struggling to save their relationships. The schema formulation is taught to assist you in predicting problematic avoidance behaviors that are likely to arise in the couple's interactions and the therapeutic work and to guide you in helping couples become more aware of dysfunctional patterns of behavior so as to prevent them from being repeated.

Healing in the relationship comes through engaging in values-guided behavior rather than schema-guided behavior.

More specifically, Lev and McKay open the book by writing about the utility of schema formulations with respect to couples' interactions. The understanding of behavioral patterns this gives us is then used to explain interpersonal events, answering such questions for couples as, "Why is this happening between us?" Avoidance of schema activation is then explored. You are asked to consider the ways in which individuals create stories about themselves, based on their history, that lead to cause-and-effect relationships, regardless of the actual causality of the stories. For instance, an individual who grew up with a parent who was depressed might form an emotional deprivation schema. The story that could unfold, in this case, might be one of how this person's partners could never meet his or her emotional needs. Seeing a relationship through the lens of this story may distort this individual's actual experience and lead him or her to misinterpret the behavior of a partner in ways that hurt the relationship. Assessing and understanding the individual's and couple's schemas is presented, then, as a method of organizing problematic stories that negatively impact romantic interactions so that it is easier to work with them. The coping behaviors that regulate and manage schemas are explored in terms of how they contribute to the cycle of reinforcing and maintaining the negative dynamic. You are then guided through the application of ACT processes: engaging values clarification; working through control of internal experience as the problem; and offering acceptance, defusion, and perspective taking as the alternative. Values-guided committed action is presented with the goal of building healthy relationships in the present.

Additionally, and importantly, you will find information that is not just topical but foundational. The intervention presented in this book is supported with empirical data, detailed in one of the book's appendices. And there is a plethora of clinical examples, handouts, and exercises as well as an eight-step process for working through the intervention to help you implement the therapy with ease. Finally, the book is written in a style that is well-suited to good clinical work—the voice of a compassionate therapist is used throughout.

In a more personal note, I have seen the work of Drs. Lev and McKay—Abby and Matt. They are dedicated clinicians who have a true and heartfelt desire to assist couples in connecting—helping them to see their partner beyond the stories—and in growing relationships through flexibility and values: through love. This book will guide you in applying ACT with couples, using schema formulations to organize and understand patterns of behavior in a way that lays the path to helping couples look "together in the same direction" and build healthy relationships based on values.

—Robyn D. Walser, PhD
Co-Author of *The Mindful Couple: How Acceptance and Mindfulness Can Lead You to the Love You Want* and *Learning ACT: An Acceptance and Commitment Therapy Skills Training Manual for Therapists*
Trauma and Life Consultation Services; National Center for PTSD; University of California, Berkeley

Introduction

Romantic relationships bring unavoidable pain that is inherent to intimacy. All relationships come with risk, but in a romantic relationship we can't get away from the inevitable pain that shows up in moments of deprivation, loneliness, disappointment, hurt, insecurity, and disconnection. As a result, we long to merge and be seen and accepted by our partner, while we also fear being rejected, abandoned, engulfed, or judged.

Because we both yearn for intimacy and fear it, we are drawn into a dance of moving toward connection while at times running away in order to protect ourselves. Learning to observe and face the unavoidable pain of intimacy, without using relationship-destroying strategies, is the focus of this book.

Although romantic relationships bring up universal human pain, a couple's unique history and life experience will also shape specific beliefs and negative expectations about what happens in an intimate partnership. These expectations are *relationship schemas*, a concept that exists across virtually all couples therapy approaches, albeit in different language. Imago Relationship Therapy, emotion-focused couples therapy (EFCT), enhanced cognitive behavioral couples therapy (CBCT), and Gottman Method couples therapy all agree that partners have mental representations of relationships that are programmed from childhood experiences. And that some mental representations may form toxic expectations that lie at the heart of relationship distress.

In EFCT, for example, maladaptive schemas are described as *attachment injuries* that derive from violations in human connection. These injuries shape people's expectations about what will happen and how to respond in relationships (Johnson, 2004). Imago Relationship Therapy posits that *early psychological wounding* (maladaptive schemas) can predetermine the kind of partner chosen, as well as the themes of relationship distress (Luquet, 2006). Gottman's term for schemas is *enduring vulnerabilities*, which are defined as painful past events that continue to impact partners' thoughts, emotions, and relationship interactions (Gottman & DeClaire, 2001). In CBCT, as Gurman (2008) notes, a major task is to help couples observe and evaluate schemas that develop from experiences in past relationships. These schemas become a lens through which couples see the conflicts and events of their current relationship.

Schemas Defined

The mind is wired to create stories, to make meaning, and to build connections among events. Schemas are stories developed about the self and relationships (McKay & Fanning, 1991). They are a neural network of relational frames that forms the basis of expectations, fears, and predictions across human encounters. A schema thus provides a cognitive structure to explain interpersonal events and develop predictions about likely future events. For couples, they help answer three eternal questions: What is happening between us? Why is it happening? What will happen next? As a result, schemas have survival value. They explain and help define threats. Plus, they function as tea leaves to forecast future threats, and they help partners prepare a self-protective response (*schema avoidance behaviors*).

The problem with schemas is that they are products of the mind and are not reality. Schemas presented by troubled couples often have a negative bias, are associated with significant emotional pain, and tend to trigger destructive avoidance strategies. For example, a partner with an abandonment schema may interpret a small, critical remark as rejection and potential abandonment. He or she may then feel very afraid and subsequently engage in maladaptive emotion-avoidance behaviors such as withdrawing or clinging.

Putting ACT and Schemas Together

We've incorporated schemas into the ACT protocol for couples in order to help clinicians recognize these maladaptive patterns more efficiently. The object of ACT-based couples therapy is not to change or challenge the veracity of schemas but rather to help therapists and couples identify schema beliefs and emotions when they arise, see the maladaptive avoidance behaviors, and use ACT processes to support alternative, values-based responses. Identifying these large themes and patterns ultimately helps partners observe schema-driven thoughts and emotions but not act on them.

The goal is to develop behavioral flexibility in the face of pain, because schema thoughts and affect are largely unavoidable and unlikely to go away. As Hayes states in *Acceptance and Commitment Therapy for Interpersonal Problems* (McKay, Lev, & Skeen, 2012 p. vi), "The act of looking for larger patterns [schemas] helps clients take a more defused and mindful look at their own behavior, and it can empower the search for ways to create new forms of adjustment."

A schema formulation has a second advantage. It helps clinicians distinguish *primary*—unavoidable—pain from *secondary* pain caused by avoidance behaviors. For couples, avoidance behavior designed to protect them from the primary pain of schema thoughts and feelings creates secondary pain, such as alienation, loss of intimacy, hostility, hurt, aloneness, and relational despair.

The third advantage of a schema formulation is that it clearly establishes a focus for treatment. The ACT processes of mindfulness, exposure, and defusion all target the avoidance of primary pain—schema-driven thoughts and affect—as opposed to secondary pain (the alienation, hostility, and hurt that result from maladaptive avoidance). There is a reason for this. Schema-driven thoughts and affect are the major barriers to flexible, values-based interpersonal behavior. Moving toward values inevitably triggers schema pain. Consequently, the thrust of couples therapy must be facing, rather than running from, these old, unavoidable thoughts and feelings.

The final advantage of a schema formulation is that it helps clinicians better recognize and describe the schema avoidance behaviors that occur in session. The process of specifying the avoidance behaviors helps clinicians to better identify these interpersonal processes as they show up and have a language to describe them. A schema formulation can help clinicians predict what avoidance behaviors are likely to arise, given that certain schemas tend to have common coping responses. Partners with mistrust/abuse schemas, for example, tend to behave accusationally, partners with self-sacrifice schemas tend to give in or surrender, and partners with entitlement schemas tend to get angry or make unilateral decisions. Staying focused on damaging schema avoidance behaviors guides clinicians to be more attuned to what to look for in the room.

In summary, schemas provide a map to clearly and quickly describe the particular interpersonal cycle for a couple and the way it gets maintained. The pattern—specific schema pain, followed by strategies for avoidance, followed by more pain—perpetuates and deepens the couple's struggle. The basic formulation is as follows:

- Couples are vulnerable to schema activation. Early maladaptive schemas are a primary and unavoidable pain in relationships.
- Relationship dysfunction is the result of destructive avoidance responses and patterns that couples use to protect themselves from schema pain.
- These avoidance responses, learned in early childhood, were once adaptive. But now the attempt to avoid schema pain lies at the root of a couple's distress.
- ACT couples therapy doesn't aim to change core beliefs, thoughts, or feelings but rather to help partners change behavior despite the presence of schema pain.

ACT Interventions for Couples

Once schemas and maladaptive schema avoidance behaviors have been identified, the couples therapy process is entirely ACT based. Partners are encouraged to develop a new relationship to the schema pain by:

- Mindfully observing and defusing (distancing) from schema-driven thoughts
- Mindfully observing and exposing oneself to schema-driven affect
- Learning to accept and hold schema pain rather than avoiding it with maladaptive coping
- Identifying alternative, values-based behavior to replace schema-driven avoidance and committing to that new behavior
- Mindfully noticing the moment of choice when schema pain is triggered and choosing either values-based actions or emotion avoidance

- Learning to recognize avoidance versus engagement, moment to moment, in the couple relationship and developing communication skills that maintain engagement in the face of emotional (schema) pain

Empirical Support for ACT-Based Couples Therapy

The authors (Lev, 2011; McKay, Lev, & Skeen, 2012) examined the effectiveness of ACT (using a schema formulation) for interpersonal problems. A randomized controlled trial, using the dependent variable of the Inventory of Interpersonal Problems (IIP-64), yielded a large effect size (Cohen's *d* of 1.23) for the ACT intervention. Lev and McKay adapted this intervention for couples. A randomized controlled trial, using dependent variables that included the Relationship Assessment Scale (RAS), the Inventory of Interpersonal Problems (IIP-64), and the Experiences Questionnaire (EQ) yielded medium to large effect sizes (Cohen's *d* of .94, .71, and 1.05) and significant differences between the treatment and control groups. See appendix A for a detailed description of the study, which, at the time of this book's publication, is under review.

CHAPTER 1

Where Couple Conflicts Start

We have come to recognize that the roots of interpersonal discord lie in schemas and schema avoidance strategies. Maladaptive schemas become relational time bombs, formed in childhood but activated by current threats, conflicts, and stressors. They create negative expectations about self and others, and drive partners to avoid schema pain with maladaptive coping responses (McKay, Lev, & Skeen, 2012).

Interpersonal Schemas

We have identified ten interpersonal schemas from Jeffrey Young's (1999) much longer list that shape partners' beliefs and responses to each other, and become fodder for chronic couples pain and antipathy. In the early, happy days of romantic relationships, schemas are often in a state of dormancy. But as time goes by, conflicting and unmet needs—and the failed, often-aversive strategies to meet those needs—give new life to old schemas. The result: these deep beliefs get repeatedly triggered, and along with them comes enormous emotional pain. Detailed descriptions of the key interpersonal schemas—and schema-driven emotions—are provided in the next chapter. But for now, let's look at an example of the schema activation process.

Example

Regina is just beginning her career as a nurse at a major university hospital. She's worked hard to get where she is, including struggling at school with any perceived criticism from professors or supervisors. She describes criticism as "feeling like I've been shot." Immediately, Regina becomes overwhelmed by feelings of being "bad" or "not good enough."

She traces this vulnerability to her father, who "never found anything good about me, no matter how hard I tried or what I achieved. He had X-ray vision—he could always see the worm in the apple."

Regina married Antoine, a French transplant, in her junior year of college. They were intensely attracted and enjoyed a passionate relationship during the remainder of their college days. But when Regina started nursing school, things changed. The courses were hard for her, and she got negative feedback about her grasp of biological science. Regina buried herself in her books, while Antoine began to complain about the lack of intimacy.

"He'd say I wasn't romantic; I wasn't giving. And I felt he must be right. I was so scared of screwing up at school, and then I got scared of screwing up with him. The more he complained, the more I felt bad. So I just kinda went into a tailspin and withdrew."

Regina has a name for her schema pain. She calls it the "I'm bad emotion" and claims Antoine could make her feel—with the mildest request—just like she did with her father.

Schema-Driven Pain

Schema-triggered emotions, while painful, are not what forces couples apart. It's just a fertile field in which discord grows. It would be a mistake to see schemas—and schema-driven emotional pain—as something that must be changed. Negative schemas are ubiquitous—everyone has them to some degree. And they are very hard to modify (see chapter 2). The object of couples therapy is not to stop schemas from being triggered, or even to reduce schema pain, but rather to change how partners respond to schema pain. The case of Sean clarifies this.

Example

Sean has felt a sense of aloneness most of his life, alleviated only when he has a strong, close relationship. His second wife, Anita, was initially very responsive to his need for closeness. She spent hours commiserating with him about his ex-wife's withdrawal, which had compounded the scars from his mother's aloofness and early death from cancer.

The core of his struggle, Sean says, is "the feeling that I wasn't okay by myself. And I was afraid that the people I counted on wouldn't take care of me, either, even Anita. She seemed annoyed after a while that I wanted to do things together all the time. And that I tried to persuade her not to go up to Boise when her mother was sick."

Sean describes his schema pain as emptiness, and numerous things Anita does seem to trigger it. However, the core belief that he can't survive emotionally on his own, and the emptiness that accompanies periods with less connection, is not the driver for this couple's problems. It is merely a vulnerability, a source of pain. A beginning.

What drives Sean and Anita's increasing sense of alienation is what Sean *does* in response to this pain. He gets angry, he demands, he clings. All of which makes Anita wish sometimes she'd never married him. She then withdraws—which only makes Sean's emptiness worse.

Schema Coping Behaviors

As demonstrated by Sean and Anita, behavior is what destroys relationships, not schemas. The schema pain is real. It is often intense. But relationships are impacted by what partners do in reaction to the pain—maladaptive ways of coping—rather than the pain itself.

Notice what happens when Sean's schema-driven fear—that he can't take care of himself—is activated. Anita gets annoyed (distant) or goes to Boise, Idaho, and Sean ends up feeling empty. The schema tells him that only Anita can help with this pain; he's helpless to cope himself. His behavioral response is to get angry, make demands, and cling—hoping to induce Anita to move closer to him. It is Sean's coping behavior—not the schema or the schema pain—that destabilizes their relationship.

It is common for couples to develop rigid behavioral coping responses (experiential avoidance) and patterns, which are driven by old stories, predictions, and expectations in relationships. These coping responses provide short-term relief for interpersonal distress but result in long-term relationship damage. These include experiential avoidant behaviors such as clinging, withdrawing, attacking, reassurance seeking, defending, explaining, controlling, or demanding.

ACT for Couples Therapy—Case Formulation

The case formulation involves identifying how the mutual activation of schemas, and each partner's response, continues to maintain the cycle. These are the key elements of a formulation for ACT therapy for couples:

1. *Negative interpersonal schemas are a part of the basic weave of human consciousness.* Most of us have one or more of these core beliefs, and they get activated by threats, conflicts, or unmet needs. Schemas, and the pain that accompanies them, are unavoidable relationship stressors. In ACT terminology, schemas constitute *primary*, or *clean*, pain. They cannot be fixed, modified, or alleviated. They show up as an inevitable part of living and relating.

2. *Schema pain drives partners into pain-avoidance strategies* (called schema coping behaviors—see chapter 3) that map exactly onto the key transdiagnostic mechanism of experiential avoidance (Hayes, Strosahl, & Wilson, 2012). Experiential avoidance, from an ACT perspective, is a major cause of human suffering—*secondary*, or *dirty*, pain. Like many avoidance strategies, schema coping behaviors backfire. What is intended to relieve pain in intimate relationships instead sows seeds of hurt and disenchantment. Once again, the behavior (pain avoidance/schema coping) creates the problem—not the schema (*primary* pain) itself.

3. *Schema coping behaviors (experiential avoidance) are aversive, reduce mutual reinforcement, reduce the ability to problem solve, and are toxic to relationships.* Schema coping behaviors, by using strategies that are hurtful or manipulative, are designed to pressure a partner to stop schema-triggering behavior, but the inevitable outcome is to make the relationship more painful. As negative experiences increase between partners, the relationship is less positively reinforcing and yields fewer agreements (problem-solving decisions). The result: increased conflict, discord, and couple pathology.

4. *Schema coping behaviors (experiential avoidance) are the target of treatment.*

What Do We Do with Schema Pain?

It is tempting to say nothing. From an ACT vantage, it's possible to argue that schema pain is uncontrollable and, because it cannot change, there's nothing to be done with it. But while schema pain is difficult—often impossible—to change, our relationship to the schema can change dramatically. Changing our relationship to schema pain involves shifting the way we relate to the thoughts and feelings connected to our schemas by increasing willingness and acceptance of schema-driven affect and creating distance from schema-driven thoughts and stories. Identifying and naming the schema is a form of *defusion* (see chapter 6). It provides distance from the thought and makes it less believable. It *explains* the schema as a story about the world learned in childhood—one that may be less of a fit for the larger, multifaceted world of adults. And it reconceives schema pain as *a byproduct of that story*, something connected to a thought as opposed to reality. So while this treatment won't make schema pain go away, it may help couples take a more compassionate stance toward the emotional pain and create distance from the story, which allows for more flexible responses in relationships.

By making avoidant partner behavior the target of treatment, as opposed to thoughts and beliefs, ACT for couples gives therapists the tools to change what is easiest to see and alter—how we behave toward the intimate other.

ACT for Couples: Goal of Treatment

The main goal of treatment is to help couples cultivate psychological and behavioral flexibility in order to be able to choose effective actions in moments of schema activation. This is established through the six core ACT processes: values, committed action, cognitive defusion, self-as-context, contact with the present moment, and acceptance. These six processes are skills that lead to increased behavioral flexibility and a decrease in experiential avoidance.

1. **Values**: Identifying values with couples helps clarify the kind of partner one wants to be. Values are a chosen direction that encompasses what each partner wants to stand for in the relationship and what matters most. Values guide and drive behaviors. Clarifying values with couples provides guidance about the behaviors they want to enact in relationships and provides motivation to try new behaviors.

2. **Committed action**: Committed actions are specific values-based actions that are used to replace old schema coping behaviors. They are intentional behaviors that are in the service of one's values.

As partners attempt to take values-based actions, barriers come up. These include painful schema-driven thoughts and feelings that stop partners from doing new behaviors. Couples may also lack the necessary skills to take effective action. Skills are taught to help couples learn strategies for effective communication. The following two ACT processes are used to work with schema-driven thoughts that act as barriers to values-based actions in relationships:

3. **Cognitive defusion**: Cognitive defusion techniques are used to create distance from schema-driven thoughts that pull partners into old avoidance behaviors. Cognitive defusion helps partners disengage from schema-driven thoughts that act as barriers to values-based actions. This decreases the influence that these thoughts have on behavior.

4. **Self-as-context** (perspective taking): *Self-as-content* describes getting caught up in the stories connected to one's schemas and perceiving oneself as equivalent to those schemas. These concepts and narratives about oneself and others cause difficulties in relationships. *Self-as-context*, on the other hand, is about cultivating an observer self and observing internal material and thoughts about oneself and one's partner as transient and continuously changing. As an observer, one can notice and stay in contact with all of one's internal experiences, including schema-driven thoughts and feelings, and have distance from the story. Self-as-context aids partners in taking a flexible perspective toward their narrative about self and partner. The goal of this process is to assist partners to have a flexible and compassionate perspective on one another without buying into a narrative about who the other is and what his or her intentions are.

These last two ACT processes are used to work with schema-driven emotions that act as barriers to values-based actions in relationships.

5. **Contact with the present moment**: *Contacting the present moment* refers to the ability to stay fully in contact with one's experiences as they occur. It means being present and willing to observe all of the experience, both internal and external, nonjudgmentally. This process encourages partners to stay present and experience each other more directly, rather than through the lens of their schemas. It allows for behaviors to be more flexible and based on workability rather than old patterns of responding. When in contact with the present moment, one is less fused with the conceptualized past and future self, and more aware of the choices one has the freedom to make in the moment. This creates the space to test new behaviors and directly observe outcomes of alternative responses.

6. **Acceptance**: Acceptance involves fully taking in and receiving, without judgment, all of one's internal experiences, including thoughts, feelings, urges, memories, and sensations. Acceptance involves contacting the present moment fully and having willingness to stay present with one's internal experience without attempting to change or control distressing private events. ACT suggests that building acceptance decreases avoidant coping behaviors and increases values-based actions (Twohig, 2007). Therefore, ACT promotes exposure to schema-driven pain for the purpose of living a valued life. Acceptance is the process of

letting go of our struggle to control our experiences and being willing to have all of our experiences, so that we can freely choose our actions. Acceptance in couples therapy is particularly important because it helps partners cultivate an accepting stance both toward themselves, just as they are, and toward their partner—dropping the struggle to attempt to change oneself or one's partner.

Mindfulness and exposure are techniques for cultivating the ability to fully and consciously stay in contact with all of one's present-moment experiences with openness and curiosity. Mindfulness and exposure foster and help facilitate these six ACT processes.

Steps of treatment

The steps of treatment do not correspond to individual therapy sessions. Some will take one session; others may take two to four sessions, depending on the couple and their ability to integrate the material. This protocol is not a session-by-session description of the therapy process but rather a sequential description of the necessary steps in order to get the couple to the place where they can utilize ACT skills in their everyday life.

1. Identifying schemas and triggers (chapter 2)
2. Identifying experiential avoidance strategies: these are the SCBs that each partner uses to avoid schema pain (chapter 3)
3. Describing the formulation of the cycle the couple gets stuck in and how this leads to secondary pain (chapter 3)
4. Workability and creative hopelessness (chapter 3)
5. Values clarification (chapter 4)
6. Identifying values-based actions and moments of choice (chapter 4)
7. Identifying barriers to values-based actions (chapter 5)
8. Practicing defusion to decrease the influence that schema-driven thoughts have on behavior (chapter 6)
9. Cultivating acceptance and mindfulness to work with schema-driven emotions that act as barriers to values-based actions (chapter 7)
10. Practicing effective communication techniques to increase conflict-resolution skills (chapter 8)
11. Applying values-based problem solving with couples (chapter 9)
12. Developing flexible perspective taking with couples (chapter 10)
13. Combining all treatment processes in session (chapter 11)

CHAPTER 2

Learning About Schemas

Because schemas drive most couple conflict, it's important to identify each partner's key schemas early in therapy. In this chapter we describe the process of identifying partners' schemas, explaining what schemas are, where they originate, and how they influence the relationship. We also discuss how to assist couples in recognizing schema triggers, as well as list common emotions that get activated in connection to particular schemas. Worksheets and handouts are provided to help couples track their triggers and observe schemas outside of session. You may photocopy the handouts directly from this book's appendix D, or find them in PDF format for free download at http://www.newharbinger.com/34800.

Understanding Schemas

According to Jeffrey Young, schemas are core beliefs and stories that we have constructed about ourselves and our relationships. A schema is a deep-rooted cognitive structure or framework that helps us organize information and make sense of the world. A schema is like a lens through which we view the world, organize our experiences, and interpret events.

Schemas are stories that we have constructed about ourselves throughout our life. These stories distort our perceptions and experiences with others and can lead to self-fulfilling prophecies in relationships. Schemas develop in childhood from early experiences we have with our family and peers, and they continue to get perpetuated in our current relationships.

Our minds are built to create cause-and-effect relationships and make connections between events, even if there isn't much of a correlation. Making these correlations is advantageous in many ways, but schemas can become maladaptive when we interpret events in the world as causal connections about our identity and sense of self. We build stories about ourselves based on experiences in early childhood when our needs were not met. We build stories and theories about ourselves as to why it is that our needs weren't met. We form schemas as we attempt to understand events in the world and make sense of why they happened. For example, if a person grew up with a parent who was depressed and who wasn't able to meet his emotional needs, he might develop an emotional deprivation schema and believe that his partner will never meet his emotional needs. He may even convince himself that if he were just different or if he were better, then his needs would have been met. He may build a story that his emotions are too intense and that he was the cause of his parent's depression. This may lead him to suppress and inhibit his emotions in relationships, resulting in further feelings of deprivation.

Schemas are like sunglasses that distort how we take in information and how we make meaning of events. For example, an individual with an abandonment schema is predisposed to interpreting others as rejecting or abandoning, and she is more likely to reach the conclusion that she is being abandoned even if there is little evidence to suggest it. These lenses distort our perceptions and experiences with others, and can lead to self-defeating patterns in relationships. Schemas are hard to give up because they help us organize our experience and create an illusion of safety and predictability in the world. They are hard to challenge because they create the impression that we can make predictions about the outcome of our relationships and protect ourselves.

Maladaptive schemas may lead to self-defeating themes and patterns that continue to repeat throughout our adult relationships. These schemas that were formed in childhood continue to get triggered throughout life in stressful situations, and the way couples respond when triggered can create the very thing they fear. Once a schema gets triggered, it brings up a whole experience including powerful schema-driven thoughts, feelings, sensations, memories, and urges.

Schemas can influence interpersonal behaviors and interfere with one's ability to satisfy basic needs in current relationships. When our schemas get triggered in relationships we tend to use certain coping behaviors (see chapter 3) learned in childhood to try to control or block the pain connected to our schemas. These coping behaviors can end up reinforcing and maintaining schemas by creating a self-fulfilling prophecy. For example, if someone with an abandonment schema copes by seeking excessive reassurance, getting clingy, acting jealous and possessive, or blaming or accusing, these behaviors may actually increase the likelihood that others will withdraw or abandon. Individuals may also select partners based on what Jeffrey Young calls "schema chemistry": we select what is familiar and known to us (Young, 2012). People can choose a partner with a schema that is the mirror reversal of their own. Thus, a person with an abandonment schema may be drawn to partners who tend to feel engulfed or trapped in relationships, such as those with a subjugation schema, and vice versa.

Introducing Schemas

You have started to identify specific core beliefs (schemas) for the partners. And you will continue to do so using the Thoughts Journal and Couples Schemas Questionnaire that follow. At this point, it's good practice to pause and briefly explain what schemas are and how they work.

Either explain the properties of schemas as discussed or provide the Understanding Couples Schemas handout (available in single-page format in appendix D and at http://www.newharbinger.com/34800).

Understanding Couples Schemas

A schema is a core belief about yourself and your relationship. It creates a feeling that something is wrong with you and/or your intimate connection. Schemas are formed in childhood and develop as a result of ongoing dysfunctional experiences with caregivers, siblings, and peers.

Schemas come from repeated messages that we have gotten about ourselves (for example, "You're bad" or "You can't do anything right") or from specific traumatic events. Once a schema is formed, it's extremely stable and becomes an enduring way to see and understand yourself and your relationships.

Schemas are like sunglasses that distort all of your experiences. They color the way you see things, and they influence assumptions and predictions that tell you the schema is true or will turn out to be true. Schemas formed during childhood are triggered throughout your life. Common triggers include conflict, strong needs, and difficult thoughts and feelings. Once a schema gets triggered, it brings up extremely painful feelings (shame, loss, sadness, fear, anger, etc.). Schemas interfere with your ability to feel safe in a relationship, your ability to get your needs met, and your ability to meet the needs of others.

Characteristics of Couples Schemas*

They are experienced as self-evident truths.

They are self-perpetuating and resistant to change.

They seem to predict the future, particularly what will happen in your relationship, because they create the illusion that you can see what's coming and prepare accordingly.

They're usually triggered by stressful events, typically something painful in your relationship, that activate old beliefs about yourself.

They are always accompanied by high levels of emotion.

Thoughts Journal

For the first several weeks of therapy, have each partner keep a Thoughts Journal (provided here, in appendix D, and at http://www.newharbinger.com/34800) for times of conflict. This can be mined for cognitive themes and distilled into relevant schemas. It's also a good source of data about what drives particular conflicts.

* Adapted from *Acceptance and Commitment Therapy for Interpersonal Problems* (McKay, Lev, & Skeen, 2012).

Thoughts Journal

Event with Partner	Feelings	Thoughts

Example Dialogue

Therapist: Bill, I notice in your journal several thoughts about Cheri withdrawing. And here's one anticipating that Cheri may give up on the relationship. How do those impact you?

Bill: I get scared.

Therapist: Is there a belief behind those thoughts—about what's happening or will happen to the two of you?

Bill: I think she's kind of leaving all the time—and eventually maybe she'll just *go*.

Ten Relationship Schemas

Sometime within the first or second session, you can introduce the list of ten schemas for couples. Provided below is a detailed description of them, plus the primary pain that accompanies them. Following the list is a handout (also provided in appendix D and at http://www.newharbinger.com/34800) that you can give to couples.

1. **Abandonment/instability**: Individuals with this schema have a core belief that others are too unreliable or unstable to consistently be there for them. They fear that they can't count on others, that people are too unpredictable and will ultimately leave. Individuals with an abandonment schema believe that they are likely to get abandoned and rejected in relationships, and that any false move could lead to the relationship ending. These individuals may be attracted to cold and distant partners including ones who have a subjugation schema (and tend to feel engulfed) or an entitlement/grandiosity schema.

2. **Mistrust/abuse**: Individuals who have a mistrust/abuse schema believe that others are untrustworthy and will intentionally hurt and/or damage them. They have an expectation that others will lie, deceive, or take advantage of them. Individuals with this schema may set up tests for their partner to prove that he or she is trustworthy. They are suspicious of other people's agendas and motives, and fear that they will be manipulated and/or deceived by others. These individuals are attracted to partners who are either untrustworthy or who seek approval and take responsibility for the mistrust in the relationship. Their partners may include those with an entitlement/grandiosity schema, a failure schema, a defectiveness/shame schema, or a self-sacrifice/subjugation schema.

3. **Emotional deprivation**: Individuals with an emotional deprivation schema expect to be disappointed and deprived by others. They believe that others will never be able to meet their needs or satisfy them. They fear that their partner will never be able to

provide them with the understanding, attention, attunement, validation, or support that they truly need. These individuals constantly feel that something is missing from their relationship. They often feel lonely and disconnected from their partner. It is also difficult for them to allow others to take care of them. These individuals tend to be attracted to partners who are cold and distant and are unable to meet their needs, which fuels feelings of deprivation and resentment. Their partner types include those with an entitlement/grandiosity schema, a subjugation schema, or a defectiveness/shame schema.

4. **Defectiveness/shame**: With this schema, the individual believes that he or she is somehow defective, inferior, or unlovable. People with this schema share the core belief that something is fundamentally wrong with them. They've constructed a story about themselves that they are broken, defective, or deeply flawed, and that no one would really love them if they really knew them. These individuals fear being exposed: they believe that if anyone really got to know them, their true self would be exposed as unlovable and unacceptable. They tend to be attracted to partners who are rejecting or critical and who have an unrelenting standards schema, a mistrust/abuse schema, or an emotional deprivation schema.

5. **Social isolation/alienation**: Individuals with this schema believe that they don't fit in and don't belong with anyone. They struggle with a sense of being alone while together, being unseen and misunderstood. The core pain that shows up is a feeling that one is different from others and doesn't belong. They tend to be attracted to partners—for instance, individuals with a defectiveness/shame schema, an emotional deprivation schema, or a mistrust/abuse schema who have difficulty validating different perspectives.

6. **Dependence**: People with a dependence schema hold the belief that they are reliant on their partner and wouldn't be able to get by alone. They believe that they need their partner for emotional survival and that they would not be able to take care of themselves outside the relationship. Individuals with a dependency schema tend to struggle with trusting their own judgment and intuition about what they need or what actions to take. They doubt themselves and their decisions; they overly rely on other people's feedback. The belief is that they can't survive or succeed on their own and are dependent on their partner. These individuals tend to seek out partners who are independent, take the lead, and make decisions for them. These can be individuals with an entitlement/grandiosity schema or an unrelenting standards schema.

7. **Failure**: Individuals with a failure schema have a fear of failing and have a persistent and pervasive belief that they are not good enough, that they're inadequate, and that they will disappoint and fail their partner. They worry that they will inevitably let their partner down, and they don't trust that they can succeed. These individuals tend to

choose partners who expect them to fail including those with an emotional deprivation schema or an unrelenting standards schema. This perpetuates the feeling of not being good enough.

8. Entitlement/grandiosity: People with an entitlement/grandiosity schema tend to feel engulfed or trapped in relationships, and they get easily overwhelmed or frustrated by their partner's emotional needs. The core belief is that their needs come first. They feel that they deserve to have their needs and shouldn't have to accommodate others. The typical presentation of individuals with this schema is that they are special and don't feel bound to principles of reciprocity. They experience their partner's needs as an imposition and as an inconvenience. They have difficulty taking another person's perspective. They insist that they should be able to say and do what they want regardless of the impact it has on their partner. These individuals tend to seek out partners who are willing to acquiesce to their needs including those with a self-sacrifice/subjugation schema, an emotional deprivation schema, an abandonment schema, or a defectiveness/shame schema.

9. Self-sacrifice/subjugation: People with both these related schemas place an excessive focus on meeting other people's needs at the expense of their own. The main difference between those with a self-sacrifice schema versus those with a subjugation schema is that individuals with a self-sacrifice schema experience themselves as making voluntary choices, whereas those with a subjugation schema experience themselves as being under the control of other people. Those with a subjugation schema surrender to other people's needs out of fear of retaliation or rejection, whereas those with a self-sacrifice schema avoid feeling guilty or selfish. Individuals who self-sacrifice end up feeling deprived, resentful, and angry in relationships as a result of giving so much. These individuals tend to be attracted to partners who are self-absorbed and demand a lot from their partner such as those with an entitlement/grandiosity schema, an abandonment schema, or an emotional deprivation schema.

10. Unrelenting standards: Individuals who have unrelenting standards tend to set very high standards for themselves and others. It is difficult for them to feel satisfied; they get overly critical with their own behaviors and accomplishments, as well as with others'. The core belief is that they have to be perfect; it is hard for them to accept their own and others' shortcomings or limitations. They focus on mistakes, flaws, and imperfections, which leads to chronic dissatisfaction. Individuals who have an unrelenting standards schema tend to be attracted to partners who have difficulty meeting their standards including those with a failure schema or a defectiveness/shame schema.

10 Schemas for Couples

1. Abandonment/instability: the belief that your partner is unreliable and that he or she will disconnect or leave.
2. Mistrust/abuse: the expectation that your partner will harm, abuse, or neglect you.
3. Emotional deprivation: the expectation that your need for emotional support will not be met.
    a. Deprivation of nurturance—the absence of attention
    b. Deprivation of empathy—the absence of understanding
    c. Deprivation of protection—the absence of help
4. Defectiveness/shame: the belief that you are somehow defective, inferior, or unlovable.
5. Social isolation/alienation: the belief that you don't fit, that you don't belong with anyone. The sense of being alone while together, being unseen and not understood.
6. Dependence: the belief that it would be hard to survive emotionally without your partner, and that you would not be able to take care of yourself outside the relationship.
7. Failure: the belief that you will fail in your relationship (and key aspects of life).
8. Entitlement/grandiosity: the belief that your partner should provide for your needs, and that you have a right to expect his or her constant support.
9. Self-sacrifice/subjugation: the belief that you must always place your partner's needs over your own—either because your partner's needs are more important or because you fear rejection.
10. Unrelenting standards: the belief that you, and your partner, must meet high standards of performance—in life and in the relationship. And if these standards aren't met, you or your partner are wrong and deserve criticism.

Give the schema handout to both partners. Encourage them to discuss the ten schemas in session, and note which ones might apply. They should focus on their own schemas rather than accuse each other of particular schema beliefs.

The process of assessing partners' schemas starts in the first session, when you ask partners to describe the issues in a recent conflict. Have them begin with content—what each person wants or objects to. Permit the conversation to escalate until partners display some symptoms of being triggered (defensive posture, louder voice, accusations, etc.).

At the point when partners are getting emotionally activated, shift from content to process:

What is each partner feeling at this moment, including physical sensations?

What are their automatic thoughts—about each other, their relationship, their future? What do they expect to happen in the interaction? Are they making assumptions? Judgments?

Write down each partner's key thoughts, and use the Downward Arrow technique to go deeper to uncover schema beliefs.

Assessing Schemas

There are two key strategies for assessing schemas: the Downward Arrow technique and the Couples Schema Questionnaire.

The Downward Arrow

The Downward Arrow is a simple process. Ask this question: "If ________ *[the automatic thought]* is true, what does that mean about you and your relationship?" Keep repeating the question with each new thought that comes up until you've reached a recognizable schema. Notice that you are looking for *beliefs*, not feelings.

Example Dialogue

Therapist: Cheri, Bill, let me explore with each of you some of the thoughts that came up regarding Bill's desire to work part-time to pursue his music. Cheri, you had the thought that "Bill just wants what he wants." Do I have that right?

Cheri: Yeah.

Therapist: If that were true, what does that mean about you and your relationship?

Cheri: That Bill knows what he wants and he gets it. He goes after it.

Therapist: Okay, and if that were true—he knows what he wants and goes after it—what does that mean about you and the relationship?

Cheri: That he isn't thinking about what I need; he doesn't care about it.

Therapist: I'm not saying that's true, but if it were—that he doesn't care what you need—what would that mean?

Cheri: That he's just going to do his music. That he'll take and take and use me up.

Therapist: So it's a *mistrust* thought—that Bill might take advantage, might use you unfairly. Bill, let me explore for a moment one of your thoughts: "I'm never going to have a life." If that were true, what does it mean about you and your relationship?

Bill: That she won't let me have the things that matter to me.

Therapist: And if that were true? What does that mean about you and your relationship?

Bill: That I'll never get what I need from her.

Therapist: Okay. So the thought is that you'll be *deprived* of what you need in this relationship. Notice how, as we drill down into these thoughts, there's an important belief at the root of each of them. For you, Cheri, it's the belief that you can't trust your partner not to use you. And for you, Bill, that your partner won't give you what you need to be happy.

The Couples Schema Questionnaire

You can also uncover schemas with a formal assessment. The following Couples Schema Questionnaire (also provided in appendix B and at http://www.newharbinger.com/34800), inspired by the work of Jeffrey Young, can identify key schemas for each partner.

Couples Schema Questionnaire

The following questionnaire will help you determine which schemas are most relevant for you in your relationship. After reading each statement, rate each statement according to how well it describes you, using the scale provided.

Place your answer in the box next to the question. At the end, a brief guide will help you assess your responses.

0—Disagree

1—Neither agree nor disagree

2—Slightly agree

3—Agree

4—Strongly agree

1. Ab/In

_____ 1. I don't feel like I can rely and depend on my partner.

_____ 2. I'm often attracted to partners who are unable to commit to me.

_____ 3. I feel insecure and unstable in my relationship.

_____ 4. My relationship feels fragile, like it can end at any minute.

_____ 5. I can't count on my partner to always be there for me.

_____ 6. I'm constantly afraid that my partner will leave me.

_____ 7. I often worry that my partner will find someone else they prefer to be with.

_____ 8. I get scared spending time away from my partner or when my partner needs space.

_____ 9. When my partner is not around I worry about his/her commitment to me.

_____ 10. I'm often afraid of being abandoned by or losing my partner.

2. M/A

_____ 1. I often worry that my partner is taking advantage of me or using me.

_____ 2. I worry that my partner will hurt or betray me.

_____ 3. It's difficult for me to trust my partner and give him/her the benefit of the doubt.

_____ 4. Most people cannot be trusted.

_____ 5. I need to protect myself and stay on guard in order to feel safe in my relationship.

_____ 6. I am often suspicious of my partner's intentions and motives.

_____ 7. I can't count on my partner to follow through on his/her word.

_____ 8. I have to be on the lookout for my partner lying or breaking promises.

_____ 9. I feel afraid that my partner will mistreat me or become abusive.

_____ 10. I often wonder whether my partner is deceiving me or fooling me in some way.

3. ED

_____ 1. I don't get the love and care that I truly need from my partner.

_____ 2. My partner doesn't understand me or provide me with the nurturing that I need.

_____ 3. I feel unsatisfied in my romantic relationship.

_____ 4. I wish my partner was more emotionally present and available to meet my needs.

_____ 5. It's been difficult for me to feel taken care of by my partners.

_____ 6. My partners have often responded to my emotional needs in a cold and distant way.

_____ 7. I've always needed more attention and affection than my partners have been able to provide.

_____ 8. I often feel deprived by my partner and left wanting more.

_____ 9. It's difficult for me to depend on my partner for emotional support.

_____ 10. I often feel alone or lonely even when I'm with my partner.

4. D/S

_____ 1. If my partner really knew me, he/she would be disappointed by me.

_____ 2. I worry that if my partner saw all my flaws and defects he/she wouldn't accept me.

_____ 3. I worry that if I reveal too much about myself my partner won't love me.

_____ 4. I feel fundamentally bad or broken.

_____ 5. I try to figure out what's wrong with me so I can fix myself.

_____ 6. I worry that if I expose myself fully with my partner he/she will reject me.

_____ 7. I often think my partner is too good for me and that he/she could find somebody better.

_____ 8. My partner wouldn't want to be with me if he/she knew the real me.

_____ 9. I have often been a disappointment to most of my partners.

_____ 10. I can't share my deepest insecurities with my partner.

5. SI/A

_____ 1. I don't feel a sense of belonging with my partner or my community.

_____ 2. I frequently feel left out of groups and like an outsider.

_____ 3. My partner and I struggle with fitting in well with our group of friends.

_____ 4. I feel awkward and different when I try to connect with my partner's friends and/or family.

_____ 5. I worry that my partner and I are too different or we live in separate worlds.

_____ 6. I worry that my partner doesn't want to include me in social situations.

______ 7. I feel excluded when I'm in social situations with my partner.

______ 8. I worry that my partner feels embarrassed or ashamed of me in social situations.

______ 9. I worry that I don't fit in well with my partner's friends and/or family.

______ 10. I feel embarrassed or self-conscious when I'm in social situations with my partner.

6. De

______ 1. It's difficult for me to get things done without my partner's help.

______ 2. I prefer for my partner to make most of the decisions.

______ 3. It's difficult for me to be alone for long periods of time.

______ 4. I need my partner's help with many issues that I can't handle on my own.

______ 5. It's difficult for me to make my own decisions without my partner's feedback.

______ 6. I depend heavily on my partner for help and/or advice.

______ 7. I can't handle most problems without my partner's support.

______ 8. I often feel helpless or at a loss concerning what to do.

______ 9. I need assistance and reassurance from my partner to solve everyday problems.

______ 10. I fear that I will make mistakes and reach the wrong decisions without my partner's advice.

7. Fa

______ 1. I worry that I will not meet my partner's expectations.

______ 2. I've been a disappointment to most of my partners.

______ 3. I've failed at most of my relationships.

______ 4. I don't trust myself to make good decisions.

______ 5. When my partner asks me to do something, I usually end up messing it up.

______ 6. I'm afraid I won't measure up to my potential.

______ 7. I always fall short in my accomplishments.

______ 8. I'm constantly failing and disappointing my partner.

______ 9. I don't live up to my partner's standards.

______ 10. I mess up everything I attempt.

8. En

_____ 1. I get angry when I don't get what I want from my partner.

_____ 2. I often feel that my partner needs too much from me.

_____ 3. I usually get what I want in my relationship.

_____ 4. I don't accept my partner telling me what to do.

_____ 5. I often feel frustrated by my partner constraining me.

_____ 6. I shouldn't have to put my partner's needs before my own.

_____ 7. My partner shouldn't stop me from doing what I want.

_____ 8. I feel that I shouldn't have to accept some of the limitations placed on me by my partner.

_____ 9. When it comes to the good things in life, I mostly get what I deserve.

_____ 10. I am good at convincing my partner to do things my way.

9. Su/SS

_____ 1. It's difficult for me to get my needs met in relationships.

_____ 2. I feel guilty if I put my own needs before my partner's.

_____ 3. I feel afraid to disagree with or say no to my partner.

_____ 4. I find myself usually going along with my partner's plans.

_____ 5. I often agree to do things for my partner that I realize I didn't want to do.

_____ 6. I feel afraid that if I don't meet my partner's needs he/she will retaliate against me or punish me.

_____ 7. It's difficult for me to identify what I want in the moment.

_____ 8. I try hard to please my partner, and put his/her needs before my own.

_____ 9. It's difficult for me to stand up for myself or advocate for my own needs in my relationship.

_____ 10. I have trouble making my own wants and needs known.

10. US

_____ 1. I set very high standards for my partner and myself.

_____ 2. Very little of what I do satisfies me; I usually think I could do better.

_____ 3. It's easier for me to see my partner's shortcomings than the way he/she contributes to my life.

_____ 4. I easily feel like I'm stagnating if I don't accomplish enough.

_____ 5. I get critical when my partner or I make a mistake.

_____ 6. Failure is very upsetting to me.

_____ 7. I often feel disappointed that my partner isn't meeting my expectations.

_____ 8. I notice the ways my partner could be better or could have done something better.

_____ 9. I set high expectations of my partner and myself.

_____ 10. I never get enough done.

Scores

_____ 1. Abandonment/instability

_____ 2. Mistrust/abuse

_____ 3. Emotional deprivation

_____ 4. Defectiveness/shame

_____ 5. Social isolation/alienation

_____ 6. Dependence

_____ 7. Failure

_____ 8. Entitlement/grandiosity

_____ 9. Self-sacrifice/subjugation

_____ 10. Unrelenting standards

Interpreting a Couple's Schemas

0–10: Not applicable. This schema probably doesn't apply to the individual.

11–19: Fairly low. This schema may have a marginal impact on the individual.

20–29: Moderate. This schema has a moderate impact on the individual.

30–40: High. This is an important schema for the individual.

Although the pain associated with these schemas is universal in relationships and all of us have experienced moments of mistrust, deprivation, abandonment, and so on, individuals tend to have a propensity toward certain schemas, given their history. When individuals score high on particular schemas, those schemas tend to be triggered more frequently for that individual. A score of 25 or more for any of the ten schemas for couples indicates an elevated schema and the possibility that it may be impacting the relationship. If none of the schemas are elevated, you can work on the two highest-scoring schemas. If there are multiple elevated schemas, work on only two or three. To work on more would make the therapy too complex and potentially confusing. Focus your work on schemas that are:

- significantly elevated;
- frequently show up during conflicts; and
- lead to behavior that triggers the other partner.

Once you've chosen the key schemas to work with, you'll return to them again and again throughout the sessions, noticing each time they get activated and how partners respond. It's not necessary to use the schema terminology with the couples; instead you may use the partners' own words to describe and label their schema experience.

Schemas and Emotional Pain

Schema beliefs trigger enormously painful emotions. They are so distressing, in fact, that partners are highly motivated to suppress or avoid schema pain whenever it's activated. Typical affect associated with each schema is summarized in the following Schema Affect handout (also provided in appendix D and online at http://www.newharbinger.com/34800).

Schema Affect

Schema	Affect
Social isolation/alienation	Loneliness, shame, dejection, embarrassment, isolation, desolate yearning, fear, anxiety
Self-sacrifice/subjugation	Guilt, fear, helplessness, obligation, anger
Entitlement/grandiosity	Anger, disappointment, deprivation, engulfment
Abandonment/instability	Fear, loneliness, jealousy, insecurity, longing, grief
Failure	Fear, sadness, disappointment, helplessness, anger, shame
Emotional deprivation	Loneliness, urgency, deprivation, hunger, helplessness, yearning, sadness, anger
Defectiveness/shame	Shame, sadness, fear, helplessness, anger

Unrelenting standards	Disappointment, discontent, emptiness, fear, dissatisfaction, frustration, shame
Mistrust/abuse	Fear, suspicion, loneliness, caution, doubt, anger, yearning
Dependence	Fear, uncertainty, loneliness, vulnerability, inferiority, doubt, confusion, anxiety

Review this information about schema affect with couples. Encourage partners to identify particular emotions associated with their key schemas.

Example Dialogue

Therapist: Cheri, when your mistrust schema shows up, what emotions do you notice getting triggered with it?

Cheri: When I get into thinking Bill wants to use me, I'm angry. And I feel stupid and ashamed for letting him do it.

Therapist: Okay, anger and shame. How big are those feelings?

Cheri: Huge. I just want to get out.

Therapist: It's very painful. Bill, we've talked about two schemas that get triggered for you. One is the deprivation schema, the belief you'll never get what you need from Cheri. What's the feeling that goes with that?

Bill: Kind of a despair—like I'm always gonna feel unhappy. And this resentment—like she could help me but she won't.

Therapist: The despair sounds very painful. And what about the abandonment schema we've looked at? What's the feeling when you think Cheri might leave?

Bill: I don't wanna go there.

Therapist: I know. But I'm wondering if we could at least name the feeling.

Bill: A kind of sick, scared feeling.

Therapist: Which is so big you don't want to even touch it. But here's what's important about these schema feelings. They're so big and hurt so much—like touching a hot stove—that you want to stop them, avoid them, get rid of them. Just as fast as you can. And the pain is fueling your conflicts.

This is the moment when you are first introducing the ACT concept of *experiential avoidance*—running away from pain in maladaptive ways that serve to increase suffering. Schema pain avoidance is understood, from an ACT perspective, to be the prime cause of relationship distress and dysfunction.

Explain the Origin of Schemas

Maladaptive schemas develop in early childhood when core emotional needs aren't met. According to Jeffrey Young (2004), six needs must be met for children to thrive. If neglected, these needs create schemas that are reenacted in relationships. Although these schemas are an adaptive response to one's early childhood environment, they can continue and be maintained in current relationships. Here are the six basic emotional childhood needs (McKay, Lev, & Skeen, 2012):

- **Safety.** The need for basic safety goes unmet when children aren't provided with a stable and safe environment. Children need reliable and consistent caretakers in order to feel safe in the world; they may develop an abandonment/instability schema, a mistrust/abuse schema, or both when this need is not met.
- **Connection.** Children need love, affection, empathy, understanding, and guidance from family members, caregivers, and peers. When they don't receive the love and empathy that they need, they may develop an emotional deprivation schema, an abandonment schema, a defectiveness/shame schema, or a social isolation/alienation schema.
- **Autonomy.** Children need a sense of autonomy and independence in order to have healthy separation from parents. When children aren't taught self-reliance, responsibility, and good judgment, they are likely to develop a dependence schema or a self-sacrifice/subjugation schema.
- **Self-worth.** When children receive a healthy amount of love, attention, acceptance, and respect they develop self-esteem. When this support from family and peers is absent they may develop a defectiveness/shame schema, a failure schema, or an emotional deprivation schema.
- **Self-expression.** In a nurturing environment, children are encouraged to express their needs and desires openly. When this self-expression is discouraged, children feel that they must suppress their own needs and feelings in order to stay connected to their caregivers. These children may fear being retaliated against or having their feelings and needs be dismissed. When self-expression isn't encouraged and supported, children may develop a self-sacrifice/subjugation schema, an unrelenting standards schema, or a defectiveness/shame schema, or all three.
- **Realistic limits.** When children are raised in an environment that encourages responsibility, self-control, self-discipline, and respect for others, they learn to operate within realistic limits. When parents are permissive and overly indulgent, children grow up without understanding the need to consider other people before acting. In the absence of realistic limits, children may develop an entitlement/grandiosity schema.

Once you've identified key schemas and related affect, it can be validating to connect the dots to originating childhood experiences. These core beliefs grow from specific traumas and negative encounters with caregivers during which core emotional needs weren't met. The therapist aids individuals in connecting current conflicts and schema triggers to these early childhood experiences, facilitating couples to recognize previous unmet needs and current emotional needs in relationships.

By identifying schema origins, the therapist achieves several objectives:

- The schema beliefs and pain are explained by forces that are not under the individual's control. Schemas aren't his or her fault.
- Empathy building occurs because each partner hears stories that shaped the other's fears and reactions.
- The schema can now be linked to specific events that both make it understandable and show how the person conflates past and present relationships.

Example Dialogue

Therapist: Bill, when you think back to when you were young, do you remember that despair feeling—that you'd never get what you need? Were there situations in your childhood that connect to that?

Bill: When my mother and father split, and she was running around looking for someone or something, I wanted her to hang out, do things, talk to me. But she was like—good-bye.

Therapist: You felt left alone.

Bill: I felt left. Period.

Therapist: I have a feeling that this same experience connects to your abandonment belief, too.

Bill: I tried to stay awake waiting for her. But I was always asleep when she got home.

Therapist: The schema feelings that get triggered with Cheri go back a long way, don't they? To that time when it felt like your mother had left you. [Turning to Cheri] Let me ask you the same question. The thought that people don't care about you, and the anger and shame that go with it, where do you remember that showing up in the past?

Cheri: Lots of times. An example? My father was running for county supervisor, and he suddenly took an interest in me. He thought it would win votes if he showed his daughter off—make him look like some kind of family man. [Waves her hand dismissively] And if I didn't want to go campaigning with him, he bullied me until I agreed to go and "put a smile on my face."

Therapist: But he didn't pay attention to you otherwise?

Cheri: No.

Therapist: I can see how that would make trusting someone feel dangerous.

How Schemas Impact Relationships

Now that the couple has been introduced to schemas, and identified one or two core beliefs that influence each partner, it's time to recognize schema-triggering situations that typically occur in the relationship. These triggers will vary according to the particular schema. The following handout (also provided in appendix D and online at http://www.newharbinger.com/34800) can be used to begin a discussion about what triggers whom.

Schema Triggers for Couples

Schemas tend to distort our view of relationships, particularly in situations when each partner's needs are different. When our schemas get triggered, we react in ways designed to protect ourselves from the emotional pain that results. Triggers are unavoidable in our relationships. However, if you can identify the triggers for your main schemas, you'll be one step closer to changing the reactions that fuel fights and conflicts. Here are some of the typical triggers for each schema:

Abandonment/instability: This schema is likely to be triggered for you when your partner is withdrawn, shut down, or unavailable. It can also be activated when your partner is critical, seems dissatisfied with the relationship, or has directly or indirectly threatened to leave.

Mistrust/abuse: This schema is often triggered when your partner says or does something that hurts you, when you perceive your partner as not caring, or when your partner pushes for things that don't seem good for you.

Emotional deprivation: This schema can get triggered if you feel lonely, if your partner seems detached, or if you don't feel understood, protected, or loved.

Defectiveness/shame: Activation of this schema can follow being criticized, or when you feel that you aren't living up to your partner's expectations. Messages that you aren't worthy, or aren't good enough, are also highly triggering.

Social isolation/alienation: This schema can be triggered when you feel different from your partner or your partner's friends or family (in values, interests, tastes, etc.), or don't feel seen and understood. Sometimes it can be activated by feeling alone while sharing the same space as your partner.

Dependence: This can be triggered when facing difficulties or challenges and your partner seems withdrawn and unavailable. Any situation when you need your partner and he or she isn't there—emotionally or physically—can be triggering. Any threat to the relationship can also activate this schema.

Failure: This schema is likely to be triggered by mistakes, criticism, or the message that you aren't living up to your partner's expectations. The suggestion that something is lacking about your accomplishments, talents, competence, or intelligence will also activate this core belief.

Entitlement/grandiosity: This can be triggered when your partner doesn't do what you want or need, or when a partner chooses his or her own needs or desires over yours.

Self-sacrifice/subjugation: This schema can be triggered whenever your partner needs something from you and you feel compelled to give it. It can also be activated by the sense that your partner's needs control you, forcing you to go along whether you want to or not.

Unrelenting standards: This can be triggered when either you or your partner doesn't live up to standards you hold for how to behave in an intimate relationship. This schema can also be activated by criticism, conflict, or feelings of dissatisfaction.

Once partners have discussed some of their typical triggers, you can have them observe and monitor triggering situations *as they occur* during the week. Give each partner a copy of the following Schema Triggers Log (also provided in appendix D and online at http://www.newharbinger.com/34800) and encourage them to use it whenever something in their relationship activates a key schema. This is extremely important homework because it allows partners to map what happens when they are triggered. The right-hand column (Behavior [What You Did]) will provide vital data on how they cope with schema activation. These responses—schema coping behaviors—are the focus of the next steps in treatment (see chapter 3).

Schema coping behaviors (SCBs) are the means by which schemas damage relationships, and the couple will begin to realize this as you examine (in the next chapter) consequences of their behavior. For now, it's enough for partners to observe and record triggering events and responses.

Homework

Homework for this early phase of therapy involves having partners (1) fill out the Thoughts Journal for each conflict, (2) complete the Couples Schema Questionnaire, and (3) fill out the Schema Triggers Log whenever a key schema is activated in the relationship.

Schema Triggers Log

Triggering Situation	Schema	Emotion	Behavior (What You Did)

CHAPTER 3

Schema Coping Behaviors and the Role of Avoidance

After exploring each partner's schemas and their triggers, and validating the primary pain that continues to show up for each partner in the relationship, you can start the process of identifying the schema coping behaviors (SCBs)—behavioral strategies that we utilize in relationships as a way to try to control, eliminate, or block our schema pain—that each partner engages in. Begin by providing psychoeducation on what SCBs are, how we learn them, and how they get maintained in relationships. Then proceed to identify the specific SCBs that each partner uses in the relationship, and provide the couple with a *formulation of the cycle*: a description of the unique pattern that the couple gets stuck in and that highlights how each partner's SCBs contribute to maintaining the dynamic.

Seen through an ACT lens, SCBs are *experiential avoidance* behaviors that we have learned as a way to avoid painful internal experiences and schema activation. These avoidance behaviors may, at times, provide temporary relief or delay the schema pain, but they end up causing more pain, suffering, and relationship damage in the long run.

We learn these SCBs in early childhood from our interactions with others in our environment, such as from watching our parents and other family members interact and cope with pain. We may have learned that if we got loud or hysterical enough, our depressed parent would pay attention to us; or if we withdrew and became very quiet, our intrusive and critical parent would give us the space we needed. We might have learned that if we accommodated our parents' every need, then we could temporarily avoid feelings of guilt or blame. We learned strategies that were adaptive for us at some point in life but now are damaging our current relationships and preventing us from getting our needs met.

Now, as adults, we have become conditioned to use the same avoidance strategies we learned in childhood in our current relationships as we attempt to avoid schema pain. The problem is that although these strategies may at times provide short-term relief, in the long run these behaviors hurt our relationships and may actually create a self-fulfilling prophecy that reinforces both partners' schemas. This creates a pattern in our current relationship that resembles our childhood.

For example, if someone with an abandonment schema gets triggered, he may cope with this experience by seeking excessive reassurance, clinging, acting jealous or possessive, or blaming or inducing. He might call his partner over and over again to get the attention that he needs, or he might use guilt to stop his partner from spending time with others. These behaviors may provide relief from feelings of rejection in the moment, but in the long run these coping behaviors take a toll on the relationship and may actually increase the likelihood that his partner will pull away or withdraw, which continues to reinforce and trigger the experience of abandonment.

The way an individual responds when a schema gets triggered in turn triggers the partner's schemas and SCBs—and this cycle is what maintains self-defeating patterns in the relationship. Use the handout that follows (provided in single-page format in appendix D and online at http://www.newharbinger.com/34800) to help partners identify the specific SCBs they use when they get triggered.

10 Common Schema Coping Behaviors in Relationships

The following is a list of 10 common maladaptive coping behaviors that couples engage in when triggered:

1. Attacking: blaming, criticizing, aggressive speech, belittling, accusing, imposing intentions
2. Demanding: controlling, insisting, making excessive requests, and requiring attention, support, or caretaking
3. Surrendering: giving up, giving in, complying, self-sacrifice, being passive or submissive
4. Clinging: dependence, seeking attention and help with problems, seeking reassurance
5. Withdrawal: silence, disconnection, stonewalling, or retreating emotionally, physically, and sexually
6. Stimulation seeking: avoiding by seeking excitement and distraction through compulsive shopping, sex, gambling, risk taking, overworking, and so on
7. Addictive self-soothing: avoiding by numbing with alcohol, drugs, food, TV, Internet, and so on
8. Manipulating: threats to do or not do something, derailing, seduction, dishonesty, guilt-tripping
9. Punishing: taking away, passive-aggressive procrastination, lateness, complaining
10. Discounting: suggesting or asserting that the other person's needs are unimportant, minimizing, defending, explaining, justifying

Identifying SCBs and their Outcomes

Once both partners are clear about what SCBs are and how avoidance of schema pain contributes to the cycle of maintaining and reinforcing the negative dynamic in the relationship, continue clarifying the different SCBs that each partner utilizes by reviewing recent conflicts and the outcomes of the SCBs in the relationship.

Each partner may engage in different SCBs for different schemas or even different SCBs for the same schema. For example, a partner with a subjugation schema may oscillate between different extremes of coping behaviors. He or she may at times respond to the experience of subjugation by complying, submitting, or accommodating, and at other times he or she may jump to the opposite extreme, responding with rebellion and demands. All of these SCBs serve the same function: to avoid the pain associated with the subjugation schema.

It's important to clearly identify all the SCBs that each partner uses in order to assess their workability. There are two parts to this process. The first is exploring the *workability* of the SCBs by identifying the negative outcomes they create in the relationship, and the second is *creative hopelessness*, an ACT process that undermines the couple's agenda to attempt to control and eliminate schema pain. Workability helps partners identify how their SCBs lead to negative outcomes in the relationship. Creative hopelessness is the realization that both partners' schema pain is unavoidable and will continue to get triggered in the relationship. The following steps can be used to continue clarifying the specific SCBs that each partner tends to use.

1. Show partners the handout with the list of SCBs and explore which behaviors they engage in. Encourage partners to review their Schema Triggers for Couples log to answer some questions:

   How do you behave when your schema is triggered?

   When you feel schema pain (hurt, rejected, abandoned, helpless) what do you do?

   When your ________ schema gets triggered, how do you behave?

   When your partner does ________ [specific SCB], how do you respond?

2. Check in with each partner regarding whether he or she agrees with the SCBs described, and then get feedback about his or her partner's SCBs.

3. Review a recent conflict and connect each partner's schemas, triggers, and coping behaviors to the specific conflict, clearly identifying the cycle.

These steps assist in labeling and recognizing the SCBs that each partner uses in the relationship and help predict the SCBs that will show up in session. As you're identifying SCBs with couples, you're also checking in and determining which SCBs will be the targets for treatment.

Workability of SCBs—Providing Couples with a Formulation

When reviewing a recent conflict, help each partner identify the outcome that the SCBs have for him- or herself, for his or her partner, and for the relationship. Note the ways SCBs trigger the other partner, reinforce schema belief, and deepen pain. Provide a formulation for how this contributes to a cycle that maintains and exacerbates both partners' schema pain. The formulation distinguishes between unavoidable pain that gets triggered and secondary pain created by SCBs.

The difficult part of providing a formulation to the couple is in presenting it as an amalgamation of both partners' responses to schema pain. In the case of Mike and Michelle, neither one of them can tolerate the pain that shows up for them around disappointment. Michelle can't tolerate the experience of deprivation and aloneness when she's disappointed, and Mike can't tolerate the experience of having disappointed her. He feels inadequate, helpless, and ashamed. Every time this experience arises for the couple, they respond with a pursuer/distancer pattern that exacerbates their pain and disappointment. One function of the formulation is to externalize the problem in a way that neither partner is at fault, while showing how both are responsible for changing it. The therapist describes the problem as a pattern that has been created by both partners' responses to unavoidable pain (in this case disappointment) in the relationship. Both partners' SCBs have contributed to maintaining the problem, and both partners are responsible for changing the dynamic.

Help the couple recognize that in every conflict the same schemas and SCBs continue to show up. The SCBs end up reinforcing and maintaining pain (both partners' schemas) by creating a self-fulfilling prophecy. The following is an example of how you might begin to identify each partner's SCBs and provide a formulation of the cycle.

Example Dialogue

Therapist: We have looked over the list of SCBs and have a pretty good idea of which ones you both engage in. If you're both willing, let's discuss a specific recent conflict, maybe one that occurred this week or the previous week, when one of your schemas got triggered. What behaviors did you use and what were the outcomes?

Mike: Well, yesterday Michelle started nagging me about the dishes again and I got extremely angry about it.

Therapist: Walk me through the entire situation.

Mike: I was watching TV, and Michelle got home from work. The first thing she said to me was, "I can't believe the dishes are still dirty! You always do this. You said that you were going to clean the damn dishes and, of course, you didn't. I just can't count on you for anything." That made me irate. She does this every day. The first thing she does when she gets home from work is criticize something I've done.

Therapist: And when Michelle said that, what did you do?

Mike: I said, "Nothing is ever good enough for you," and I walked away.

Therapist: What happened next?

Mike: Well, she can't ever leave me alone, so she started following me to the bedroom and telling me what a horrible person I am, and then I got so angry that I exploded and left the house.

Therapist: Michelle, what was happening for you at this moment?

Michelle: I just feel like he never listens to me or cares about how he impacts me.

Therapist: I think you are trying to describe to me that you are feeling very alone and maybe hurt? But do you notice how you are describing it? Do you think you might be engaging in a coping behavior right now? Let's look at the list. [The therapist identifies the coping behaviors in the moment and reframes the partner's statements using nonjudgmental language.]

Michelle: I'm being critical, blaming? I just don't know how to get through to him.

Therapist: Let's try to understand what's going on for you and how you attempt to get through to him. Can you describe to me what happened between you two? How did you feel when you got home?

Michelle: I walked in the house and saw what a mess it was and that the dishes weren't done and Mike was just watching TV, and I felt disappointed and alone.

Therapist: Your deprivation schema was triggered?

Michelle: Yes. I felt completely alone and that none of my needs will ever get met in this relationship.

Therapist: You felt alone and deprived? And you had thoughts about how your needs will never get met?

Michelle: Yes.

Therapist: And what did you do? How did you behave in that moment when you were triggered? Look at the list of coping behaviors and see if you can identify which SCB you used.

Michelle: I criticized. Blamed.

Therapist: Yeah. You started feeling alone and deprived, and in your attempts to get Mike to understand your pain, you got critical and blaming with him. Is that correct? Mike, do you think you got triggered at that point? What schemas were triggered for you? What coping behaviors did you use in that moment?

Mike: I was annoyed and frustrated and tired of having the same argument over and over again and being reminded of what a bad husband I am.

Therapist: Let's notice any judgments and come back to your experience. Did you feel hurt? Helpless? Inadequate? What was going on for you? Which one of your schemas was triggered at that moment?

Mike: I guess the defectiveness/shame one was triggered for me. Feeling like I'm never good enough. I'll always disappoint her.

Therapist: And what did you do in that moment when you felt inadequate and not good enough?

Mike: I walked away. I withdrew like I usually do because I feel like I can never please her.

Therapist: And what happened after you walked away? How did Michelle respond?

Mike: She just kept following me all around the house and kept nagging and criticizing even more.

Michelle: Every time he walks away I just feel so discarded. So I try to tell him how much he's hurt me and why it's important to me. It's not just about the dishes, it's about the fact that I can't depend on him for anything, and he doesn't care about how he makes me feel.

Therapist: [To Mike] So the more you tried to withdraw and escape the feelings of inadequacy and shame, the more intense it became—the more you tried to escape the nagging, the louder she got?

Mike: Yeah, she just wouldn't stop until I exploded and left the house.

Therapist: [To Michelle] And the more that you tried to get Mike to understand how hurtful this was to you, the more he withdrew and distanced himself? You wanted him to hear you and understand you, but the more you tried to explain how bad it made you feel, the more he withdrew and the more deprived you felt?

Michelle: He wouldn't listen to a word I said; he just kept walking away and telling me he'll do them later, which just made me feel more upset.

Therapist: And then when you felt more upset, what did you do then?

Michelle: I told him that he clearly doesn't care about me or my feelings, and that I can't count on him for shit.

Therapist: So you got more critical and more demanding? [Turning to Mike] What did you do after Michelle said that?

Mike: I said that if I can't ever do anything right, then maybe we shouldn't even be together, and I left the house.

Therapist: You felt inadequate and helpless. You wanted to escape this experience so much that you gave an ultimatum, and then you withdrew?

Mike: Yeah. I just feel like there's nothing I can do at this point. I already disappointed her, and she hates me, and there's nothing I can do.

Therapist: So the way the cycle escalates looks like this: It starts with one of your schemas getting triggered; in this case, Michelle's deprivation schema got triggered when she saw that the dishes weren't done. Then she felt deprived, and she tried to avoid the despair of ever getting her needs met by getting critical, demanding, and blaming. In turn, that triggered Mike's feelings of defectiveness and inadequacy. When Mike felt helpless he pulled away. Which in turn triggered Michelle's feelings of loneliness and deprivation. Is that correct? The more Mike pulls away and withdraws, the more alone and deprived Michelle feels, and the more deprived Michelle feels, the more she criticizes and demands, which increases Mike's sense of defectiveness and pulls him to withdraw?

Both: Yes.

The therapist labels all SCBs that each partner uses and identifies the ways each partner's SCBs trigger the other's schemas and schema pain. This provides a concise formulation of how each partner's SCBs contribute to the negative cycle in the relationship. You will notice that the same schemas and SCBs tend to show up in a couple's conflicts, even if the cycle appears in different contexts. These behaviors become the main focus and target in treatment, and it's important to continue to clarify the formulation of every conflict with the couple. The problem in the relationship is not in the content of the conflict but in the avoidance strategies that are employed. Struggling to escape unavoidable pain is at the root. After helping the couple formulate the problem as one of avoidance, the therapist helps partners cultivate both acceptance of the unavoidable pain and ways to respond to it differently.

Tracking SCBs and Outcomes Outside of Session

After identifying SCBs and their outcomes in session, couples continue to track and monitor their SCBs and their outcomes outside of session by using the SCBs Outcomes Log (provided in appendix D and online at http://www.newharbinger.com/34800). This log builds on what partners learned from the Schema Triggers Log (chapter 2), where they began monitoring SCBs. Now, with the SCBs Outcomes Log, you are gathering more-specific data about schema-driven thoughts and, most important, the relational and emotional outcomes from using avoidance strategies. Have each partner fill out the log for homework and review it in session.

When introducing the SCBs Outcomes Log, explain the following to the couple:

Therapist: Every time one of you gets triggered, you have a choice to engage in a new behavior or an old SCB. Each behavior you engage in will have an outcome for you and your relationship. It is important to mindfully observe the outcome of your behaviors and assess whether it led to the situation getting better or worse. This worksheet can help you continue to identify which SCBs you use most frequently and assess the short- and long-term costs of the SCBs. I would like for you both to fill out this worksheet this week. Would you be willing to do that? You can fill it out at any sign of conflict or moment of trigger that occurs this week.

First describe the specific event that triggered you. This is a description of a specific behavior or event that was triggering and should be stated as facts, not judgments. For example, "Jason said he wanted to end the relationship" is stated as a fact. "Jason threatened me" is a judgment.

Next, write down all of the emotions that came up for you when you were triggered. Again, make sure that you are using words that describe emotions, not judgments. "I felt hurt" is an example of a feeling. "I felt uncared for" is a judgment. You can use the List of Feeling When Needs are Unmet in Relationships [in appendix D] if you need help. After labeling the emotions, write down all of the thoughts that you had about yourself and your partner when you were triggered.

Then, write down the specific behavior you did when you were triggered. Clearly stating what you did in that moment is important because that's what we're working on changing in therapy. Finally, describe the outcome of your behavior. What happened right after you did the behavior? Did you feel better? Did you feel worse? Did you feel more connected or more alone? Write down all the outcomes of your behavior.

SCBs Outcomes Log

Trigger	Feelings	Thoughts About Myself	Thoughts About My Partner	Schema	Behavior	Outcome

Example: SCBs Outcomes Log

Trigger	Feelings	Thoughts About Myself	Thoughts About My Partner	Schema	Behavior	Outcome
Mike didn't return my text for an hour	*Loneliness, fear, anger*	*I can never count on people. I will always be alone.*	*Mike is a jerk. He doesn't care about me. He doesn't make me a priority. I am not important to him.*	*Emotional deprivation and abandonment*	*I called him over and over again and kept texting him. I told him I can't count on him, and I said he's unreliable .*	*He became angry with me and felt more distant. He said I always blame him. We argued and yelled at each other.*
Mike said he couldn't pick up the kids from school because he was running late	*Rage, deprivation, loneliness, hopelessness*	*I'm alone in this relationship. I have to do everything myself.*	*I can never count on him. He is selfish. I can't depend on him.*	*Emotional deprivation*	*I picked up the kids from school and didn't express how I felt. Ignored him for the rest of the evening.*	*Felt more alone and distant*

The worksheet will help partners track conflicts that arise during the week, including their triggers, SCBs, and outcomes. Couples are asked to fill this out every week and review it in session until values and intentions are clarified. Once values and intentions are clarified (about three or four sessions), you can switch to using the Weekly Triggers Log (chapter 4) to track SCBs that are triggered outside of session.

Creative Hopelessness

Once you have clarified the formulation of the cycle that the couple gets stuck in and identified the negative outcomes that SCBs have for each partner and the relationship, it's time to make the shift from *workability* to cultivating *creative hopelessness*.

Creative hopelessness is a crucial process in ACT because it helps partners recognize the futility of trying to use avoidance strategies in attempts to eliminate pain, which is unavoidable in life—including in relationships. Experiences connected to our schemas—such as feelings of disappointment, fear, hurt, rejection, and aloneness—are a part of our programming and will continue to show up for us in all of our relationships. Creative hopelessness is the first stage toward an alternative way to respond to that pain.

SCBs lie at the root of relationship problems and continue to maintain the maladaptive cycle in the relationship. The thoughts, feelings, sensations, memories, and urges connected to our schemas are out of our control. Our partners' schemas and behaviors are also out of our control. The strategies we use as attempts to control and escape the unavoidable deep-rooted pain that gets triggered in all our romantic relationships end up creating and exacerbating the very pain we fear. These maladaptive strategies and attempts to try to suppress, numb, manage, and control the schema pain that is unavoidable in relationships are the problem, not the solution.

Whenever we try to avoid or block the primary pain connected to our schemas, our relationships are damaged. Creative hopelessness offers an alternative way to respond to pain. Pain is maintained and exacerbated when we continue to struggle with changing what is uncontrollable, rather than focusing our efforts on what is within our control—our behaviors and how we respond and relate to our schema pain. Our internal experiences are not the problem—how we respond to them is the problem.

Here are several questions you can ask the couple that will move you toward the creative hopelessness process:

> How often has this feeling connected to your __________ schema come up for you this week? This month?
>
> In how many other relationships has this experience come up for you?
>
> Have you had a romantic relationship in which the thoughts and feelings connected to your schema did not come up at all?
>
> In what other relationships does this pain show up? Has this come up for you with your mom, dad, siblings, coworkers, bosses, or friends?

Do you respond in a similar way when your schema gets triggered with others? Do you use similar SCBs? What are the outcomes in other relationships?

How common is this experience for you?

How long has this experience been with you?

How old are the thoughts connected to your schema?

What is one of the first memories you have of this pain? When was the first time this experience showed up for you?

These questions help couples recognize that this pain has been with them their whole lives and shows up in many different contexts. Assist couples in recognizing that all of their attempts to relieve their schema pain have not permanently eliminated this pain—and in fact have made it worse. The idea is that the more we try to get rid of the pain or eliminate it in the short run, the more damage it creates for us and our relationships in the long run.

Creative Hopelessness Metaphors

The metaphors that follow aim to help partners recognize that the strategies they've used in the past have done little to decrease their relationship pain, and that the more they try to avoid pain the stronger it becomes.

Although this concept may seem bleak or hopeless at first, it is actually promising. This concept encourages individuals not only to practice self-compassion, acceptance, and loving-kindness with their own schema pain but to take a compassionate, loving, and accepting stance toward their partner's schema pain. Use the following examples to guide how you might frame the metaphors when working with couples.

SCRATCHING THE ITCH

This metaphor describes the way SCBs may create a temporary relief from pain but end up making the pain worse in the long run.

Example Dialogue

Therapist: Trying to eliminate and soothe your schema-related pain by using SCBs can be likened to scratching parts of your body that have been exposed to poison ivy. It may be that your hand got in contact with poison ivy and feels incredibly itchy. Scratching this itch with your other hand may feel relieving and soothing for a moment, but now your other hand is contaminated, and everything you touch with your hands will get contaminated. The more you scratch, the better it feels in the moment but the worse it gets. The more you scratch, the more the rash spreads and spreads.

The alternative to coping with poison ivy is analogous to coping with schema pain: facing the pain; noticing where the itch is, where it hurts most; mindfully observing what the pain feels like; and watching your thoughts, feelings, and urges to scratch and not acting on those urges. The more you try to get away from your emotional pain using your SCBs, the deeper you dig yourself in. The more you try to escape and struggle, the more you get stuck.

What would happen if you stopped resisting and struggling? Have you ever allowed yourself to go with your emotions rather than fighting them? What would it be like if you allowed yourself to just notice the urges to struggle and escape? What if you dropped the struggle and gently observed the pain with curiosity, compassion, and kindness? Notice the moment when it starts slowly shifting or diminishing on its own.

THE SKY METAPHOR

This exercise can be used as a *self-as-context* exercise (discussed further in chapter 10) and/or as a creative hopelessness metaphor. This exercise highlights the transitory and unavoidable nature of schema pain by comparing thoughts and feelings connected to schemas to the weather: The belief that we can control the thoughts, feelings, and sensations that are connected to our schemas is like believing that we can control the weather.

Ask partners if it's possible, given that their pain has always been with them, that their pain is unavoidable. Just like bad weather is an unavoidable part of life, schema pain is also an unavoidable experience in relationships. Just like bad weather comes and goes, schema pain also shows up and then passes. It's not permanent, but it always comes back. The pain will continue to show up—it will get triggered by negative interpersonal events and will bring up specific thoughts ("I'll always be deprived," "He doesn't care," "My needs will never get met," "I'm alone in this relationship") and feelings (shame, loneliness, anger, hurt, disappointment) connected to schemas. Every day we have dozens of emotions and thousands of thoughts. So thoughts and feelings are not permanent states; they are temporary events that keep shifting and changing just like the weather. To help clarify the temporary nature of our thoughts and feelings, you might present the following metaphor of being the sky, not the weather (Hayes, Strosahl, & Wilson, 1999).

Example Dialogue

Therapist: Having different kinds of weather is necessary in life. After all, we wouldn't take the same delight in a beautiful sunny day if every day were bright and blue. Plus, we need rain and snow to supply us with water. Similarly, we need difficult emotions to remind us when we've gotten off course, when we are unhappy with something in our life, or when we have lost track of what's important. Although the weather is sometimes cloudy and dark, sometimes snowy and rainy, and sunshine comes and goes, the sky remains the same. The sky never changes; it remains the same, receiving each change in weather with perfect willingness.

The sky is not equal to the weather, just like you are not your thoughts or feelings. You may feel lonely, but it doesn't mean you're alone; you may feel guilty, but it doesn't mean you've done something wrong. You may have the thought that you failed, but it doesn't mean you are a failure. You, like the sky, are the container for all the different weather. The difficult thoughts and feelings that come up when your schema gets triggered are like a terrible, scary storm with thunder and lightning. But eventually the storm quiets and the air clears. Nothing has to change; we don't have to take any action to change the weather. The sky simply holds these storms and watches them fade away.

Do you think you could observe all of your different weather conditions without struggling or trying to change them? Could you just observe the sensations in your body, the thoughts that pop up in your mind, and the emotions that surge up and recede? Sometimes you're happy, sometimes sad, sometimes you're fearful. Would you be willing to notice all of your experience as it unfolds in the moment? Could you learn to just watch the experience as it comes and goes, staying aware of the fact that the experience is not a reflection of who you are or of your relationship? Just observing as the painful thoughts, feelings, and urges show up and then fade away?

THE CRYING BABY METAPHOR

This metaphor helps articulate the unavoidability of schema pain and suggests an alternative way to relate to one's own schema pain and one's partner's schema pain.

When partners are able to recognize that all the strategies they have used to try to avoid feeling deprivation, loneliness, disappointment, hurt, rejection, guilt, and so on in relationships haven't worked, continue the process of suggesting an alternative way to respond and relate to schema pain. Pose the following questions:

If trying to avoid and escape the pain connected to your schemas hasn't worked, could it be that the answer lies in something quite different? Something you haven't tried before?

What if the solution doesn't lie in running away from this pain but rather in the pain itself?

What if the answer lies in facing the pain and letting yourself truly feel and connect with all the difficult emotions connected to your schema?

Example Dialogue

Therapist: Imagine your schema pain is like a baby. Sometimes the baby feels hungry, confused, scared, or helpless. The baby doesn't know what it needs or how to meet his own needs. The baby just cries, screams, and yells. If you're in the same room with that baby, you may have an urge to avoid these screams and cries, to move away from the baby or push him farther away. But if you did that, the baby would get louder and more distressed. Instead you bring the baby closer, and even though the screams sound louder and the anxiety is more intense, you rock the baby and hold him tight. You hold him with kindness, compassion, and tenderness. You listen to the baby and soothe him, perhaps even saying, "It's okay," or "You're scared," or "I'm here for you," or "Don't be so sad." You may get curious about the pain and wonder if the baby is hungry or thirsty, or if he needs to be changed. You validate the fact that there is a need underneath this screaming and yelling. That there is valid pain and fear. If you move away from the baby or ignore the screams, he may cry even louder, but if you hold him closely with love and affection, sooner or later the crying will cease.

Our schema pain is the same way. Like a crying baby, at times it gets triggered and feels hurt, rejected, or abandoned. But if we are willing to sit with it and hold it gently with loving-kindness and compassion, it will pass. If we relate to it with harshness, impatience, and intolerance—instead of holding it with kindness and curiosity—it will always intensify.

Your schema pain—and your partner's—is going to continue to get triggered in your relationship, whether you intended it to or not. Can you relate to your own schema pain and your partner's pain as if it's a crying, deprived, and helpless baby? Can you be with it and stay patient, accepting, and loving? Does this pain have to be the enemy, or is it something you can have, observe, and hold kindly?

Creative hopelessness is accepting that this pain is unavoidable and that it will continue to show up in the relationship. It means committing to learning how to relate to one's own schema pain with more compassion and to make space in the relationship for the schema pain that shows up for one's partner as well. A partner's schema pain doesn't have to be the enemy. It doesn't have to be taken personally—no one needs to be blamed for it, and it doesn't need to be fixed or altered. Couples can learn to incorporate and welcome schema pain as it surfaces, making room for it in the relationship, and relating to it with curiosity, acceptance, and compassion.

What Do We Have Control Over?

It's important to help couples realize that the agenda of emotional control is the problem. Struggling to control the internal experiences connected to one's schema—feelings, thoughts, sensations, and urges—is the problem. The more we don't want to have an experience, the stronger it becomes. The more we try not to think of something, the more likely it will stay in our head. Have you ever gotten a song stuck in your head that you didn't like? The more you focus on how much you want to get rid of it, the longer it stays stuck in your mind. As soon as you accept that it's there, it suddenly disappears with no notice.

Another technique for helping couples understand the futility of attempting to control thoughts and feelings is to ask them to check in with their own experience in moments when they are struggling to control an internal experience. Inform them that you are going to give them a number between 1 and 10, and ask them: "Try your best not to think of the number that comes after number 1 and before number 3. Don't let this number come to your mind. Do your best not to think of the number between 1 and 3." Pause for a couple of seconds, and then say: "Do you know the number I'm referring to? Struggling to control your schemas makes them stronger and more intense. Trying to control the thoughts, feelings, sensations, and memories connected to your schemas only makes them more powerful. Trying to control your partner's behaviors so that your schemas don't get triggered doesn't block your schema pain—it damages your relationship. If control doesn't work then what are your options? What is in your control? What can you do to make things better?"

Remind couples about what is in our control and what's not:

Out of Our Control

- Universal relationship pain: All relationships come with some pain—deprivation, rejection, loneliness, helplessness, disappointment, hurt, insecurity, and so forth.
- Schema activation: Triggering situations will activate thoughts, feelings, sensations, and urges connected to our schemas. We bring our schemas with us into all of our relationships, including romantic ones.
- Our partner's schemas, behaviors, and reactions

Within Our Control

- Our behaviors
- Our values

What Are Our Options?

Given that our internal experiences are out of our control and that struggling to change what is out of our control is what keeps us stuck, what are our options? When we are unhappy with an aspect of our relationship or with our relationship as a whole, these are our options:

1. *We can change our own behaviors that contribute to damaging the relationship.* We can make requests instead of demands, increase appreciation and affection while decreasing hurtful behaviors, and/or assert ourselves by setting limits and boundaries.

2. *We can accept our partner or his or her behavior exactly as is.* We can choose to let go of the struggle and accept ourselves, our partner, a behavior, or the relationship without demanding change.

3. *We can recognize that our relationship is unacceptable to us and leave the relationship.*

4. *We can continue the struggle.* We can carry on responding in the same ways, doing the same behaviors, trying to control and change our partner rather than our own behaviors, and continue feeling unhappy in our relationship.

The goal is to replace maladaptive behaviors—which are under voluntary control—with behaviors that are consistent with the couple's values. This can help partners heal and learn new, effective ways of meeting their needs. Rather than focusing on overcoming schema pain, ACT focuses on replacing old behaviors with values-based actions, despite our schemas.

In the next chapter we help you clarify each partner's values as well as identify specific, alternative, values-based responses for each partner when he or she is triggered. You will work on helping couples identify specific behaviors that are based on their values and the kind of partners they want to be. You will also help couples track and monitor the outcomes of these new behaviors.

CHAPTER 4

Values Clarification for Couples

Once couples are better able to notice triggers, SCBs, and the thoughts, feelings, and urges connected to their schemas, the emphasis of treatment shifts toward practicing new interpersonal behaviors based on values.

The ACT approach uses values to help identify alternative behaviors that can replace SCBs, especially in moments of activation. This process begins with clarifying each partner's core values in the relationship and then converting these general concepts into specific behaviors that are congruent with their values (aka *values-based actions*). Throughout all of this work, it is important to continuously distinguish between new values-based actions and old SCBs.

This process can be undertaken in three steps. Initially, the focus is on understanding what values are and what they are not. The next phase consists of each partner clarifying his or her own values in the relationship. The last step is to identify specific values-based actions that each partner wants to practice in the relationship. As they practice new values-based actions, it's necessary to continue assessing whether these new behaviors are aligned with their set of values. There are numerous exercises and examples for each phase of the process listed in this chapter. In practice, you should assess which exercise would be most relevant and effective for each couple. It's not necessary to use every one.

Defining Values: A Chosen Meaningful Direction

Values reflect our deepest desire for how we want to be in the world, how we want to behave and interact with others, what matters to us most, and what we want to stand for. They guide and motivate our actions in our relationships, as they represent the kind of partner we aspire to be. In order to explore values on an individual level, begin by explaining what values are in a general sense.

Example Dialogue

Therapist: Your values define who you want to be and how you want to act. Your values assist in actualizing the kind of partner you want to be and what you want to stand for in your relationship. The importance of identifying core values lies in their power to guide actions in the moment. Every moment offers us an opportunity to take actions that bring us either closer to the kind of partner we want to be or farther away.

Values are like a compass, as they provide us with a sense of direction. There is an important distinction to be made, though, between a value and a goal. Where a value provides direction, a goal provides a destination. Values can never be "accomplished" in the same way a goal can, as they are a way of living and a way of being.

What Values Are and Aren't

Because values are such a crucial component throughout treatment and help clarify alternative behaviors to SCBs, it's important for therapists to understand what values actually are and what they aren't:

- **Values are not goals.** *Goals* are tangible, achievable destinations that may or may not be reached. *Values*, on the other hand, are a constant companion. They are neither tangible nor achievable. There is no scenario in which a value is met or accomplished; values merely inform our direction and orientation as we move through the world. This means that although we may never reach an ideal version of ourselves, we can choose at every moment to take steps that bring us closer to becoming that person. If an individual has a value of being appreciative, he or she will never be 100 percent appreciative all the time but will have moments of choice to get closer or farther away to being appreciative. An example of a goal that may bring that individual closer to the value of being appreciative may be to say "thank you" more often.
- **Values are freely chosen.** This means that values are not based on rules that we hold about ourselves, others, the world, relationships, or how things "should be." Rather, they are freely chosen representations of our deeply held principles. Because values are choices, they are not dictated by social norms or external expectations, nor do they necessitate defense or justification. Similar to one's individual musical taste or preference in food, values can never be wrong. They are valid because they are dictated by and for oneself. At times, partners may seem to choose values that they believe they "should" work on, or that they believe their partner wants them to work on. When you recognize that partners are choosing values based on rules and assumptions of what they "should be," challenge their rules and help them connect with their genuine ideals. Two exercises that you can use with couples to help them connect to their authentic values are the My Clone Exercise and the Perfect Partner Exercise (in chapter 4).
- **Values are not emotions or thoughts.** Feelings—such as happiness, confidence, or anxiety—are not values. They are *emotional states*, which are highly

variable. Values are a way of being in the world and are not contingent on external circumstances and limitations. If a partner states an emotion as a value, such as feeling safer or more trusting, ask him or her, "If you felt safer and more trusting in this relationship, how would you behave differently? How would it manifest? How would your partner know that you are feeling safer and more trusting in the relationship?" The answers to these questions will help you identify the partner's specific values-based actions and underlying values.

- **Values are not needs or wants.** The characteristics and traits we long for in a partner are not our values—they are the *needs* that we have in relationships. Values represent the kind of partner we desire to be and inform our actions and behaviors. Needs, on the other hand, are what we desire from our partner or how we would like him or her to be. Needs are out of our control; we can gently ask for a need to be met or make a request of our partner, but ultimately it is up to our partner whether he or she is willing to meet our need. Values, on the other hand, are always within our direct control. You can read more about the difference between values and needs in the section "Underlying Needs vs. Wants" in chapter 8.

- **Values are not contingent on outcomes.** Values-based actions are appraised based on their workability in the long run. There may be initial discomfort when changing behaviors; however, values are not contingent on a particular outcome. They are about and for the individual and his or her process of getting closer to the kind of person he or she wants to be remembered as. For example, if a partner has a value of being assertive and takes a step toward that value by making an assertive request or saying no, she may not get the outcome she desires. Her partner may not meet her request or may be angry at her for saying no. But she still took a step that brought her closer to her value of being assertive.

- **Values are not deficits.** Values are not a way of labeling our weaknesses or deficits. Identifying partners' values is not about assessing what they are lacking or needing to improve on; it's about clarifying what matters most. Even if we are already acting consistently with certain values, it still helps to identify them because values guide our actions. Therefore, clarifying values promotes intentional awareness of our actions in the moment and helps us assess the degree of alignment between our behaviors and our values.

- **Values rarely conflict.** It may appear that there are certain values that are in conflict or in competition. This conflict is usually not between values but between prioritizing the values' *domains*. Domains are categories in life where values can be actualized. Examples of values domains may be work, romantic relationships, friendships, health, and so on. These domains may reflect similar values or different ones. For example, Elizabeth maintains both the value of being productive as well as the value of being present with her family. This might seem like a conflict between values, but it's actually a conflict between two different domains, work and family, which are in competition for her time. It isn't possible to be 100 percent engaged in every domain all of the time. It is thus necessary to prioritize values across relationship domains (see Values Domains Worksheet, chapter 4). We may also prioritize different domains at various times in our life. For example, in adolescence we may prioritize friendships and romantic relationships, and as we get older, we may find that health and family become more of a priority. Helping partners rate the importance of different domains may assist in resolving what may seem to be a conflict in values.

Values are not a means to an end—they *are* the end. Our values are always under our control regardless of circumstance. They are choices, not conditions, and can be actualized at any moment.

Identifying Values with Couples

Once the concept of values has been explained and understood, have partners compose a list of their own individual values. Use the following exercises to help narrow down these key principles. You can start by asking couples the following questions:

What kind of partner do you want to be remembered as? (For example, a partner who is spontaneous, appreciative, affectionate, accepting, emotionally available, expressive, assertive, etc.)

What do you want to stand for in your relationships?

What's important for you in relationships?

What kind of partner do you want to be when your ________________ schema is triggered?

What kind of partner do you want to be when you feel sad?

What kind of partner do you want to be when you feel inadequate and/or insecure?

What kind of partner do you want to be when you're angry?

What kind of partner do you want to be when you feel doubt or ambivalence about your relationship?

Values in Relationships

These are examples of values in relationships to help couples clarify key values.

Accepting
Adventurous
Altruistic
Appreciative
Assertive
Attentive
Attuned
Available
Committed
Compassionate
Composed
Considerate
Consistent
Contributing
Curious
Decisive
Deliberate
Dependable
Determined
Empathic
Encouraging
Engaged
Expressive
Fair
Firm
Flexible
Forgiving
Forthright
Fun
Generous
Gentle
Genuine
Grateful
Honest
Humorous
Independent
Inquisitive
Kind
Loving
Loyal
Mindful
Patient
Persistent
Present
Productive
Punctual
Reliable
Respectful
Romantic
Self-advocating
Self-aware
Self-compassionate
Self-disciplined
Sensitive
Sensual
Sexual
Spontaneous
Supportive
Tactful
Trustworthy
Understanding
Validating
Vulnerable

Wedding Anniversary

This exercise is adapted from the work of Russ Harris (2009). Ask the couple to imagine writing their own wedding vows from the perspective of their partner. What would they want their partner to say about them, their character, their behaviors, and their most appreciated qualities? Remember this is not about what one partner really would say about the other but rather what he or she would most want to hear.

Funeral

This exercise was developed by Hayes, Strosahl, and Wilson (1999). Ask couples to imagine that they have passed away and are witnessing their own funeral. Ask what they would want to hear their partner say about them. What would they want to be remembered for by their partner? What would they want their family and friends to say about their relationship and the kind of partner they were? Again, this is not about what would be said in reality but what they would ideally like to hear.

Talking to Grandchildren

Ask the couple to imagine teaching their grandchildren about values-based relationships. Have them begin by describing their relationship. What would they want to share with their grandkids? What would they want to express to them about what each person stood for in the relationship and the kind of partner each was?

Describe Someone You Admire

Have the couple think of someone they admire in order to help them explore the qualities and characteristics of the ideal partner. It can be a friend, relative, or a fictional character from a movie. Start a discussion about what that individual represents and embodies. Ask what qualities they admire about the person, what characteristics and values he or she has that they appreciate. How does he or she communicate? What does his or her body language look like? How does he or she behave during a conflict with a partner? How does he or she behave when triggered? When he or she is angry? Bored? Lonely? Mistrustful? Hurt?

This exercise will help couples identify shared core values that can then be connected to specific behaviors that they practice in the relationship. Oftentimes, individuals who have difficulty identifying the kind of partner they want to be have a much easier time recognizing these qualities by describing someone else.

Example Dialogue

The following dialogue illustrates how to begin the process of identifying core values with couples:

Therapist: I'd like to talk a little bit about values today. Values represent the kind of partner you want to be and what you want to stand for in your relationships. The values that we will identify today will continue to guide our work together for the rest of our sessions. Moving forward, we will explore your behavior in terms of whether that behavior is consistent with your values. We will want to watch whether the behavior brings you closer to or farther away from the values that we're identifying today, and we will explore how you want to behave differently. What are your thoughts about that?

Lauren and Mark: [Nodding in agreement]

Therapist: Imagine that we are time traveling into the far future and that you are observing your own funeral. Your partner, kids, grandkids, and all of your closest friends are there, and they're all describing the kind of partner that you were and the kind of relationship that you had. What would you most want to hear? Lauren, what would you want most to hear from Mark about what kind of partner you were and what you stood for and how you behaved in your relationship? And Mark, what would you want to hear the most from Lauren?

Lauren: I would want him to say that I was loving, accepting, compassionate, kind… I'm not sure what else.

Therapist: Well, imagine someone you really admire, someone who represents an ideal version of the kind of partner you want to be. Do you have someone in mind? What kind of qualities does that person have? How does he or she behave when scared, abandoned, or lonely?

Lauren: She is curious, she asks questions, and she tries to be flexible and open. She remains patient, but she also expresses her needs and communicates her feelings clearly.

Therapist: Do some of these values resonate with you? Are flexibility and curiosity important values for you? Do you want to express your feelings and needs openly?

Lauren: Yes. I would like to be able to do that, but it's hard to do when I feel mistrustful and suspicious.

Therapist: It's difficult to recognize your values in moments when you're triggered. The fear pulls you toward doing old behaviors.

Lauren: [Nodding in agreement]

Therapist: What about you Mark? What do you want to stand for in this relationship? What kind of partner do you want to be when you feel engulfed and trapped?

Mark: Well, I don't want to withdraw. I want to be able to stay and hear her, but it's very hard when she's so demanding.

Therapist: I think there will be times when it is hard, and it's not unusual for our minds to want to point to where things won't work. But can you notice that your mind is trying to pull you away? Can you still describe your values? Let's go back to your own funeral. Imagine Lauren describing the kind of partner you were, and it's exactly what you would like to hear—what would that sound like? You can take a look at this list of values to help you. [Hands him the Values in Relationships list.] Do any of these resonate with you?

Mark: That I am supportive, fair, that I consider her feelings. I want to be able to listen to her and take care of her but also still be able to take care of myself and assert myself when I need to. I would want her to say that I'm reliable and caring. Also that I'm compassionate and make an effort.

Therapist: So what I'm hearing is that some of your values [to Mark] include being supportive, fair, considerate, and compassionate? And some of your values [to Lauren] include being curious, flexible, expressive, and open? Is that correct?

Mark and Lauren: [Nodding in agreement]

Therapist: Would you like to take a look at the triggers that came up for you this week? We can look at how you behaved when you got triggered, explore whether it was consistent with your values, and clarify how you would like to behave differently the next time you get triggered.

Mark and Lauren: Okay.

This dialogue is the beginning of the process of identifying partners' values. After general values are identified, the next step is turning these values into specific actions that are consistent with all the values mentioned.

Clarifying Values Across Relationship Domains

During the course of a session or two, help partners identify core values and behaviors that are consistent across important relationship *domains*. Values domains are categories of different areas in life where values can be enacted: in work, friendship, health, recreation, and so forth. In this book we focus only on certain domains within the arena of intimate relationships. For each domain, have partners rate the importance of the domain, then write down the core values for the domains that the couple rated high in importance. (Partners don't have to fill out values for all domains; they can choose to focus on the domains they both find most important.)

Finally, have partners identify a specific action that is congruent with all the values in that particular domain. The goal is to help couples identify specific actions that they would like to practice in particular situations that are consistent with multiple values in the domain. This process helps partners recognize new ways of relating to each other that are based on what truly matters to them, rather than using old SCBs as a short-term strategy for avoiding pain. You can use the following worksheet (also provided in appendix D and online at http://www.newharbinger.com/34800) to assist in this process.

Values Domains Worksheet

Relationship Domains	Importance (0–10)	Values	Values-Based Action
Communication			
Sex			
Parenting			
Money			
Affection			
Work			
Conflict			
Decision Making/ Negotiation			
Friendship/ Extended Family			
Shared Activities			

Example: Values Domains Worksheet

Relationship Domains	Importance (0–10)	Values	Values-Based Action
Communication	*10*	*Expressive, open, kind, honest, flexible, compassionate, cooperative, assertive*	*Express appreciation and gratitude, reflectively listen to my partner, stand up for myself, and say no when I don't want to do something*
Sex	*8*	*Spontaneous, fair, appreciative, loving, flexible, altruistic, respectful, assertive, encouraging, adventurous*	*Give feedback about what I enjoy, reciprocate and ask for feedback about what my partner enjoys, discuss a new thing we would like to try in bed*
Parenting	*10*	*Fair, kind, assertive, firm, curious, compassionate, supportive, encouraging, consistent*	*Collaboratively decide consequences for the children, agree with each other next to the kids and then discuss disagreements in private, discuss the pros and cons of private school vs. public school for Katy*
Money	*8*	*Fair, generous, flexible, open, collaborative, expressive, supportive, contributing*	*Discuss any expenses that are more than $1,000, hire a housecleaner once a month, discuss bank account structure*
Affection	*10*	*Sensual, loving, tender, gentle, cooperative, inquisitive, assertive, expressive, romantic*	*Ask for a hug or a kiss, give my partner a massage, ask my partner if he wants a hug*

Work	*8*	*Productive, assertive, balanced, persistent, consistent, determined, fair, flexible, firm*	*Work a maximum of 8 hours a day, only return e-mails on weekdays*
Conflict	*10*	*Honest, open, fair, considerate, firm, compassionate, curious, understanding, empathic, gentle, kind*	*Ask for a time-out when I am triggered, say "I feel hurt" when I feel angry, write down my needs and feelings after a fight*
Decision Making/ Negotiation	*10*	*Persistent, determined, firm, fair, open, flexible*	*Check in about a decision that has been made, ask for help, make pros and cons list together about schools, brainstorm ideas for anniversary*
Friendship/ Extended Family	*9*	*Considerate, cooperative, patient, assertive, supportive*	*Spend time with Tom and Mary once a month, have grandparents visit once a month*
Shared Activities	*8*	*Fun, humorous, spontaneous, open, cooperative, considerate*	*Go for a walk together once a week, go to the gym together once a week, go to a movie once a month*

After filling out this worksheet and discussing it with the couple, explore with them which values they would like to focus on during the week.

The next step is to identify alternative behaviors based on values that partners will commit to practicing. When helping partners commit to values-based actions, it's beneficial to be as precise as possible—to identify the specific behavior they will do, what values they're connected to, and when they will engage in the behavior. For example, if Mike wants to focus on the communication domain for the week, he may identify practicing reflective listening with Amanda on Thursday night for fifteen minutes with the intention of moving toward being a supportive partner.

Identifying Values-Based Actions

Identifying values-based actions involves (1) combining several values into a congruent behavior, and (2) clarifying what alternative behaviors to SCBs would look like. Values-based actions are specific behaviors and steps that allow partners to actualize their chosen values. Two important parts of this process are helping partners (1) identify precisely how the behavioral manifestation of their values appears in any given situation, and (2) prioritize their most important values in moments when particular schemas are triggered.

Continuing with the example of the previous couple, let's look at what Lauren has identified:

Appreciative: Say "thank you" every time Mike makes dinner; give an authentic compliment every day.

Assertive: Say "let me think about it" to any request, or say no, ask for help, or express discomfort.

Vulnerable: Share a fear, express an emotion, or ask for help.

The following worksheet helps partners clarify what values-based actions they will practice, when they will practice these, and what potential barriers may show up.

Values-Based Actions Worksheet

Value	Importance (1–10)	Values-Based Behavior	Thoughts That Act as Barriers (stories, expectations, predictions)	Feelings That Act as Barriers (shame, guilt, fear, helplessness)	When will I practice this new behavior?	Am I willing to have these barriers and still take steps toward my value?

Values-Based Actions Worksheet

Value	Importance (1–10)	Values-Based Behavior	Thoughts That Act as Barriers (stories, expectations, predictions)	Feelings That Act as Barriers (shame, guilt, fear, helplessness)	When will I practice this new behavior?	Am I willing to have these barriers and still take steps toward my value?
Curious	*9*	*Ask open-ended questions.* *Listen*	*He's lying.* *I'm going to be fooled.* *I can't trust him.*	*Fear* *Anger* *Suspicion* *Anxiety*	*When I feel disappointed or suspicious or have an urge to withdraw*	*Yes*
Assertive	*9*	*Say no.*	*I'm selfish.* *I don't want to be demanding.* *He'll be disappointed.*	*Guilt* *Responsibility* *Obligation* *Fear*	*When I feel ambivalent about something* *When I feel uncomfortable or obligated*	*Yes*
Vulnerable	*8*	*Express a feeling.* *Makes a request.*	*I'm going to be disappointed.* *e won't follow through.* *I'll get dismissed.*	*Fear* *Guilt* *Anxiety*	*When I feel hurt* *When I feel alone* *When I need support* *When I have the thought Mike doesn't understand me*	*Yes*
Independent	*8*	*Go to the gym.* *Have a friends' night out.*	*What is he doing?* *Is he flirting with other people?* *I can't trust him.*	*Fear* *Suspicion* *Doubt* *Loneliness* *Longing*	*Every Thursday Once a week When I feel guilty*	*Yes*

The following exercises help couples identify the specific behaviors that they would like to increase and decrease in the relationship. These exercises can facilitate the process of turning general values into specific actions that can replace SCBs.

The Perfect Partner Exercise

This exercise has been adapted from the book *ACT with Love* (Harris, 2009). It is very useful in helping couples see the relationship between values and actions.

First, have both partners make a list of all the things they want their partner to change. You might say, "Write down all of the behaviors that your partner does that upset you. Write down at least ten specific behaviors that you want your partner to change. What would you want him or her to do less or do more of?"

Once partners have completed the list, ask them to imagine that a miracle has happened and their partner has made all the changes that they wanted him or her to make—every single negative behavior mentioned on the list has been changed. You might say, "Now your partner is the perfect partner for you and meets all your needs and wants: never criticizes you, is never late, always follows through, is a great listener, is expressive and loving. Now, turn the paper around and on the other side of the paper write down all of the ways you would behave differently if your partner changed. How would you behave in this relationship if your partner no longer did the negative behaviors you mentioned on the other side of the paper? Write as many specific behaviors that you would do differently if your partner made all the changes you long for."

If partners wrote down feelings such as, "I would feel happier or calmer or safer," then ask them, "If you felt happier and calmer in this relationship, how would you behave differently? How would your partner notice that you feel happier and calmer? What behaviors of yours would change? What would your partner notice? If there was a camera watching you, but the camera had no audio, only video, how would your partner notice you acting differently?"

Keep the discussion going. Ask partners if any of the ways they would behave differently are behaviors that are connected to their values.

Have them write down the specific values that these behaviors are connected to.

Ask each individual whether there is a gap between the partner he or she wants to be and the partner he or she is being.

This exercise presents couples with the option to choose to behave consistently with these values, regardless of how the other person chooses to be. It demonstrates that behaviors and values are not contingent on the other partner's behaviors and values. Nothing has to change in order for a person to start taking steps toward improving the way they relate in their relationships. One's thoughts, feelings, sensations—and even one's partner—don't have to change in order to start doing new behaviors.

Flip Card Exercise

Begin by having each partner write down all the negative thoughts and feelings that come up for them connected to their schema. Then ask them to write down all of the negative thoughts and feelings that come up about themselves, their partner, and the relationship as a result. If couples have difficulty identifying these, have them either look at their triggers log and use thoughts and feelings from the log or think of a recent conflict and recall the thoughts and feelings that came up in that conflict.

Now have partners turn the paper over and, on the other side, write down all of the specific things that these thoughts and feelings have stopped them from doing in the relationship. Ask them, "Is there anything important that any of these thoughts or feelings have stopped you from doing in this relationship this week? This month? This year? Has the feeling of ______________ ever stopped you from doing anything important in this relationship? Has the thought ______________ ever stopped you from taking important actions connected to your values?"

Help the couple connect these behaviors to specific values that each has in the relationship, and write these values down. The purpose of this is to help partners recognize that pain and values are on the opposite sides of the same coin, and that you can't push negative experience further away without also pushing values further away. Invite partners to bring the side of the paper with the negative thoughts and feelings close to their face. Ask them, "What do you usually do when this experience shows up? How do you relate to this experience?"

Help partners identify the old schema coping behaviors they do to avoid and get rid of the negative thoughts and feelings connected to their schema. Every time they identify a coping behavior, ask them to move the paper farther away from their face to show how they try to move away from this experience. When the paper is far away from their face, help them recognize that the values on the other side of the paper are also farther away from them. This illustrates that the more they use SCBs to get rid of their experience, the farther away they are from their values and the kind of partner they want to be.

Follow the above with further exploration of engaging values-based behavior rather than schema-driven behavior. You can ask partners a number of questions:

> Would you be willing to bring these negative thoughts and feelings closer to you and still do the important behaviors that you identified on the other side of the paper?
>
> Would you be willing to bring all the schema-driven pain closer to you, and stay loving and curious with it, if it means that you will be closer to your values (on the other side of the paper)?
>
> Would you be willing to have these negative stories about your partner and yourself, and still take a step toward one of these values-based actions?
>
> Would it be possible to take steps that bring you closer to these values without bringing some of these negative thoughts and feelings (on the other side of the page) closer?

If partners are willing to bring the pain closer to them in order to move toward their values, bring the paper physically closer to them, and have them gently hold it and look at it. Have them notice what it feels like to look at the thoughts and feelings on the paper with curiosity and compassion.

My Clone Exercise

One exercise you can use with couples to help them connect to their freely chosen values is presenting them with the following scenario: "What if you had a clone of yourself or a robot that was an idealized version of you. Your clone can do everything you do, but better. It can accomplish all of your tasks and activities perfectly. What are the parts of your relationship that you would reserve just for yourself? The things you love so much that you would not want your clone to do instead of you? What are the things that you would want your clone to do instead of you? What are the behaviors that you fear or avoid doing that you would still prefer to do, over having your clone do them for you?"

Using the Triggers Log to Identify Values-Based Actions

Using the log that follows, discuss the behaviors of each partner upon being triggered during the week. Next, discuss and observe the outcomes of these behaviors. Explore the degree of consistency each incident had with each partner's set of values, and identify alternative values-based actions that each would like to practice in the future. (Note that when partners respond to triggers in a manner consistent with their set of values, they will not need to identify alternative vales-based behaviors or moments of choice.) It is important to highlight the moment of choice, when old schema-driven thoughts and feelings present, in order for there to be marked change in the future.

Weekly Triggers Log

Trigger	Thoughts (thoughts, stories, expectations, predictions, etc., that acted as barriers)	Feelings (feelings that acted as barriers: shame, fear, guilt, etc.)	Behavior (What did you do?)	Values (What values is this behavior connected to? Was your behavior consistent with those values?)	Values-Based Action (How would you have liked to behave differently?)	Moment of Choice (When did you have a choice to behave differently?)

Example: Weekly Triggers Log

Trigger	Thoughts (thoughts, stories, expectations, predictions, etc., that acted as barriers)	Feelings (feelings that acted as barriers: shame, fear, guilt, etc.)	Behavior (What did you do?)	Values (What values is this behavior connected to? Was your behavior consistent with those values?)	Values-Based Action (How would you have liked to behave differently?)	Moment of Choice (When did you have a choice to behave differently?)
Bill's mom bought us a couch for our new home without informing us.	*He never sets boundaries with her.* *He doesn't respect me.* *She's going to keep intruding in our life.* *He always takes her side.*	*Angry* *Disappointed* *Helpless* *Guilty* *Fearful*	*Blamed Bill.* *Got angry.* *Demanded that he stand up to her.*	*Flexible* *Curious* *Empathic* *Assertive* *No*	*Express my feelings and needs to Bill.* *Ask him to negotiate how we want to set boundaries with his mom.*	*Next time Bill makes a decision I disagree with.* *When Bill's mom makes a decision for us.* *When I feel helpless.*
Bill discussed our fight with a mutual friend.	*He doesn't have boundaries.* *Our friends are going to judge us.* *He doesn't respect me.*	*Embarrassed* *Ashamed* *Angry* *Helpless*	*Yelled at him.* *Blamed him.* *Threatened him.*	*No* *Compassionate* *Assertive* *Fair* *Flexible*	*Ask him questions and try to understand his needs.* *Express my feelings and needs.* *Request to negotiate solutions.*	*When Bill and I have a disagreement.* *When I feel angry or helpless.*
Bill canceled our plans so he could help his mom.	*He never prioritizes me.* *I'm not important.* *I'm alone in this.*	*Deprived* *Angry* *Alone* *Disappointed*	*Expressed my disappointment and hurt.* *Validated his feelings and needs.*	*Yes* *Assertive* *Fair* *Flexible*		

Clarifying Alternative Behaviors Based on Values

Now that both partners are clear about their values in the relationship, they will be able to identify new values-based actions and detect moments of choice when they might act according to their values. If partners have difficulty expressing themselves in a values-consistent way due to skills deficits, teach them skills from chapter 8 to help them communicate effectively.

The following dialogue is a continuation of Mark and Lauren's from the previous example. Earlier in the chapter the couple identified their values in the relationship. The dialogue assumes that key communication skills have been acquired.

Example Dialogue

Therapist: Did any triggers or conflicts come up for you this week that you would like to discuss in today's session?

Lauren: I got very triggered on Thursday night because Mark went out with his friends and told me that he would be back at 10 p.m. and didn't get home until 11:15 p.m.

Therapist: What schema got triggered for you?

Lauren: That feeling that I'm alone, that I'll never be able to rely on anyone to be there for me.

Therapist: At what moment did you notice this experience get triggered?

Lauren: I started noticing it around 9:45 p.m. I already started feeling very anxious and anticipating that he wasn't going to get home on time. I had a lot of scary thoughts like: I'm not important to him, he's going to be late again, I can't count on him, I'm alone in this relationship.

Therapist: In that moment when you noticed yourself feeling triggered, what did you do?

Lauren: I called him and texted him. I tried to reach him a couple times, but I didn't hear back from him, which made me more upset.

Therapist: [To Mark] What was going on for you at that time?

Mark: I responded to her first message and I told her that I'm running a little late. Then she started guilt-tripping me about how I'm never there for her and I'm unreliable, so I got very annoyed. Then she continued to text over and over again asking when I'm going to get home and who I'm with and why they are more important than she is. At that point I was so angry that I just ignored her messages.

Therapist: What experience got triggered for you?

Mark: I felt angry, guilty, trapped, suffocated.

Therapist: So the experience of engulfment showed up for you, and the way that you coped in the moment was to avoid her messages?

Mark: [Nodding head in agreement]

Therapist: And the way you [turning to Lauren] coped with it in that moment was to continue seeking reassurance and reaching out to him—is that correct?

Mark and Lauren: Yes.

Therapist: Would you be willing to rewind and walk through this moment again and clarify your values and how you would have liked to behave differently?

Mark and Lauren: Yes.

Therapist: Mark, when was the moment that you noticed that you might be running late? What happened for you at that moment?

Mark: I was working on a project with my colleague and I realized around 8 p.m. that it would probably take us longer than I thought it would. I started feeling guilty and anxious about how Lauren would react.

Therapist: If you were able to accept guilt and anxiety—to be present to those feelings without them dictating your actions—what values would you want to go toward? What do you want to be about when guilt and fear about Lauren's reaction show up?

Mark: I want to be considerate and honest, and I also want to be able to stand up for myself.

Therapist: What might that look like in that moment?

Mark: Calling her as soon as I realized that I might be late and explaining to her that we had some problems with the computer and that it's taking longer than anticipated.

Therapist: What would standing up for yourself look like in this situation?

Mark: I would want to assert myself by explaining that this project is very important to me, and I'd ask her if she would be okay with me staying an extra hour so that we can finish up.

Therapist: Lauren, how would you want to react if Mark called you and explained that?

Lauren: It just makes me so angry when he's late. He never makes me a priority.

Therapist: I can imagine that when you get into that place, that it feels very hard, just as it does for Mark to choose something else. The feelings are powerful and seem to take on a life of their own… Being willing to experience them and choosing a different response feels challenging, but in some ways necessary given what you want in the relationship… If the feelings of anger and loneliness were not in charge, how would you want to behave? What kind of partner do you want to be when this experience shows up for you?

Lauren: I want to be able to hear him out without getting so reactive, but I also want to be assertive. I don't want him to think it's okay to be ignoring me and showing up late.

Mark: I'm rarely ever late and I was working on something important. I can't stand it when you're so controlling. This is why it's better to just ignore you, because there's no negotiating with you.

Therapist: What got triggered right now?

Mark: I'm the bad guy again. It's always my fault. I feel bad. I'm in a lose-lose situation.

Therapist: You feel stuck? Helpless?

Mark: Yeah. I guess I feel guilty. Like I always do the wrong thing.

Therapist: It's difficult to recognize how you want to behave when you feel that every move you make is wrong. The fear becomes very overwhelming.

Mark: [Nodding head]

Therapist: Let's see if we can notice how overwhelming this is and still check in on your values. What do you want to stand for right now in this moment? Let's remember the values you've described including consideration, honesty, assertiveness, and curiosity. What can it look like to do something that brings you closer to these values right now?

Mark: Lauren, I understand that it's difficult for you when plans change and that it feels very unstable and you feel alone, but can you understand that in this particular case, this was very important for me and I just needed a little more flexibility from you?

Lauren: I know this project was really important for you. I understand that, but when I try to reach out to you and I don't hear back from you, it really hurts me. I feel scared and confused and angry. I need more consistency and feedback from you.

Mark: I want to discuss these things with you in the moment and negotiate with you. But it's difficult for me when I feel guilty and attacked.

Lauren: I'm willing to negotiate with you and understand that there are circumstances when you need to change plans. Are you willing to communicate better with me in the future? Let me know ahead of time if you think you're going to be late and reassure me of the time that you will be home?

Mark: I'm willing to do that. I don't want to ignore you. I want to be honest and consistent with you.

Therapist: Lauren, would you be willing to experience that feeling of loneliness and fear, and still take steps toward curiosity and flexibility the next time your experience of abandonment gets triggered?

Lauren: Yeah. I'd like to be more curious and flexible when I feel like this. It's hard to be understanding in those moments. I forget that he is doing his best and I start feeling suspicious and scared.

Therapist: What specific behavior can you do the next time that you feel suspicious and alone, and you start having thoughts that he is selfish and bad?

Lauren: The next time I start getting suspicious of Mark, and I have an impulse to call him selfish, I'm going to ask him a question instead and try to understand what's happening for him.

Therapist: What about you, Mark? What do you want to do when you have the urge to avoid Lauren and withdraw from her? What can you do during those moments that will bring you closer to being consistent, considerate, and assertive?

Mark: Next time I have an urge to avoid Lauren's calls or texts, I'm going to let her know that I'm starting to feel guilty and overwhelmed and try to negotiate with her more clearly.

The therapist uses the discussions of recent conflicts to clarify triggers and alternative behaviors, and to identify the cues when there's a moment of choice to engage in values-based actions. The therapist specifies what behavior each partner will practice in the future and when he or she will practice it.

Values and Schema Pain

Our pain tells us about what we value, and our values give us information about our pain. For example, anxious feelings prior to an exam are emotional indicators that the exam is important. Angry feelings may reveal that boundaries have been crossed. Schemas function similarly. Individuals who have a social isolation/alienation schema often find community and friendships to be important. Individuals with a self-sacrifice/subjugation schema often find fairness and consideration important. Those with an abandonment/instability schema often find consistency, connection, and reliability to be a priority. Oftentimes values-based actions contrast directly with schema coping behaviors.

Observing this pain can reveal information about what an individual finds important and meaningful. After identifying all the thoughts and feelings that are connected to a particular schema, asking couples the following questions will assist in finding the meaning of their pain and their underlying values:

> Is there something important that this pain is trying to tell you?
>
> Have these thoughts and feelings ever stopped you from doing something important? What have these thoughts and feeling stopped you from doing in your relationships?
>
> If all of these thoughts and feelings connected to your ______________ schema were permanently gone, and you never had these experiences again, what else would be gone? Would something important be missing?

You might say, for example, "If the guilt associated with your self-sacrifice schema disappeared and you never felt guilty again, how would that impact your relationships? What does the guilt tell you about what's important to you and what matters to you in relationships? Can it be that this experience is reminding you of something that matters to you?" Help the individual notice that the function of guilt is to help individuals feel empathy. It encourages them to be collaborative and fair, and stops them from doing harm to others or taking unethical actions.

All feelings have an important function. Shame is a reminder that community and belonging are important, anger indicates that boundaries have been crossed, and anxiety presents in conjunction with things or events of great importance. Getting curious about our pain can help us decipher what really matters to us.

It is common, however, for individuals to mistake their SCBs for values. They may confuse values and wrongly identify a value that actually assists in their avoidance strategy. In other words, they may be acting out an SCB under the guise of a values-based action. For example, someone with an abandonment schema who tends to cope with a fear of abandonment by giving in, accommodating, and surrendering might identify "acceptance" as a value. In this case, this value may function as a justification for tolerating and "accepting" all of a partner's hurtful behaviors in order to escape abandonment. When values are used rigidly in this way they are actually functioning as schema avoidance, with acceptance being used, in this case, as a means to avoid abandonment.

It is essential to distinguish between behaviors that bring individuals closer to their values and those that are simply alternative versions of old schema coping behaviors. It is important for the therapist to regularly check in on the function of the behavior, helping couples clarify and differentiate values-based actions from covert attempts at avoiding pain.

One way to do this is to simply ask partners whether the behavior is new or old, and whether it is moving them farther away from pain or closer to a value. Not only do these questions reveal the rationale behind a chosen value, they are also a practical exercise in introspection. Helping couples learn to discriminate between a value that is freely chosen and one that is based on rules, feelings of obligation, or avoidance of fears is a key part of success.

Assessing Degree of Alignment with Values

The three worksheets that follow can be used with couples to help them track how aligned their behaviors are with their values. They can be used throughout the week to monitor treatment progress and whether individuals feel that they and/or their partner are increasing values-congruent behaviors. (The worksheets are also provided in appendix D and online at http://www.newharbinger.com/34800.)

The first worksheet, Monitoring Values Throughout the Week, provides a general way to monitor values-consistent behaviors. Have couples rate the importance of each value and then rate themselves and their partner's level of consistency with these values from 0 to 100 percent, zero being completely inconsistent with the value and 100 being completely consistent. This worksheet is helpful to use with couples who are ambivalent about the relationship. Ambivalent partners struggle with committing to working on the relationship and tend to have one foot in and one foot out. This creates a dynamic by which neither one is willing to be the first to change behaviors, and so they remain on the fence about the relationship. Using this worksheet can help partners recognize the cost of not engaging in new behaviors. It can show them how being inconsistent with their own values makes it difficult for them to choose whether to stay in the relationship or to leave it—or even to know whether the relationship is workable—because they are not being the kind of partner they want to be.

Encourage partners to focus only on changing their own behaviors and to stay mindful and curious about whether or not their partner's behaviors change. As long as they continue *not* to change their own behaviors, they will continue feeling stuck on the fence.

Monitoring Values Throughout the Week

Thinking about the past week, how consistent have your behaviors been with your values? How consistent have your partner's behaviors been? First, begin by entering each of your values, then rate the importance of each value. For each value, rate yourself on how consistent you have been between 0 and 100 percent, 100 being that all your behaviors have been consistent with this value, and 0 being that none of your behaviors were consistent with this value. Then rate your partner.

Sample: Monitoring Values Throughout the Week

Relationship Values	Importance (1–10)	My Consistent Behaviors (0–100%)	My Partner's Consistent Behaviors (0–100%)
Kind	*9*	*60%*	*45%*
Compassionate	*10*	*65%*	*40%*
Assertive	*10*	*30%*	*80%*
Curious	*10*	*40%*	*40%*
Accepting	*10*	*35%*	*30%*
Cooperative	*9*	*70%*	*40%*
Flexible	*9*	*50%*	*20%*
Fair	*10*	*60%*	*45%*
Expressive	*9*	*25%*	*45%*
Honest	*10*	*75%*	*45%*
Open	*10*	*60%*	*70%*
Appreciative	*10*	*20%*	*30%*

These next two worksheets can also be applied to monitor partners' values-congruent behaviors throughout the week. These can inform treatment progress as well as track the specific actions that each partner engaged in that were either consistent or inconsistent with values. When reviewing behaviors that were inconsistent with values, help partners identify alternative behaviors they would like to practice instead.

While filling out the worksheets, have partners reflect on their behaviors during the week. What actions did each take that were consistent with their values? What actions did they take that were inconsistent with values?

In the first column, have partners enter each of their values. In the second column, ask them to write down the specific actions they took that were *consistent* with those values, and then have them write down how their partner responded to their values-based actions. In the next columns, have them write down the behaviors that were *inconsistent* with those values, as well as how their partner responded. Finally, in the last column, have partners rate themselves for overall consistency with their values for the week from 0 to 100 percent, 100 being that all their behaviors were consistent with that value, and 0 being that none of their behaviors were consistent with the value.

Alignment with Values Worksheet

Thinking about the past week, how consistent were *your behaviors* with your values? First, begin by entering each of your values. Then write down actions you've taken during the week that were *consistent* with those values. Include how your partner responded to your behaviors. Next, write down the actions you've taken that were *inconsistent* with those values, as well as how your partner responded. Finally, give *yourself* an overall rating (0–100%) for values-consistent actions for the week.

Relationship Values	Values-Consistent Actions	Outcome (How did your partner respond?)	Values-Inconsistent Actions	Outcome (How did your partner respond?)	Rating for Values-Based Actions This Week (0–100%)

For the following Alignment with Values Worksheet for Partner, individuals follow the same instructions as the previous worksheet but fill it out according to *their partner's behaviors* during the week. Have individuals write down the values-consistent behaviors that their partner did and how they responded, as well as the values-inconsistent actions that their partner engaged in and how they responded. Finally, have individuals rate their partner in terms of his or her values-consistent behaviors for the week from 0 to 100 percent.

Alignment with Values Worksheet for Partner

Thinking about the past week, how consistent were *your partner's behaviors* with your values? First, begin by entering each of your values, then write down actions your partner has taken this week that were *consistent* with those values. How did you respond to your partner's behaviors? Next, write down behaviors your partner did that were *inconsistent* with those values. How did you respond? Finally, give *your partner* an overall rating (0–100%) for values-consistent actions for the week.

Relationship Values	Partner's Values-Consistent Actions	Outcome (How did you respond?)	Partner's Values-Inconsistent Actions	Outcome (How did you respond?)	Rating for Your Partner's Values-Based Actions This Week (0–100%)

These two worksheets encourage individuals to remain mindful of their level of consistency with the values that they've identified for themselves. They promote taking intentional actions throughout the week and noticing moments when their partner is engaging in values-based actions in order to respond accordingly.

In summary, clarifying values is the most crucial component of treatment because values guide the behavioral changes that couples are working toward. Clarifying values involves identifying values within relationship domains and then turning these into specific actions that replace SCBs. Moving forward, the rest of treatment consists of continuing to assess the degree of alignment of behaviors with values and working with the thoughts and feelings that show up as barriers to values-based actions.

CHAPTER 5

Identifying Barriers to Values-Based Actions and Recognizing Moments of Choice

Once couples have clarified their values, they need to learn specific tools to cope with the barriers that will show up. Taking steps toward a valued direction brings up intense and uncomfortable thoughts and feelings connected to one's schemas. As soon as a partner attempts to do a new values-based behavior, old stories, predictions, and powerful emotions will arise, threatening to block more-adaptive responses. Values-based behavior inevitably triggers or runs into obstacles. This is because values-based behavior frequently (1) activates emotional pain, (2) brings up negative beliefs about the self and others in relationships, and (3) requires skills that couples may lack.

Now that you have identified each partner's values, the rest of treatment involves recognizing moments of choice to use values-based actions, remembering what values-based behavior looks like, and working with the barriers that show up when partners start moving toward a valued direction.

"Between stimulus and response, there is a space. In that space is our power to choose our response. In our response lies our growth and our freedom." —Viktor Frankl

Every important step that couples take to get closer to their values is filled with obstacles. They can't get closer to the kind of partner they want to be without facing the things that get in the way. Individuals have to be able to identify the painful experiences that get in the way and learn to relate to them differently so that they aren't driven by fear and avoidance.

This chapter will briefly introduce three types of barriers and use these to identify moments of choice between avoidance and values. In the next three chapters we discuss each of these barriers in detail and provide a methodology for working with them.

Identifying Moments of Choice

Once a schema gets triggered, it brings up automatic and conditioned stories, feelings, images, sensations, and urges that pull partners toward using old SCBs (experiential avoidance). During these triggering situations and conflicts there are several moments of choice when partners can choose to behave differently and engage in new values-based actions.

An essential part of treatment is bringing the recognition of the moment of choice closer to the triggering moment. This is done by cultivating mindfulness to notice thoughts, feelings, sensations, and urges so that behavioral flexibility can be used to act on values. Noticing and staying present with urges creates the ability to choose alternative responses.

The therapist helps partners identify the cues that a particular schema has been triggered, along with the moment of choice, when old avoidance behaviors can be replaced with new values-based responses. This process involves helping partners recognize the moment when they are triggered. Is it in the form of a thought, sensation, feeling, or image? Or does it show up after they already engaged in a coping behavior?

Recognizing moments of choice involves:

1. Identifying and predicting triggers (discussed in chapter 3)
2. Identifying and predicting barriers. These include schema-driven thoughts, feelings, and sensations that pull partners into old coping behaviors. Predicting that these barriers will continue to show up and identifying alternative responses is key (discussed further in chapters 6 and 7)
3. Noticing triggers in and outside of session (discussed in chapter 3)
4. Practicing mindfulness of barriers in and outside of session (discussed further in chapters 6 and 7)
5. Practicing mindfulness of behavioral outcomes: observing a partner's response after a behavior and remaining curious about the impact and workability of a behavior (discussed in chapters 3 and 6)

There are many moments of choice. One moment of choice occurs before an anticipated trigger. For example, if an individual has an abandonment schema and her partner goes away on a work trip, this would be a moment to predict that barriers will show up and prepare the individual to be mindful of the thoughts and feelings that pull her to use old SCBs.

Another example is if an individual has a self-sacrifice schema and has identified that one trigger for this schema is when others make requests of him. In this case, cultivating mindfulness of requests may be helpful. You can help the partner to recognize requests and slow the process down, such as by making an agreement that every time someone makes a request, the individual will respond by saying, "Let me think about it."

Recognizing when one's partner is triggered can also help slow down the process and bring the moment of choice into awareness. For example, you can ask individuals what they need when they are triggered, and how their partner can help them recognize when they are triggered. You might say, "If Mike notices that your deprivation schema is triggered, what can he say to you during those moments that can help remind you of your values?" Schema-driven thoughts and feelings (discussed in detail in chapters 6 and 7) also indicate a moment of choice.

Last, another opportunity to respond differently occurs after partners notice that they have already engaged in an SCB, such as yelling, attacking, or inducing guilt—all of which, again, qualify in ACT terms as experiential avoidance. When partners recognize that they've engaged in an old SCB, they still have an opportunity to choose a values-based behavior.

Throughout treatment, the therapist assists couples in identifying moments of choice so they can act on new intentions in the relationship. There are several steps to this process. First, the therapist encourages partners to practice mindfulness of triggers. Second, the therapist identifies the cognitive and emotional barriers that show up when partners are triggered, and the therapist uses these as opportunities to practice new values-based actions. The therapist can identify these barriers by exploring a recent conflict (by discussing or role-playing), catching moments when partners get triggered, and identifying what blocks their values-based actions. The therapist connects certain schema-driven thoughts and feelings to particular values partners have identified. You can do this by asking partners questions such as:

> When you feel angry, what value do you want to act on? What triggers your anger?
>
> What values do you want to keep in mind when the deprivation comes up? What triggers the deprivation? What are the cues that indicate that your deprivation schema is triggered?
>
> When you have the thought that Mike will never understand you, what do you want to do during those moments? How do you want to behave?
>
> What do you want to do when you feel the urge to distance yourself from Mike? Notice moments during the week when this urge feels strongest.
>
> How do you want to behave in this relationship when you feel ambivalent and hopeless? How can you help each other recognize when this experience shows up?

Identifying Barriers

Explore with partners what is stopping them from taking certain values-based actions in their relationship right now. What are the stories, predictions, or fears that block them from acting consistently on their values? What particular thoughts and feelings have the strongest pull to move them away from their values? Here are sample questions to get at this material:

> What thoughts and stories connected to your schemas stop you from taking steps toward _______________ value?
>
> What feelings stop you from taking steps toward _______________ [values-based action]?
>
> What predictions come up as you imagine taking a step toward _______________ [being more vulnerable, appreciative, loving, compassionate, etc.]? Are you willing to test this hypothesis in your relationship?
>
> What uncomfortable sensations come up as you attempt to take steps toward _______________ [the valued direction]?

What values feel hardest to work toward?

Do you feel that your partner needs to change before you can start taking steps toward being the kind of partner you want to be?

Three Common Types of Barriers

Barriers to acting in a values-based manner generally fall into three categories:

COGNITIVE BARRIERS

When an individual's schemas get triggered in session, it will bring up all of the automatic thoughts connected to the core belief. His or her mind will turn into a convincing machine. Every thought will try to pull him or her away from doing a new behavior in order to protect him- or herself from that schema pain. For example, if a person with a mistrust/abuse schema calls her partner and doesn't hear back, her schema will likely get triggered. In that moment, many thoughts that arise will function to protect her from fear of betrayal. These thoughts will pull her toward seeking out her partner, accusing her partner, or demanding reassurance from her partner—all to avoid the schema pain that is being triggered in the moment. Not acting on these urges, and choosing to do a values-based action instead, will bring up feelings of uncertainty and anxiety in the moment but will also bring her closer to the kind of partner she wants to be.

When individuals attempt to do a new behavior and take a values-based action, they are doing something new, something uncomfortable and unfamiliar. They are taking a risk. Therefore, values-based actions will unavoidably trigger powerful schema-driven thoughts. The therapist's role is to elicit verbalization of fused thoughts, in the moment, and label them as barriers. In chapter 6, we discuss common types of thoughts that tend to pull partners away from values-based actions and identify thirteen key techniques for defusing from these thoughts.

EMOTIONAL BARRIERS

As with defusing from schema-driven thoughts, partners also need to face the schema affect that can block values-based actions. Such emotional pain may include feelings of shame, helplessness, loneliness, and deprivation, as well as the physiological arousal that accompanies this affect. Values-based behavior triggers schema pain because doing something new brings up turmoil, fear of the unknown, fear that the schema will get confirmed, fear of rejection, or fear that the new behavior will leave oneself vulnerable to more pain.

Helping couples learn to observe and describe this pain without acting on it is crucial. This process involves supporting individuals to label the emotions, make space, and move through the emotional wave. This requires developing acceptance, willingness, and compassion toward the difficult emotions that show up when schemas get triggered. ACT provides specific strategies to achieve this. These include using mindfulness to help partners observe and describe the pain nonjudgmentally, and conducting emotion exposure to induce emotions through the use of imagery or by reviewing a recent conflict. These techniques are described in detail in chapter 7.

SKILLS-BASED BARRIERS

Values-based interpersonal behavior often requires skills that couples lack. Partners may be able to defuse from schema-driven thoughts and stay present with painful affect, but they may not know how to respond differently. They may lack assertiveness skills or skills such as *reflective listening* and *nonviolent communication*. They may not know what an effective alternative behavior looks like. These types of deficits can act as barriers to effective values-based actions. The skills training for couples is described in chapter 8.

Predicting Barriers

Predicting the specific barriers that will show up when each partner attempts a new values-based behavior is a key intervention. You don't want partners to be unprepared for the barrier and not anticipating it. Specifically naming and predicting the thoughts and feelings that will show up as barriers helps build awareness of the moment of choice, prepares partners for likely reactions, increases "buy in" and willingness, and allows partners to decide whether to withdraw or avoid the pain, or move toward it.

Practicing Mindfulness of Barriers Outside of Session

Continue to have partners fill out the SCBs Outcomes Log and Weekly Triggers Log (both provided in appendix D and online at http://www.newharbinger.com/34800) to track and monitor the triggers, thoughts, and feelings that occurred during the week. Using these worksheets, explore with partners some moments of choice that led to a decision to behave differently. Reviewing these worksheets every week helps the therapist and the couple identify the choice to use values-based actions. It also encourages partners to practice these alternative behaviors in and outside of session.

The therapist should encourage partners to mindfully observe the next time they get triggered. Then, using the worksheet record of each incident, ask these kinds of questions:

How did you recognize that you were triggered?

Was it a sensation in your body that made you realize that a schema got triggered?

Was it a particular thought that came up that made you realize that you were triggered?

Was it a feeling or memory that made you realize that you were triggered?

At what moment did you realize that a particular schema had been triggered?

Recalling the very first moment you realized you were triggered, how would you want to behave differently during that moment?

What values do you want to remember during those moments?

Practicing Mindfulness of Barriers in Session

The therapist remains mindful of the thoughts and feelings that both partners have identified as barriers, and labels those as they arise in session. The therapist connects the specific barriers to corresponding values and suggests that when those thoughts and feelings arise, they can be cues to act on a specific value. For example, suppose the therapist has identified the schema-driven thought, "My partner will never understand me." If this thought is seen as a barrier to making a request, sharing a feeling, or expressing a need, the therapist can remind partners that here is a moment of choice to do any of these behaviors instead of yielding to the urge to use SCBs.

In summary, the therapist listens for thoughts and feelings that act as barriers, then reminds partners that there is a moment of choice. The therapist helps partners identify the intentions they want to act on during moments of choice, helps partners connect values to particular schema-driven thoughts and feelings, and helps clarify which values-based actions to apply instead of SCBs.

Example Dialogue

Daniel and Ashley are trying to negotiate the fact that their friend's graduation is occurring the same week that Ashley is having surgery. Ashley is getting her gall bladder removed, and she is taking a week off of work to recuperate and heal. She wants Daniel to stay with her while she is recuperating. Daniel doesn't want to miss the graduation, and Ashley's desire has triggered his self-sacrifice schema. As the schema gets activated, he feels afraid and guilty, and he copes by surrendering, giving in, accommodating, and withdrawing. This leads to a growing resentment and the feeling that the relationship is unfair. Daniel's withdrawal triggers Ashley's mistrust schema—she's afraid he won't make taking care of her a priority. She responds with anger, attacks, threats, and blame.

Therapist: I wonder if we can try to negotiate the plan for Saturday by first identifying what the ideal situation is for each of you, then identifying what is intolerable for each of you, and then brainstorming some solutions. How does that sound?

Ashley: That makes sense.

Daniel: Sounds good.

Therapist: Before we start negotiating, I'd like for all three of us to stay mindful and notice any moments when schemas get triggered. It's likely that certain aspects of this negotiation will trigger both your schemas. What are your thoughts about that?

Ashley: Yeah. I think negotiating our different needs is very difficult for us.

Therapist: Well, let's see if we can notice moments of choice and the triggers that show up so that we don't get pulled into old behaviors and fight.

Both: Okay.

Therapist: For you, Ashley, let's pay attention to any moments when you start feeling alone or become suspicious of Daniel. Or when the story that you can't rely on Daniel and that he doesn't care about you shows up. Would you be willing to watch for that?

Ashley: Yeah. I already feel it coming up. I'm worried that Daniel won't take care of me and be there for me when I need him.

Therapist: Let's notice during our negotiation that there will be a moment when this experience shows up and pulls you toward old behaviors such as getting angry or attacking. In this moment, you'll have a choice to either respond in the old, automatic ways or to stay mindful, focus on your values, and choose a new behavior.

Both: Okay.

Therapist: For you, Ashley, let's try to catch and notice the moment right before you get angry or attack. Let's try to catch the first powerful thought, feeling, or sensation that you notice.

Ashley: Okay.

Therapist: Daniel, do you think it's likely that your self-sacrifice beliefs and feelings of helplessness might get triggered during this negotiation?

Daniel: Yeah. I already feel nervous about even describing my ideal situation because I know it's going to make Ashley angry.

Therapist: That's important. I'm glad you labeled that. And as we negotiate, and as each of you identifies your ideal situation, see if you can notice any urges to pull away, surrender, give in, or disconnect.

Daniel: I'll try to watch for that.

Therapist: Now, when you recognize a moment of choice during this negotiation, what values would you like to focus on and come back to, Daniel?

Daniel: I want to be compassionate, assertive, and fair.

Therapist: And Ashley, what values do you want to stay focused on?

Ashley: I want to be empathic, flexible, and understanding.

Therapist: Okay. Let's start the negotiation and keep our focus and attention on any thoughts or feelings that come up and pull you toward old avoidance behaviors. And when urges to avoid show up, let's notice the moment of choice to try something different. This is hard, but it starts with just paying attention and being able to recognize it.

Both: [Nodding]

Therapist: Daniel, what would be the most ideal situation for you, under this circumstance?

Daniel: I don't know. I don't want Ashley to be stuck alone, but I also wish I could attend the graduation.

Therapist: I know it's a difficult predicament, but can you give us an idea of what you'd like to do on Saturday?

Daniel: Well, Ashley is having her surgery on Thursday, and I took Thursday and Friday off of work to be with her. Ideally I would like to go just to part of the ceremony on Saturday and not stay for the whole thing. I would like to be able to stay for two or three hours just to—

Ashley: [Yelling and cutting Daniel off] Three hours plus the ride over there and back, and I'm going to be stuck—

Therapist: Ashley. Let's slow it down. What's happening right now?

Ashley: He doesn't give a shit about—

Therapist: What are you feeling right now? What's the feeling?

Ashley: I feel scared that I'm going to be alone and he doesn't care.

Therapist: Feeling alone and deprived got triggered for you?

Ashley: Yes.

Therapist: How do you want to be with Daniel when this experience shows up? What are the values that you want to act from?

Having predicted cognitive and emotional barriers, and having noted the values each partner wants to use while negotiating, the therapist quickly stops Ashley's schema coping behavior. Immediately, the schema-driven emotions are identified, and Ashley is asked to reconnect to her values and recognize it as a moment of choice to respond differently.

In summary, running into barriers to values-based actions is unavoidable. Given that barriers will inevitably show up when couples engage in new behaviors, it is advantageous to prepare partners by predicting and identifying these barriers. As treatment progresses, barriers will continue to show up, and working with these barriers is a continuous process in therapy.

In the next chapter we discuss strategies for helping couples defuse from thoughts that act as barriers toward values-based actions, and in chapter 7 we discuss strategies for working with emotional barriers to values-based actions. Chapter 8 covers communication skills training for couples. We begin first with working on cognitive barriers, because when you start working on emotional barriers, schema-driven thoughts tend to come up and pull partners away from the emotional experience. Keep in mind that in your actual work with couples, using defusion and mindfulness of emotions usually happens simultaneously, and you will have to switch back and forth between the two when conducting emotion exposures.

CHAPTER 6

Cognitive Barriers to Values-Based Actions

In order to help partners move toward their values and make changes in their relationships, they need tools to relate to their *cognitive barriers*. Cognitive barriers are thoughts that pull partners toward using old SCBs and prevent them from taking positive, values-based action. Schema-driven thoughts, in particular, act as barriers because they occur more often and instantaneously come up in moments of activation. One ACT tool, called *defusion*, assists couples in mindfully observing their schema-driven thoughts so that their thoughts have much less control and influence over problematic behaviors.

Defusion Training

Cognitive fusion is the process by which we yoke words to experiences. Therefore, as soon as a schema gets triggered, it brings up automatic thoughts connected to that schema. When we are fused with a thought, we get entangled with it as if it's reality. We view the thought as an absolute truth rather than a product of our mind. Because schema-driven thoughts are connected to core beliefs, they tend to show up more frequently, are more deeply fused, and have a stronger pull on partners' actions.

Cognitive defusion is an ACT process that facilitates the recognition of and detachment from one's thoughts. It is a practice of observing the process of thinking and then distancing (Hayes et al., 1999) from thoughts such that they have less influence on behaviors. According to Luoma and Hayes (in press), "Cognitive distancing consists of encouraging clients to detect their thoughts, and to see them as hypotheses rather than objective facts about the world."

With defusion, the goal is to help partners see the ongoing process of thinking and to relate to thoughts as experiences one has rather than as experiences that are necessarily facts or truths. ACT offers a variety of defusion techniques, which help change one's relationship to the mind. Helping couples defuse or disentangle from thoughts allows thoughts to function less as barriers. Defusion creates a useful level of detachment from mental content. It allows partners to view thoughts as they are—as thoughts—creating a space where thoughts can be taken less seriously and viewed as part of an old learning history. It is from this space that couples can choose to behave differently rather than responding reflexively to thoughts and treating them like they are causing problematic feelings, sensations, and actions. In ACT for couples, therapists can use these techniques to help partners distance themselves from schema-driven thoughts—defuse from the content of those thoughts—and take steps toward a valued direction, regardless of what their mind is telling them.

Provided in this chapter are a variety of exercises and metaphors to help couples cultivate and practice detachment from schema-driven thoughts. The exercises will cover each of the four components of cognitive defusion skills: noticing thoughts, labeling thoughts, distancing from thoughts, and letting them go.

Defusion is also a stance that the therapist models by taking every opportunity to notice and hold lightly partners' schema-driven thoughts, stories, justifications, reasons, interpretations, and assumptions. Taking a defused stance also means helping partners view schema-driven thoughts as hypotheses that can be explored and tested rather than as facts that control one's behaviors. Holding thoughts lightly allows partners to check in on the outcome of their behaviors in the present moment rather than what their mind predicts will happen. The therapist should stay curious about schema-driven thoughts and bring awareness to the process and function of thinking.

The therapist will also want to mindfully listen for fused thoughts that pull partners to use old SCBs. When a thought emerges that acts as a barrier, the therapist labels it and, if appropriate in terms of timing, assists the couple in defusing by using one of the techniques described in this chapter. With defusion, it does not matter whether the thought is true, or whether the therapist agrees with the thought, or whether there is evidence for the thought—the only questions to ask are, "What is the function of the thought? How does the thought impact partners' behaviors? Does the thought act as a barrier or a motivator to values-based actions?" When thoughts act as barriers, use the following defusion techniques to help partners create distance from them.

Cognitive Defusion with Couples

When a schema gets triggered, it can turn our minds into a "convincing machine," pulling us to protect ourselves with old patterns of behavior. For instance, if a person has an abandonment schema, those thoughts are about how he or she will be abandoned, and they seem to push him or her into trying to figure out how to avoid abandonment. In moments of schema activation, most thoughts will involve interpretations and predictions consistent with the schema. When you notice that a partner's thoughts largely focus on the same conclusion and fuel attempts to avoid a feared emotional experience, then it is safe to assume that the individual is fused with an activated schema.

This is also true when partners try new behaviors. As soon as partners attempt to take a new values-based action in the relationship, their minds will inevitably seek to talk them out of it. Minds often crave predictability and certainty. Given this, they will try to prevent actions that can create uncertainty and fear. When you recognize that a particular common thought shows up for individuals in various domains, help them realize that they can choose not to let that thought govern their behavior. Point out how prevalent it has been; for instance, note how it has shown up in multiple relationships. You can predict that this thought will show up when attempting values-based behavior. When individuals are alert for these thoughts, they can observe how the thoughts seem to pull them toward old SCBs.

However, partners can also notice that they can still choose new responses, gently being aware of the thought without acting on it. They can choose not to buy into the thought and instead relate to it in a way that allows for more behavioral freedom. Continue to work with the process of defusion in session by illustrating the ways in which thoughts aren't always helpful and are largely out of our control.

Defusion Metaphors

You can utilize the following metaphors to highlight the point that thoughts aren't always helpful and are largely out of our control:

POPCORN MACHINE METAPHOR

Our mind is like a popcorn machine (Hayes et al., 1999) that continues to pop thought after thought, judgment after judgment. We have little control over these thoughts. Our minds are hardwired to come up with reasons and hypotheses that explain why things happen to us. They function to try to protect us from danger. The problem is that usually this danger doesn't exist. Trying to stop this process of thinking doesn't work. Our mind is a machine that continues to generate thoughts and judgments that don't help our relationships.

THOUGHTS AS SALES REPRESENTATIVES

Suggest to couples that minds can be just like sales representatives trying to sell products that aren't necessarily good for us (Vuille, n.d.). For example, minds tell us things like, "I'm unlovable," "I can't trust anyone," "If anyone really knew me they would stay away from me," "I'm different," "I don't belong," or "I'll never be good enough." If we gently observe these thoughts without entertaining them, they will rise and pass, and rise and pass, without much struggle or persistence. Certain thoughts, especially if entertained, can be rather pushy. If they are fully engaged, they pull out all of the hard-selling strategies. Some thoughts, like seasoned sales reps, are very compelling and keep coming up over and over again.

Have partners ask themselves which thoughts connected to their schemas are really good salesmen, which thoughts act as the most powerful barriers, and which thoughts they tend to buy into the most. Encourage partners to notice that, instead of arguing with these sales representatives, they can simply say, "Thank you, but I'm not going to buy this product right now." This doesn't mean the thought will go away, necessarily; it means it doesn't have to serve as a barrier to values-based action.

THOUGHTS AS BULLIES

Thoughts can sound like and be bullies. The kind of bullying referred to here isn't schoolyard bullying, where the bully has bad intentions. Rather, it is the kind of bullying that has good intentions but bad methods. That is, these thoughts may be trying to lead us in a good direction, but they are not very effective at communicating this plan. These kinds of bullying thoughts are often accusing, beating us up with the intention of creating a better person, for example, "You're lazy," "You need to work harder," "You're selfish," or "You need to get your life together."

Invite couples to examine this experience and consider whether anyone has ever been able to bully him- or herself into being a better person, and whether it's possible to bully somebody else into being a better person. Bullying usually doesn't work, nor does it move us closer to self-improvement; rather, bullying creates fear and self-doubt. When bullying thoughts show up, help partners notice what this bully is trying to pull them toward or protect them from. Rather than being a victim to the thoughts or fighting the bully, encourage partners to understand the underlying message and to stay in a compassionate stance with their mind.

TUG-OF-WAR METAPHOR

Suggest that trying to argue with or dispute schema-driven thoughts is like getting into a tug-of-war with the mind (Hayes et al., 1999). The more we pull on one side of the rope, resisting a particular thought, the harder the mind pulls on the other side of the rope. The mind can always come up with great rebuttals, and it is impossible to win this game. The mind will try to convince us, providing more judgments, predictions, and disputations. The only way out of this struggle is to simply drop the rope.

Encourage partners to hold thoughts lightly, letting them come and go without resistance. Any effort to try to control, reason with, convince, or argue with our mind is just like picking up the rope again and returning to that tug-of-war. Even though you drop the rope, the thought on the other side does not go away, but the fight is no longer taking energy—freedom is there to choose effective responses.

DON'T THINK OF...

Suggest to partners that the more they don't want to have a particular thought, the stronger and more powerful it can become (Luoma, Hayes, & Walser, 2007). You can offer an exercise to test out this hypothesis. Here is what you might say to introduce this activity: "I am going to tell you a number between one and ten, and I am going to ask you not to think about that number. Ready? Whatever you do, don't think about the number that comes after one and before three. You can think of any other number you want just as long as it doesn't have the number that comes after one and before three in it. Do you know which number I am referring to?"

Everyone will know exactly what number you are referring to. The more you explain to them that this particular number is dangerous and shouldn't be allowed to enter their mind, the stronger that number becomes. This is the same for most thoughts. You can also ask couples not to think about their favorite flavor of ice cream, favorite song, or even a pink elephant and have them notice that the harder they try to avoid thinking of this thing, the more intrusive the thing becomes.

The previous exercises help partners recognize that thoughts are not literal, they don't necessarily represent reality, and they don't always reflect the truth. If we struggle with them, we make them more powerful. Instead, we can notice thoughts, allow them to be there, and respond to them with curiosity. We don't always have to take thoughts seriously or literally. We give our minds permission to have whatever thoughts show up, allowing them to fade as a new thought appears.

Schema-based thoughts that have served as barriers to values-based behavior do not need to continue to have this kind of control. It's not necessary to permanently rid our minds of certain thoughts in order to feel better or relate to our partners in different ways. Instead, we can learn to relate to our mind in such a way that it is not our enemy. We do not need to buy every product our mind tries to sell. Partners no longer have to be held hostage by the bullies that our thoughts can be. We can learn to simply notice the thoughts our minds create, label these thoughts for what they are, and let them go without needing to struggle with them or figure them out.

In conclusion, our minds are not always our friends (Walser & Westrup, 2009). They are not our enemies either. Relating to the mind from an observing, defused position can help partners to "see" thinking, recognizing it for the ongoing process that it is and noting how it regurgitates the same old stories connected to our schemas. Defusing from reflexive conclusions that may no longer be relevant, but may continue to inhibit behavior, can create the freedom to engage in values-based actions in service of loving relationships.

In the sections that follow, we'll explore the four components of cognitive defusion with couples: noticing thoughts, labeling thoughts, distancing from thoughts, and letting them go. For each component, we provide key techniques for fostering defusion.

Key Techniques for Fostering Defusion

When you recognize that partners are fused with particular thoughts that seem to be preventing them from moving forward, you can work with and explore the following processes and techniques to help them defuse from these barriers (remember, defusion itself is not a technique, it is a process; the techniques support the process).

Noticing Thoughts

One of the starting points in teaching couples the process of defusion is helping them learn how to "watch" their minds. When a powerful cognitive barrier surfaces, the first step is to simply notice it. Catching moments of fusion is particularly challenging, especially when a thought is connected to a core schema. In order to help partners build awareness and mindfulness, the therapist maintains a defused stance by pointing to thoughts that act as barriers—including stories, justifications, reasons, interpretations, and assumptions—while working with couples to practice defusion. By doing so, the therapist is less likely to get caught up in the content and is more able to remain focused on the workability of thoughts.

COMMON COGNITIVE BARRIERS IN RELATIONSHIPS

The following is a list of common thoughts for therapists to be aware of that act as barriers in relationships:

Jumping to Conclusions. This is an attempt at mind reading, whereby an individual assumes he or she knows the reasons behind a particular behavior that a partner is doing. This occurs when an individual builds a hypothesis about an event, or a partner's intentions, and is convinced that the hypothesis is correct. One of the primary indicators that individuals are making assumptions or jumping to conclusions about a partner is when they use the word "because" when referring to their partner's behavior:

Bill is quiet right now *because* he is mad at me.

You didn't do the exercises *because* you don't care about me.

We don't have sex anymore *because* you're not attracted to me.

He said that *because* he wants to hurt me.

She is trying to manipulate me *because* she wants everything her way.

Predictions. This cognitive barrier includes stories and predictions about the future, and about how an individual imagines a partner will respond to him or her. These thoughts are difficult to manage and often act as significant barriers to values-based actions. A common indicator of predictions is the construct: "If I do this…that will happen."

Examples of predictions include:

If I say no, Lisa will be angry with me.

If I share my feelings, they will be used against me.

Nothing is ever going to change anyway.

He's never going to follow through on our agreements.

If we start this conversation, we'll get upset and we'll be up all night and never resolve it.

Judgments. Judgments are the most common type of barrier and the most seductive, as our minds often confuse judgments for actual facts or descriptions. When we describe something, there is no evaluation. Judgments, on the other hand, impose an evaluation or a subjective opinion on the thing or event being evaluated. We discuss the difference between judgments and descriptions further, in chapter 8, but here are some examples of judgments:

His communication style is toxic.

She needs too much. Nothing is ever good enough for her.

He's demanding.

She's abusive.

He has no capacity for empathy.

Memories of past hurt and resentments. This shows up when partners continue to bring up resentments from past events that they seem to be unable to let go of or forgive. They continue to process and bring up the same story over and over again. They may be holding on to a particular memory, responding emotionally as if it were occurring in the present moment. The problem with continuing to bring up the same resentments from the past is that these situations have already been discussed, they can't be undone, and as such, partners are powerless to resolve them in the present moment. Another major problem with bringing up hurts from the past is that partners use the past hurts as reasons not to engage in values-based actions in the present. Here are some things they might say:

The last time I opened up to Bill and shared my feelings, he used it against me.

Why should I pick you up from the airport? Last time I came back from vacation, you didn't pick me up.

I can't trust anything you say since last December, when you lied to me about going to John's party.

How can I feel safe with you after last year, when you stormed out and left me?

Reason giving. This behavior is characterized by individuals providing reasons, explanations, and excuses as to why they believe they are unable or unwilling to take actions toward becoming better partners. When reason giving shows up in session, it often sounds like "If…then…" statements. Here, the implication is that something outside of them needs to change before they can start acting on their values.

I would be able to share my feelings with Kevin if he was more empathic.

I would follow through more if she wasn't always complaining and nagging me.

I would be more appreciative if Mike would actually follow through on his word.

I wouldn't be so angry if Katy wasn't always pressuring me and trying to control me.

Rule making. As children, we learn rules about how to behave in relationships, about what's appropriate. However, some rules can be problematic and lead to feelings of resentment, self-righteousness, obligation, and pressure. When rules are not explicitly agreed upon, they come across as demands rather than requests. And rules can overemphasize how things "should" be rather than what is. Creating norms in a relationship is a collaborative process, whereas dictating how others "should" behave without negotiation is projecting an assumption that may not be shared. This rigid thinking inhibits negotiation, expression of individual needs, and problem solving. Have partners take a moment to notice any rules they have about what relationships "should" look like and how their partner "should" behave. Notice when they use this term, and have them recognize this manifestation of fusion. Examples of rule making include:

I shouldn't have to change.

Bob should be a better listener.

Relationships shouldn't be this hard.

She should follow through on her promises.

We should be having more sex.

Help partners explore the workability of being fused with rules, recognizing that even if they get caught up in believing that judgments or stories are true, it still hasn't helped the relationship.

Be familiar with these common types of cognitive barriers, and notice when they show up in session. Consider using the following questions to work with fusion in session (remember to be compassionate and curious, as these questions are not intended to be delivered from a "one-up" position):

How does getting caught up in these thoughts or stories impact your relationship?

How do you behave when you get caught up in these stories?

Have any of these thoughts, or actions driven by these thoughts, helped you change your partner for the better?

Has buying into these thoughts helped you change yourself for the better?

Does getting caught up in these stories make you feel closer and more connected to your partner? Or farther away?

As you ask partners these questions, help them explore the workability of particular thoughts. Note that if the thought leads to positive outcomes in the relationship, then it is not necessarily a barrier. If the thought leads to negative outcomes and pulls them farther away from their relationship values, then help partners explore the costs of buying into these thoughts and suggest the practice of defusion. After exploring thoughts and costs, be prepared to engage in and foster defusion work in session.

Labeling Thoughts

After noticing a thought that seems to act as a barrier, help couples label the thought as a product of their mind in order to better let it go. The following three skills are about labeling thoughts, which can help partners to see thoughts as thoughts:

LABELING BARRIER THOUGHTS

One powerful technique is simply to label thoughts. With distance from the internal narrative, it is possible to acknowledge the appearance of a thought without fusing with it or integrating it into a perception of reality. Labeling observations sound like: "I notice that my mind is telling me ________________," "I'm having the thought that ________________," or "Now my mind is having a ________________ thought." Have couples use the cognitive barriers elaborated in the section "Common Cognitive Barriers in Relationships," in chapter 5, as they label thoughts here, such as "My mind is reaching conclusions" or "My mind is having a prediction." This helps create distance from the thought, thus diminishing its power.

CONNECTING THOUGHTS BACK TO SCHEMAS

When you recognize a schema-driven thought in session, connect that thought back to the schema. Ask, "What schema is this thought connected to? How old is this thought? When was the first time you had this thought? Has this thought shown up for you in other relationships?" You may inquire about the origin of the thought and how often the particular thought shows up for the partner: "How often has this thought come up for you this week or this month?"

Connecting schema-driven thoughts back to the schema helps individuals recognize that this thought has been with them for a long time, that it precedes the relationship, and that it shows up in almost all relationships. This process helps label a particular thought as a schema-driven thought. When partners can recognize that this thought is in them—that they bring this thought with them into all of their relationships, and that it is not necessarily a reflection of reality—it enables them to let it go.

NAMING THE STORY (SCHEMA)

Similar to connecting thoughts back to schemas, this process helps individuals name their schemas and create distance from the idea that the story is caused by their partner. Examples of this technique include statements like, "I'm having a thought connected to my abandonment story," or "There's my abandonment schema," or "There's the 'my partner will leave me' story." Help each partner use his or her own words to label thoughts that fit into particular themes, stories, and schemas, such as, "There's my 'I can't trust my partner' story." This helps couples interact with these stories in a lighter way rather than a fused and potentially problematic way.

Distancing from Thoughts

Certain defusion exercises are especially effective for creating space between the self and the thought. Practicing distancing techniques helps couples learn to take thoughts less seriously, holding thinking lightly and accepting it as an ongoing experience. Distancing processes have a common element: they help partners to embrace painful thoughts while, paradoxically, allowing them to diminish in power. Encourage couples to experiment with the following exercises to see which techniques are most effective in supporting the relationship.

EXPLORING THE WORKABILITY OF A THOUGHT

Urge partners to consider how a particular thought is working for them. Ask, "How do you usually behave when this thought comes up? Has this thought managed to protect you from the pain connected to your schemas? Has it helped you feel safer in this relationship in the long run? Does it pull you toward engaging in behaviors that lead to positive outcomes in the relationship?"

CONNECTING THE THOUGHT BACK TO VALUES

Here, discuss what particular values-based action the thoughts inhibit. It is important to keep in mind the kind of partner they want to be in the relationship and to connect their thoughts to this choice. Ask, "Has this thought stopped you from doing something important in this relationship? Has this thought stopped you from being ______________ [value, such as vulnerable, open, or assertive] in other relationships? Does this thought seem to keep you from doing those things that are important to you? If yes, are you able to see the thought and choose differently?"

More important, ask partners if they would be willing to have that particular thought or set of thoughts and still act on their values in the relationship. Would they be willing to bring that thought along and still take a step toward the kind of partner they want to be? For example, you might say, "Would you be willing to have the prediction that you will be disappointed and deprived, and still express a need right now if it brings you closer to being the expressive and honest partner that you want to be?"

IDENTIFYING THE FUNCTION OF THE THOUGHT

Most schema-driven thoughts function to avoid some kind of imagined pain or emotional experience. For example, if Ryan has a deprivation schema and believes that others are incapable of meeting his needs, he may believe that it's better not to express any needs at all than to make a request and have it be rejected. This may inhibit Ryan from making requests or expressing needs as a means to avoid feeling an imagined disappointment or hurt.

If Sonia has a failure schema and believes that she will fail regardless, then Sonia may believe that it isn't worth trying to reflectively listen or validate her partner's experience. It may feel safer not to try at all than to face the disappointment of trying and failing over and over again.

Ask partners: "What painful experience is this thought trying to protect you from? What is the function of this thought? What is your mind trying to achieve? Is it attempting to protect you from something? Protect somebody else? Keep you safe?" You may even state, "I wonder if your mind is trying to protect you from the disappointment of expressing a need very clearly and still not having it be met. It feels even scarier to imagine that you may express yourself very clearly and still feel the same disappointment and deprivation that you feel now." If partners are able to identify the primary pain that the particular thought is meant to protect them from, but the thought still stops them from acting on values, return to creative hopelessness and cultivating willingness. Explore the unavoidability of the primary pain, the fact that SCBs have not managed to eliminate this pain, and the choice to act on values instead.

REPEATING THOUGHTS

The process of repeating negative thoughts, known as Titchener's Repetition (Titchener, 1916), is based on the discovery that repeating any word fifty or more times begins to diminish its meaning. On the occasion that an individual expresses a barrier thought, have him or her repeat that word or sentence out loud for at least one minute. Following this exercise, discuss what happened to the meaning of the word or phrase. Oftentimes the result is that the word or sentence begins to feel empty or meaningless, more like a sound or gibberish than a word or words. It makes it sound more absurd and less connected to reality. You can also have partners try saying these thoughts in silly voices or in a singsong fashion—anything to defuse from schema-related thoughts that seem to be interfering with positive movement in the relationship.

PHYSICALIZING THOUGHTS

One way to help couples distance themselves from problematic thoughts is by objectifying or imagining them as physical objects (Hayes et al., 1999). This technique can be utilized by asking partners to imagine a thought as an object, identifying its color, size, shape, texture, and so on. Ask how heavy their thought is right now. If this thought had a shape, what would it be? It might feel silly at first; however, the more the physical properties of the thought are identified, the easier it is to relate to it differently and from a less fused place.

HOLDING THOUGHTS LIGHTLY

Have couples write down negative thoughts and fears that they have about themselves and the relationship. Have partners fold their paper in half and hold it in the palm of their hand. Have them try to hold these thoughts lightly and loosen their grip on them (Harris, 2009). You can also have the partners exchange papers and practice holding each other's thoughts lightly and gently with compassion and kindness. Discuss what it feels like to hold these lightly and with compassion.

AGREEING WITH THE THOUGHT

If a partner is fused with a thought about him- or herself that isn't too harmful to the relationship, you can also experiment with taking the thought to be true and being willing to test it as a hypothesis. Just take it as a fact and bring it back to values. Say to the partner, "If this thought were true, now what? What kind of partner do you want to be, given this circumstance?" For example, if a person has a mistrust/abuse schema and he is fused with the thought, "If I am vulnerable with my partner she will use it against me," you can ask him, "If this thought were true, would you still be willing to try being vulnerable right now? Would you be willing to express a feeling even though your mind is predicting a negative outcome? Maybe your mind is right, maybe it isn't—would you be willing to test it out?" This technique helps cultivate willingness and behavioral flexibility when partners get confronted with difficult thoughts.

Letting Go of Thoughts

Once partners have gained distance from schema-driven thoughts, you can teach them a variety of techniques to release the thoughts and let them go. You can experiment with several of the following exercises to see which are most effective for the couple.

THANKING YOUR MIND

Explain that the mind is always vigilant, constantly trying to defend against danger. It's working to shield us from hurt, deprivation, loneliness, disappointment, and rejection. It's continually coming up with strategies to escape negative feelings and fears. Unfortunately, the mind is not very accurate, and sometimes it finds danger where there isn't any. One way to respond to the mind when it is coming up with these thoughts is to thank it for its efforts.

As each painful schema-driven thought shows up, encourage partners to use the mantra "Thank you, mind, for that thought," and then let it go. The therapist should be careful not to use this technique in a dismissive way, which may minimize partners' experiences. Remind couples that their mind is doing its best to protect them. It is also effective to thank the mind while labeling the thought. Say, for example, "Thank you, mind, for that prediction" or "for that judgment" or "for trying to protect me from hurt, deprivation, disapointment," and so on.

CARD CARRYING

In this defusion technique, each partner writes down on a card his or her schema-driven thoughts as they come up in session. Ask partners, "Has this thought ever stopped you from doing anything important in this relationship?" Have partners write the values-based action that this thought acts as a barrier to on the other side of the card. At this point, whenever the thought comes up in session, have partners turn over the card and take a step toward that value. Then, whenever these painful thoughts continue to show up, partners can look at the card, remind themselves that it's a barrier, let it go, and still act on their value.

VISUALIZING: PUTTING THOUGHTS ON OBJECTS AND LETTING THEM GO

The following exercises can help partners release and let go of schema-driven thoughts. The purpose of these exercises is to notice the ongoing flow of thoughts and to assist with observing thinking. The goal is to drop the struggle with thoughts, not to have the thoughts cease.

- *Leaves on a stream.* Have partners imagine a gently flowing stream. Ask them to visualize their thoughts as autumn leaves and watch the thoughts fall down from the tree, land in the stream, and get carried away downstream. Thoughts may return, but again, have each one placed on a leaf and carried away. The point is not to make the thoughts disappear down the river but to notice the ongoing flow of thoughts.
- *Clouds or balloons.* Have couples visualize the beautiful bright blue sky with lots of fluffy clouds passing overhead. Ask them to visualize placing each thought that shows up onto the cloud and simply watch the thoughts drift away on the cloud. You can also try this visualization with balloons.
- *Computer pop-ups.* Have partners imagine that their mind is like a computer screen, and each thought is an advertisement that continues to pop up. Encourage partners to briefly notice each thought that pops up and then let it disappear until the next pop-up appears. Have them continue to do this without getting pulled into paying attention to any of these advertisements.
- *Billboards.* Have couples imagine driving down a highway toward a very important destination. As they're driving, ask them to visualize each difficult thought that enters their mind appearing on a billboard ahead. Encourage partners to briefly observe the thought on the billboard and then continue driving toward their destination without allowing that thought to pull them in a different direction.
- *Physically letting go.* Practice having partners discuss a recent conflict while holding out their right hand, palm up. As each schema-driven thought and judgment shows up during the discussion, have partners imagine putting the thought in the palm of their hand, rotate their hand, and drop the thought down until it is out of sight. After each thought that drops, have partners imagine returning their hand to the palm-up position to receive the next

thought, and continue to keep physically dropping each thought that acts as a barrier to values.

Any of these techniques can be used in and/or outside session during moments of fusion. As soon as you notice a thought that acts as a barrier, intervene using one of these techniques and come back to values. Don't spend too much time engaging in the content of these thoughts; let thoughts go and bring partners back to the present moment and what they want to stand for in the relationship.

Example Dialogue

The following dialogue is a continuation of the exchange between Mike and Michelle from chapter 3. There, both partners were able to identify their schemas, schema coping behaviors, and values. Here we see them using defusion with cognitions that act as barriers to values-based actions. Notice how most of the thoughts that arise during this session stem from each partner's schemas—Mike's defectiveness/shame and failure schemas and Michelle's emotional deprivation schema.

Therapist: We've been talking about your values and the barriers that come up for both of you in the moment. Should we go over your Weekly Triggers Log from this week and discuss any triggers that occurred?

Michelle: Yeah. Mike had agreed to cook dinner and do the dishes, and then after dinner, when I reminded him to do the dishes, he exploded on me and ruined the whole evening.

Mike: Well, of course as soon as she gets home from work, the first thing she does is criticize every move I make. I already had dinner cooked and ready for us on the table, and the first thing she does is start complaining about how everything is not done right. No "Thank you, Mike," no appreciation. It's never, ever good enough for her. Nothing ever satisfies her. She'll never be happy with anything I do.

Therapist: Mike, let's notice that you're having a prediction that no matter how hard you try, you can't get it right, that Michelle will still be unsatisfied. What does it feel like when you buy into this prediction? When your mind tries to sell you this product, what does it pull you toward? When you take this prediction as a fact, does it help you take actions toward being collaborative, curious, and flexible?

Mike: It makes me feel hopeless. Like there's no point in trying anything.

Therapist: Well, maybe that's true. Maybe if you try a new behavior Michelle will still be dissatisfied. But maybe she'll feel appreciative, surprised, or grateful. We just don't know until after we've tried.

Michelle: I would be happy with any effort that he makes if I could just explain what I would like and be able to give him feedback. If he could just hear some feedback, maybe he would actually meet my needs, but he just won't take any kind of feedback. He just hears everything I say as a criticism. I can't say anything to him.

Therapist: Let's slow it down and check in. What schema is that thought connected to, Michelle? Where does the idea that Mike will never understand or listen to you come from?

Michelle: I guess I expect that people just won't listen to me or get me. That's the deprivation schema.

Therapist: Mike, when Michelle says that you never understand her, what gets triggered for you when you hear that?

Mike: I feel frustrated and inadequate. The defectiveness schema and failure. I'm just never good enough for her. I can never get anything right in this relationship.

Therapist: Mike, let's just notice that you're having the thought that you can't do anything right. We've talked about how this thought shows up for you at work, with your friends, and with your mom. This is a pretty familiar thought, isn't it?

Mike: Yeah. It's a common thought that I have.

Therapist: And when this thought shows up for you in these different areas, you start feeling helpless and inadequate. The experience becomes so overwhelming that choosing different behaviors is difficult. If we made space for the experience of helplessness and inadequacy, what would you want to do in those moments? What values would you want to recall? What kind of partner do you want to be when your mind tells you that you'll never be good enough?

Mike: I want to be compassionate. I want to be a better listener, more open. I really tried to be open to feedback the first three criticisms that Michelle mentioned, but by the tenth one I started getting really angry. I just realized I'm never going to meet her standards. She's impossible to please.

Therapist: When your mind tells you that Michelle is impossible to please, what choices do you have in that moment? Would you be willing to experience this thought and still choose to behave in a way that feels consistent with your values? Can you watch that thought and still take steps toward being compassionate and open?

Mike: That's really hard. It feels so true.

Michelle: You see what he does? He just continues to insist that I'm a perfectionist and my standards are too high, and then he never has to actually listen or understand what I need. He never actually listens to me. Maybe if he actually heard me he'd get something right, but anything that comes out of my mouth just sounds like a criticism to him.

Therapist: [To Michelle] It's very scary for you right now. It feels hopeless. Like your needs will never get met in this relationship.

Michelle: Mike doesn't actually take the time to understand what I need. I'm completely alone in this relationship. He has no empathy.

Therapist: You're yearning for Mike to understand your needs and to connect with you. And as soon as that longing to feel closer to Mike comes up, your mind starts replaying that familiar story about how you're always going to get deprived and your needs are not going to get met. Has that thought stopped you from expressing your needs kindly in other relationships?

Michelle: Yeah. It pretty much shows up in every one of my relationships. I really don't know how to make requests when every request I make sounds like a criticism to him. I'm never going to be understood in this relationship.

Therapist: What do you usually do when your mind tells you that every request that you make doesn't get heard and is seen as a criticism?

Michelle: I get angry and critical, or I just give up.

Therapist: And if that thought wasn't in charge, if you were willing to have that thought and try something new, what could that be? How do you want to behave when your mind tries to convince you to give up?

Michelle: I want to express my needs clearly. I want to be assertive in an effective and calm way.

Therapist: Would you be willing to express a need right now? What would you like to express to Mike?

Michelle: Even if I make a request right now, he'll just agree to it and not follow through.

Therapist: I am noticing this is an old story, a kind of place where your mind is doing what it thinks its job is… Would you be willing to give a gentle nod, a kind of thank-you, to your mind as it tries to protect you, while still staying curious and making a compassionate request right now? Would you be willing to try that? Would you be willing to go toward your value of being assertive and express a request right now with Mike?

Michelle: [Nods her head in agreement]

Therapist: Mike, would you be willing to try to work on this right now? Would you be willing to hear Michelle's request?

Mike: As long as it doesn't turn into a criticism and an attack on my character.

Therapist: Now it seems your mind is trying to protect you from that feeling of inadequacy and disappointment by predicting that Michelle is going to respond critically. See if you can hold that thought very lightly, let go of the story a bit, and stay present with your experience right now. Would you be willing to reflect back Michelle's request? Would you be willing to just notice what a powerful product this thought is trying to sell you right now, and still stay curious and open?

Michelle and Mike: Yes.

In summary, taking steps toward valued directions can be new and scary. Therefore, as couples start taking steps toward their values, they inevitably run into cognitive barriers. These thoughts and stories pull them toward using old SCBs and away from values—when they are fused with them. When these barriers show up, help partners defuse from this content and bring them back to the present-moment process. Identify what their values are and what they want to stand for, and assist them in engaging in new values-based actions in the moment.

CHAPTER 7

Emotional Barriers to Values-Based Actions

The previous chapter discussed using defusion strategies to work with thoughts that act as barriers to values-based actions. In this chapter we'll explore how to work with emotions that also act as barriers to values-based actions. When emotions get in the way of values, ACT targets these barriers with *mindfulness* and *emotion-exposure* techniques. The purpose is to get couples to see beyond emotions, as they see beyond thoughts, to identify moments of choice and the opportunity for values-based responses.

Mindfulness is the skill of being in full contact with one's present-moment experience, both internal and external, while remaining curious and nonjudgmental. It is building the awareness and ability to watch thoughts, feelings, sensations, and action urges so that they have less influence over each partner's behavior. When partners don't get swept away and caught up with thoughts and feelings, they can better notice moments of choice and make decisions about how to respond. Mindfulness aims to increase the ability to stay purposefully aware of the present moment and to act on values rather than emotion-driven urges.

Emotion exposure involves deliberate schema activation to induce significant emotional arousal in partners so that they can learn to integrate several processes at once. These processes include present-moment contact, defusion, connecting to values, enacting values-based actions, maintaining flexible perspective taking, and acceptance of self and other.

During emotion exposure, the therapist induces a triggered state in couples and helps them stay present with the experience. The therapist fosters acceptance by guiding couples toward expressing their experience over content. The therapist encourages partners to come back to describing their experience and creating a compassionate and validating space, while simultaneously reminding them of moments of choice to respond differently while facing difficult emotions and urges. The therapist assists partners in accepting internal experiences including feelings, desires, and needs while helping them change the way they communicate about those experiences. This transforms the context in which conflict occurs. By actively modifying the context, couples build tolerance for facing difficult emotions, thereby increasing willingness to accept and remain with schema pain in future moments of activation.

The purpose of exposure is to build a broad and flexible behavioral repertoire during periods when couples are emotionally triggered (e.g., experiencing feelings of shame, fear, anger, hurt, loss, etc.), since schema-driven emotions can act as barriers to values-based actions. For example, guilt can act as a barrier to behaving assertively or saying no, shame can act as a barrier to expressing vulnerability, and fear might stop a partner from making a request or being truthful. The goal is to fully contact one's emotional experience, undermine experiential avoidance, and support effective, values-based responding in the moment. Couples thus learn to tolerate distress and focus on effective action rather than pain and distress avoidance.

Cultivating Mindfulness

Mindfulness can be acquired and cultivated. Just as going to the gym builds muscles, practicing mindfulness builds the capacity to act on values in the face of pain. Integrating mindfulness into daily life can increase a couple's ability to stay aware of schema-driven thoughts and feelings, and choose different ways to respond rather than the avoidance behaviors partners have been using. Research on the effects of mindfulness suggests that it has a positive impact on interpersonal relationships (Hoopes, 2009; Palmer & Rodger, 2009). It's no different in ACT for couples. When couples can use mindfulness to stay in contact with the present moment and observe their experiences nonjudgmentally and with curiosity, they can notice emotional waves pulling them toward old behaviors without reacting in automatic ways. Mindfulness helps partners learn to stay present with one another, untangle from past and future stories, and have more freedom to respond from a position of awareness. This "allows" the partners to choose responses that are consistent with values.

Mindfulness practice can be placed into two categories: *formal* and *informal*. Formal practice refers to what we typically conceive of as "meditation." It involves setting aside a specific time to intentionally attend to the present moment. Examples include sitting meditation, body scan, five senses exercises, and mindful breathing, to name a few. Formal mindfulness exercises are practiced in-session.

Informal practice is about bringing mindfulness into daily activities. It helps in generalizing the skills developed from a formal mindfulness practice. Although informal, it requires choosing a particular activity to engage in mindfully and using focus and concentration to attend to the activity. Informal mindfulness exercises are practiced outside of session, and support the cultivation of mindfulness between sessions. Informal mindfulness is essential to help couples strengthen their ability to observe interpersonal processes.

Formal Mindfulness

Practicing formal mindfulness with couples helps them learn to be present with one another, deepen their connection, and strengthen their bond. Mindful breathing helps partners align their breathing, become more in sync, and become more receptive and attuned to each other.

Compassionate Breathing

This guided mindfulness meditation can be utilized with couples in session to increase empathy and compassion. You can use this exercise in the beginning of a session or toward the end to wind the session down. After completing the exercise, encourage couples to share what they experienced and any learning that occurred.

Begin by having partners sit across from each other facing one another. Use a slow and gentle tone, leaving a couple of minutes of silence between each paragraph, while using the following script:

> Get into a comfortable position and let your eyes close. Take a few deep breaths to settle into this moment. Bring loving and kind attention to your breath. Bring attention to your physical sensations, and notice what you are experiencing in your body right now. Be aware of any areas of ease or tension. Whatever you notice, just let it be as it is. Notice all sensations and experiences, whether evaluated as good or bad. Just let them all be as they are.
>
> [Pause]
>
> Now see where you notice your breath most intensely or easily in your body. Do you feel it in the rising and falling of your chest? Do you feel the warmness or coolness of the air inside your mouth or in your nostrils? Do you feel it more strongly on the inhale or the exhale? Or do you feel it in your belly as it expands and contracts? If you notice yourself judging or trying to control your breath, just come back to noticing the experience and letting it be just as it is.
>
> [Pause]
>
> Now, gently open your eyes and look at your partner in front of you. Look into each other's eyes, and try to see the person behind those eyes. Look deeply into each other's eyes. What are you seeing right now? What do you imagine your partner is feeling? What do you imagine life is like for this person you are looking at, who has all the complexities and emotions of being human?
>
> [Pause]
>
> See if you can connect with this person sitting in front of you and all the complicated thoughts, feelings, and experiences that each of you have had. If you notice any judgments showing up, or thoughts about the past or future, see if you can bring yourself back to this moment and just observe the person sitting before you. What is it like to gaze into your partner's eyes right now?
>
> [Pause]
>
> Now I invite you to turn your attention to your partner's breathing. See if you can be aware of the subtle rise and fall of your partner's belly or chest as it expands and contracts. Notice the rise and fall of your partner's chest.
>
> [Pause]
>
> Notice if you have any urges to breathe in the same rhythm as your partner or an urge to breathe in a different rhythm. Notice when you and your partner

breathe differently or in sync. Notice when you break eye contact or when you're in a deep gaze. What are those experiences like for you in this moment? Notice any emotions that arise: fear, connection, love, or even engulfment.

[Pause]

Stories from the past may show up, or thoughts about the past or future. Notice these thoughts and gently return to observing the rhythm of your partner's breath, noticing what you experience when you really see each other.

[Pause]

As you're looking at your partner, notice what it feels like to see your partner. Notice your partner's face. Be aware of any changes in your experience as you face your partner. Notice the experience in your body in this moment: your breathing, your posture, your heartbeat. Notice any strong sensations. Are any emotions arising? If so, be aware of what they are. Are there feelings of longing, fear, loneliness, or relief? Make space for any emotions that may be showing up. You may feel closer to your partner or farther away. This experience may fluctuate. Simply be aware as whatever you feel rises and falls. I invite you to remain in contact with all the different experiences that you are having as you see your partner. See if you can stay curious about your feelings, sensations, and thoughts. Notice any action urges. Gently observe these urges, and allow yourself to ride the waves of these experiences.

You can also have partners practice more complex breathing exercises by adding the following variations:

- *Synchronized breaths*: Begin by having partners practice the Compassionate Breathing exercise. Next, have partners breathe together by synchronizing their breathing: inhaling and exhaling together at the same pace.
- *Breath exchange*: As one partner inhales, the other exhales, as though they are breathing each other.
- *Hand to heart*: Have partners take turns placing a hand on the other's heart as they are breathing together, sending warmth and compassion from one partner's hand to the other's heart.

While doing the above formal mindfulness exercise in session, you could also encourage couples to practice formal activities at home. Mindful breathing is ideal because it teaches partners to notice and let go of thoughts while returning attention to the breath. Chapter 10 provides another formal exercise to use with couples, in session, to promote flexible perspective taking.

Informal Mindfulness

Most people have had the experience of leaving work and finding themselves home when they were supposed to be heading to another location. This is autopilot behavior.

In this "mindless" state, we behave automatically—we are less aware, and we don't notice our choices and options in the moment. In some ways this is evolutionarily beneficial: it makes us more effective, as it allows us to expend less energy in the routine tasks of life. However, autopilot mode makes us less conscious of the choices we have in the moment. Practicing mindfulness in daily life can help couples build more awareness in interpersonal interactions and better recognize moments of choice. Couples can learn to pull out of autopilot mode by practicing mindfulness, cultivating present-moment awareness, and slowing down the process so that they have more flexible ways of responding.

The following exercises, adapted in part from *ACT with Love* (Harris 2009), can be used in session as formal mindfulness exercises or outside of session as informal mindfulness practices. They are intended to cultivate mindfulness during triggered states. These exercises help couples bring attention to the present moment and notice what their actual experience is rather than what their mind is telling them it is. One or more exercises should first be practiced formally in session, with the therapist guiding the activity. Afterward, the therapist should encourage couples to practice them at any moment informally outside of session.

Mindfulness of Facial Expression

This exercise encourages individuals to pay close attention to their partner's face and to make present-moment observations. Start by having the couple face each other. Then begin guiding the exercise:

> Bring your attention to your partner's face. Observe your partner's expressions as if you're seeing them for the first time. Notice subtle facial movements as your partner talks. Notice the lines and creases around the mouth and eyes. Focus on your partner's eyes and brows. What emotions are you seeing in your partner's face? Notice any subtle changes in his or her responses to you. As you pay attention to your partner's facial expression, see if you can also stay mindful of your own facial expressions. What are your facial gestures conveying to your partner? How may he or she be experiencing you? Pay attention to what your face feels like and how it may come across to your partner.

Mindful Listening

This exercise is about giving one's partner complete and undivided attention. You can try this in session or assign it for homework.

> The next time you and your partner are having a discussion, give your full attention and curiosity. Listen to your partner as if you are on your first date or as if your partner is one of your favorite authors or actors. Pay attention to what your partner is attempting to express. What is he or she saying about his or her feelings, worldview, underlying needs, or longings? Ask clarifying questions, maintain eye contact, reflect back what he or she is saying, and ask if you heard

it correctly. See if you can lower the volume of your own internal dialogue about what you're hearing and just listen with the intention to really understand.

Mindful Affection

This exercise uses one of the five senses—touch—to connect couples to the present moment and to each other. Talk them through the steps to practice at home:

> Set a time to mindfully connect physically through cuddling and touching. Notice all the sensory experiences. Hold and touch your partner as if you are touching him or her for the first time. Notice the areas where your bodies connect. Notice what you are seeing and hearing, what touching your partner feels like on your fingertips. What is the experience like in that moment? Notice any thoughts and feelings as they arise. Notice the experience in your body: your breathing, your posture, your heartbeat. Notice any strong sensations and emotions that show up. Are there feelings of longing, fear, connection, or loneliness? See if you can make space for any emotions that show up.

Sharing a Mindful Activity Together

Encourage couples to try walking together, doing dishes together, putting the kids to bed together, or dancing. In each of these activities, partners should bring their full attention to the physical experiences of the moment.

> While doing dishes, you could be noticing the feel of warm water, the sensations of sponge and soap, the random touch of your bodies, the feel of the hard pots and plates in your hand, and so on. You might also notice feelings of comfort, belonging, or connection as you and your partner work together.

Mindfulness of Schema Activation

Perhaps the most important application of mindfulness is teaching partners to observe schema activation. Have the couple notice moments when schemas get triggered in daily life, and have them mindfully practice observing the schema pain. What schema showed up? What was the trigger? What were the thoughts, feelings, and action urges? Did they act on the urge or not? Ask partners to use the Interpersonal Experiences Log (also provided in appendix D and online at http://www.newharbinger.com/34800) to monitor schema activation in daily life. This should be an ongoing process whereby partners are encouraged to observe moments of schema pain, noticing as best as they can the experience as it unfolds, and then recording the experience on the worksheet after *every* event. You'll be reinforcing mindfulness of schema pain during sessions by having partners describe aloud these same experiences (schema thoughts, emotions, sensations, and urges) when they are triggered.

Interpersonal Experiences Log

Event	Schema Emotions	Schema-Driven Thoughts	Sensations	Urges	Did you act on the urge?

Emotion Exposure

A central component of treatment for couples is conducting emotion exposure during schema activation while practicing values-based actions. The therapist can use emotion exposure with partners in moments when strong emotions emerge as barriers to values-based responding. If a partner's schema-driven emotions get too intense to practice values-based responding—including effective communication, reflective listening, or problem solving—the therapist should conduct emotion exposure. The therapist can also induce schema activation by revisiting a recent conflict or role-playing a recent triggering event.

The purpose of emotion exposure is to expose partners to the schema-driven pain that arises during moments of trigger while walking through the process and expressing their feelings rather than acting them out. The therapist actively coaches the partners to slow down and stay with the difficult emotions that arise. This allows partners to build tolerance and willingness to stay with difficult emotions in order to develop more flexible responses in moments of schema activation. Once a partner's emotions are less of a barrier to values-based actions, the focus shifts toward values-based problem solving.

Exposure to schema-driven emotions is crucial because of *state-dependent learning.* "State dependent learning refers to the fact that subjects are more likely to retrieve a memory when in the same affective state as when the memory was encoded. Therefore, anything we can do to help patients experience their feelings as fully as possible should speed the process of memory retrieval" (Coughlin Della Selva, 2004).

The implication of state-dependent learning is that if partners do not learn the needed skills and values-based responses while in a triggered state, they are less likely to be able to use these skills in moments of schema activation. Therefore, it is critical that the therapist encourages discussions of recent conflicts, inducing moments of schema activation in session, for the purpose of guiding partners to practice new behaviors while in an emotionally aroused state.

In traditional exposure, the therapist gradually exposes individuals to an externally feared stimulus, such as a spider. Treatment might begin by having persons look at pictures of spiders, then maybe look at movies of spiders, then gradually move on to looking at a spider in a locked box. A last step would involve having the person make full contact with the spider. Similarly, in emotion exposure the therapist "moves" the individual closer to the emotion while assisting him or her to create space to hold it.

Exposure is designed to fundamentally change a partner's relationship to schema-driven emotions. Through exposure work, the emotions are no longer intolerable and something to be avoided but instead experiences that can be observed with nonjudgmental curiosity. By embracing the pain connected to schemas (rather than evading it with SCBs), partners are free to move toward what really matters. Through slowing down the process during moments of trigger, making space for difficult emotions and responding according to values instead, partners build behavioral flexibility and the ability to engage in a broad range of behavioral options.

In summary, the goal of exposure is to stay mindful and present with the schema pain (including thoughts, sensations, emotions, and action urges) long enough to identify all the different experiences that show up, label them, identify a moment of choice, and experiment with new values-based behaviors in the moment.

Conducting In-Session Emotion Exposure

Before conducting exposure, explain to couples the purpose of exposure. The rationale for facing schema-driven emotions is to reduce emotionally driven behaviors and replace these with values-based actions. When couples are clear on the formulation and rationale for emotion exposure, secure an agreement that you will stop whatever is going on and shift into exposure any time they are triggered or are engaging in the identified SCBs.

When conducting emotion exposure, it's important to start early in the session so there's enough time for partners to work through the full exposure. It's necessary, as with exposure to feared stimuli, that the duration of the emotion exposure include the partner having made full contact with the experience; the exposure should not be terminated prematurely. You'll also need time to process and discuss reactions.

While inducing schema activation, or when schema pain gets triggered organically in session, use the following steps to conduct emotion exposure:

1. **Identify that a partner is triggered.** Label the schema that is triggered. For example, if you notice a partner engaging in an SCB such as defending, belittling, accusing, or yelling, you can say, "What's going on for you right now?" or "It seems like you're trying to defend yourself, as if you've done something wrong. Does it feel that way to you?" or "I'm noticing you're pulling away. What's happening for you right now?"

2. **Have couples describe the sensations in their body.** Ask, "What physical sensations do you feel in your body? Scan your body to see where the feelings seem to be experienced. Where do these experiences feel most intense in your body?" Have partners describe the emotion as if it's an actual object in their body. "How big is the sensation? How heavy is it? What shape does it have? What size is it? What color is it? What else do you notice about this experience? Is there movement? Or is there a feeling of pressure, weight, or tightness? Is it light and easy to hold or large and ubiquitous? Are the edges jagged, sharp, or smooth?" Have them sketch out the shape.

   As partners describe the experience, notice any subtle shifts or changes in the intensity of the emotion. For example, if a partner is clenching his fist or appears to be holding his breath, bring attention to these nonverbal behaviors as evidence of schema activation and avoidance. Encourage opening up to the experience and staying in full contact with it.

3. **Describe feelings in detail.** Label the emotions that are emerging, and help couples observe the experience with compassion and curiosity. Have partners describe their feelings. Is it hurt that's showing up? Or shame, helplessness, deprivation, loneliness, fear? If partners have difficulty articulating the emotions, use the List of Feelings When Needs are Unmet in Relationships (in appendix D and online at http://www.newharbinger.com/34800). Make sure that you have partners describe the experience and its intensity using nonjudgmental language.

4. **Label and let go of schema-driven thoughts.** As you help the partners stay with the emotions and sensations that show up, it is likely that schema-driven thoughts will emerge during the exposure and start to pull partners away from the experience. As thoughts arise, have partners notice each thought, label it, and come back to describing the present moment's emotional, sensory, and physical experience. Stop partners from getting entangled or caught up in any thoughts. Teach them to simply observe the thought, let it go, and come back to observing the emotion and describing the experience.

5. **Have partners notice and describe any action urges.** Help partners observe any impulse to act on or to suppress the emotion. Ask partners if they are feeling pulled toward old schema coping behaviors. Have them recognize and notice any urges without doing anything about them. The goal is to have partners watch, label, and describe without acting on the impulse. Notice and point out any moments of avoidance or blocking of emotions. As described, as soon as intense emotions arise, there is often a deep urge to push them away. Help partners stay with these feelings, opening up to the experience, and pointing out any moments of resistance. When you encounter resistance, help couples soften to the experience, allowing them to gently notice moments of struggle. You can help partners do this by identifying their struggle and by saying statements like: "Try opening up to this experience—take a deep breath and make space for this emotion," or "This pain has been with you for so long. Does it have to be your enemy?" or "Will you have this experience as it is right now?" You can also have individuals put a hand over their heart and send some warmth and compassion to the pain.

6. **Circle back to emotions and sensations.** Continue with exposure by frequently returning to the present-moment experience, noticing sensations, and labeling and describing emotions. When thoughts show up, ask partners to gently observe and let go, and then return to describing the experience. Periodically remind them to notice any urges or impulses to resist or act. Have partners observe their emotions as they change or morph. Invite them to remain curious about what's happening emotionally. Have them watch the waves of emotion without responding.

7. **Check in about willingness.** After partners have observed, explored, and validated the feelings in detail, ask the following key question: "Would you be willing to have this experience and still take steps toward your values?" State a specific value or values-based action here. If the answer is no, then continue with further exposure, and assess barriers as well as costs and workability. If the answer is yes, continue to the next step.

8. **Clarify values.** Ask partners what values they want to move toward when the schema pain shows up. What values do they want to bring to mind when these old thoughts and feelings arise, and how do they specifically want to act?

9. **Values-based problem solving.** This step involves practicing skills from chapters 8 and 9. Begin by identifying which skill to practice based upon the values and intentions stated in the previous step. When partners aren't hearing each other, stick to reflective listening and validating. If values about assertiveness are mentioned, have couples practice assertiveness skills: making requests, or setting limits. If partners are struggling with conflicting needs, help them negotiate a fair solution.

10. **Mindfully observe outcomes.** Often when individuals are vulnerable and reveal their deepest thoughts and feelings, it's difficult for them to remain present and curious about their partner's reaction. Schemas color and shape the way partners take in new information; all of the history and old stories from the past act as barriers to witnessing how a partner is responding to them in the present moment. They may close down, fuse with their predictions, and misperceive their partner's reactions. Therefore, part of emotion exposure is helping individuals check in with the real outcomes.

    Have partners make eye contact with one another, notice the expression on each other's face, and connect. Have them check in regarding their predictions about how the other will react versus how the other is actually reacting in the moment. When conducting emotion exposure with couples, help them bring awareness to the behavior that is occurring in the moment and not the story about how the other is reacting: Is the partner responding with disinterest, distance, and impatience? Is the partner responding with curiosity, love, and compassion? Help couples defuse from the story and check in on the evidence present in the moment.

You can initiate an emotion exposure by (1) catching a moment when a partner gets triggered in session, or (2) inducing schema activation by either having the couple discuss a recent triggering event or role-playing a recent conflict when they engaged in SCBs. Depending on the level of activation, you can either conduct emotion exposure simultaneously with both partners or conduct the exposure with the emotionally activated individual and have the observing partner watch and validate. Remind couples to focus on the process, including what the experience feels like in their body. Coach couples to keep describing sensations, emotions, and urges. If the situation escalates and partners become more triggered:

1. Validate the pain.
2. Encourage partners to observe the emotion and the SCB impulse.
3. Explore the values-based alternative.

Although it is not a difficult task to get partners into a triggered state in couples therapy, the challenge is that once one partner is triggered and engages in avoidant behaviors, it quickly triggers the other. The best course is to work with one partner's emotions while asking the other to compassionately observe. As you're conducting the exposure, physicalizing the emotion or practicing mindfulness of the emotion with one partner, you can simultaneously assist the observing partner to stay present and reflect his or her partner's experience.

The therapist first models validation and then helps each partner validate the other's pain. Once you have explored one partner's emotion, shift focus to the observing partner. If the observing partner has been triggered, repeat the exposure process by examining schema-driven thoughts, emotions, sensations, and urges. When the emotions of both partners have been explored, you'll shift again, this time focusing on values-based communication.

What makes exposure more challenging in couples therapy, as opposed to individual therapy, is that both partners may collude in resisting schema affect as soon as it shows up. When intense schema-driven affect gets triggered for one partner, the other may attempt to lessen his or her partner's emotional response. Typical strategies include defending, minimizing, problem solving, reassuring, trying to fix or take away the emotion, apologizing, rationalizing, explaining, and/or justifying. The therapist has to stay mindful and work to manage avoidance strategies from either partner in any attempt to reduce the schema affect.

As you help one partner label, observe, and describe emotions, you also help manage the observing partner's response. You model responding to an individual's intense emotions with validation, acceptance, and empathy. It will be important for you to help partners notice the effect validating responses can have, as well as the subtle shifts in emotions as a result of being responded to with compassion rather than defensiveness. Couples should learn that responding to feelings in an invalidating manner only exacerbates and intensifies the affect, while validating the experience tends to reduce activation. Feeling states tend to be transient and temporary when they are responded to with kindness and validation.

Staying present with schema-driven emotions allows for partners to have increased behavioral flexibility in the face of schema pain and makes it so that emotional states have less influence over their choices. Instead of prompting SCBs, emotions may now engender a broader range of values-based communications. Below is an example dialogue of emotion exposure.

Example Dialogue

Nick and Agnes are struggling with disappointment in the relationship. Agnes has an unrelenting standards schema and often experiences feelings of dissatisfaction and loneliness. She copes by getting critical and withdrawing emotionally. Nick has a failure schema, with the expectation that he will make mistakes and disappoint Agnes. He copes by denying, explaining, justifying, and defending hurtful behaviors. This leaves Agnes feeling more alone and unseen in the relationship. She ends up convinced that she can't share moments of hurt and disappointment with Nick. She shuts down emotionally.

The therapist begins by discussing a recent triggering event and focuses on the physical sensations, thoughts, feelings, and urges that show up.

Agnes: I had a very important work event on Friday, and I asked Nick to bring the car back at 6 p.m. so that we could get to the event at 7:30 p.m., but Nick was forty-five minutes late and we got there—

Nick: I wasn't forty-five minutes late. I was thirty minutes late and it's because—

Agnes: Damn it, Nick. Why can't you hear anything I say? I was very embarrassed when I was supposed—

Nick: I was only a half hour late and I'm trying to explain why—

Therapist: Nick, what's happening for you right now?

Nick: I didn't mean to be late. I really tried my best. It's just that—

Therapist: I wonder if the feeling of failure and inadequacy is showing up right now?

Nick: Yeah. I messed up and I feel very misunderstood right now.

Therapist: You feel very misunderstood and you have an urge to explain and defend yourself?

Nick: Yeah. I messed up again and I'm trying to explain why.

Therapist: Let's slow things down a little. Would you be willing to take a couple of breaths and just observe this experience right now? Agnes is expressing feelings of disappointment and embarrassment. What's happening for you right now as she's describing that?

Nick: I feel bad. I feel at fault. I failed her again. I always do this.

Therapist: You feel responsible? That you've disappointed her?

Nick: Yes.

Therapist: Let's stay with this for a little while. [Slowing it down.] This is a familiar experience for you. You feel like you didn't measure up, and she's disappointed. Then you start defending and justifying yourself, and Agnes ends up feeling unheard. Is that correct?

Nick: Yes.

Therapist: Would you be willing to stay with this for a little while? Would you be willing to make some space for the feeling that you've disappointed Agnes?

Nick: I don't want her to be disappointed. I don't want her to feel embarrassed.

Therapist: What is that like for you when Agnes feels disappointed? Take a deep breath, slow it down, and let's get curious about what's happening for you around disappointment.

Nick: [Starts to tear up and points his head down.] I feel ashamed. I'm not good enough for her. I always mess things up.

Therapist: Where do you feel this shame in your body right now? Where is it most intense?

Nick: My chest feels tight. I feel like I can't breathe. I have to explain.

Therapist: Something feels urgent? Like you've been bad and you have to fix it?

Nick: Yeah. I can't do anything right.

Therapist: Let's try to stay with this experience in your chest. Can you open up and make some space for this experience?

Nick: [Breathing heavily]

Therapist: Put your hand on your chest where it feels most intense. Take a deep breath and just allow this experience in. Agnes is very disappointed. She felt embarrassed and disappointed. What's happening for you right now?

Nick: [Crying] I feel scared. I'm going to continue to let her down and she's going to leave me.

Therapist: Your mind connects disappointment with abandonment? You feel afraid?

Nick: Yes. I feel like at any moment I will do something that will cause her to end the relationship and it will be my fault.

Therapist: Where is this fear in your body right now?

Nick: I feel it in my throat. I can't get air in. My throat is tight.

Therapist: What's happening in your throat right now? What does it feel like? If I were feeling this sensation in my throat right now, what would that feel like?

Nick: Like there's something stuck in there.

Therapist: Like an object is stuck in your throat?

Nick: Yes. Like something is growing and getting bigger in my throat and constricting my breathing.

Therapist: And when you feel this fear of the relationship ending and this sensation in your throat, that's when you feel the urge to start explaining and defending yourself?

Nick: Yes.

Therapist: It's difficult to listen to her disappointment when you feel this way?

Nick: Yeah. I feel panic. I need to do something to fix it.

Therapist: Let's come back to the experience in your throat. Help me understand what it feels like. Is something expanding? How fast is it growing? How big is it right now? Outline it with your hand.

Nick: [Outlining the shape with his hand] It's right here in my throat. It's big, it's filling up my entire throat.

Therapist: Is it moving?

Nick: It feels like a vacuum, sucking out all my air.

Therapist: Tell me more about this sensation.

Nick: It feels hot. It's hard to breathe in.

Therapist: How fast is the vacuum sucking out the air? Take a deep breath. Open up to this sensation. Let's get curious about how this vacuum feels in your throat right now.

Nick: Well, it's slowing down now.

Therapist: Your breathing is less constricted?

Nick: Yes. It got a little smaller.

Therapist: What's happening with the shame/not-good-enough feeling right now?

Nick: It's softer. It isn't hurting so much.

Therapist: Okay. Let's try to have Agnes continue to express her disappointment and notice the moment when the sensation in your throat intensifies or if any other sensations or emotions come up. Would you be willing to do that if it means that it will bring you closer to your value of being validating and supportive?

Nick: Okay.

Therapist: I'm going to ask Agnes to continue expressing her feelings and needs, and just notice any urges to explain or defend yourself. See if you can be aware of this experience of shame and inadequacy in your body. See if you can make space for this experience and just reflect back her feelings to her.

Nick: Okay.

Therapist: Notice when you turn toward the feeling and allow it in that you don't have to defend and explain yourself. You can just have the feeling. You can watch it—like we did—and not try to avoid it with old coping behaviors.

When conducting exposure, you will often find that multiple schemas may unfold. First, Nick's failure schema was triggered and, as the exposure unfolded, feelings of abandonment and defectiveness also emerged.

When doing exposure with couples, the therapist has to stop the interaction as soon as one of the partners gets triggered or engages in an SCB. The exposure process should begin immediately with the triggered partner. While the partner will have strong urges to engage in old SCBs, the therapist has to remain determined to bring both partners out of the content and into the present-moment emotional experience. The therapist defuses from thoughts and comes back to helping partners articulate the emotional experience. As schema-driven thoughts emerge, label the thoughts ("There's a judgment thought") and bring attention back to the emotional experience.

Couples may not recognize when they are engaging in SCBs. As a result, the therapist must continue to bring triggered partners back to describing and labeling the experience nonjudgmentally, and help observing partners notice their own experience and stay present. The key is for the couple to experience each other's pain with nonjudgmental loving-kindness.

In summary, by allowing partners to experience avoided emotions, exposure provides a bridge across the barrier of schema affect. Schema pain, because it has been experienced and tolerated, no longer blocks the road to values-based communication.

CHAPTER 8

Skill Deficits as Barriers to Values-Based Actions

Now that couples have gained knowledge about how to defuse from schema-driven thoughts and have faced schema-driven emotions, they can start learning skills to communicate more effectively in the relationship. Even when partners have clarified their values and developed the means to work with internal barriers, they may still need assistance in learning problem-solving skills for managing conflict. In this chapter we present five key communication skills that will help partners respond to conflict in effective, nondamaging ways:

Listening and validating

Asserting

Negotiating

Pausing with time-outs

Appreciating

Helping couples communicate effectively involves teaching them how to assert feelings and needs using clear communication, and then teaching partners how to listen and validate actively. We'll examine negotiation skills and how to pause (take a time-out) when partners get emotionally overwhelmed. Finally, we'll offer specific appreciation strategies for helping couples express gratitude.

This chapter is the first part of a two-part approach. It will prepare you for the work you'll do to propose values-based solutions that respond to the needs of both partners and integrate these communication skills in session. The process, in the next chapter, involves reviewing triggering events from the past week and identifying alternative behaviors to replace SCBs.

Schemas and Corresponding Skills Deficits

Before we launch into the five essential components for effective communication, let's look at common skills deficits that correspond to particular schemas. A therapist's awareness of each partner's schemas will help him or her identify which communication skills to focus on.

Abandonment/instability: Individuals who have a high score on the abandonment/instability schema may have difficulties initiating or adhering to time-outs in relationships, especially during moments of conflict. They struggle with allowing space, spending time alone, or not having an immediate resolution to a conflict. They may also use ineffective forms of expression that include blame, guilt, criticism, or threats.

Mistrust/abuse: Individuals who have a mistrust/abuse schema may have problems creating and maintaining boundaries, including adhering to time-outs. Their suspicion may also act as a barrier to active listening and providing appreciation and rewards in relationships. People with this schema are afraid to express vulnerability and may need assistance in sharing their feelings and needs.

Emotional deprivation: Partners who have a high score on this schema have difficulty making requests and expressing needs. They tend to oscillate between either holding back from making requests and asking for help or making excessive and urgent demands and threats. These individuals have a tendency to hold in their feelings and needs until the experience of deprivation becomes so intolerable that they start coercing partners to meet their demands.

Defectiveness/shame: Partners who have a core belief that they are defective typically have difficulty being vulnerable or sharing fears, hurt, and insecurities. They may attempt to hide their flaws by covering up feelings and needs. Their fear of being exposed leads them to be secretive or emotionally inexpressive. Individuals who have this schema struggle with reflective listening and validation. They tend to get triggered by a partner's feedback or expression of negative feelings. Instead of reflecting their partner's feelings and needs, they may attempt to defend themselves through overexplaining or withdrawing.

Social isolation/alienation: Individuals with a social isolation/alienation schema have a sense of being different from others, and they often feel alone even in intimate relationships. As a result, they struggle with validating a partner's different experience and appreciating a partner with whom they aren't sure they belong. Ambivalence gets in the way of expressing feelings and appreciation, and being vulnerable.

Dependence: Partners with this schema tend to have difficulty taking no for an answer. They may use demands instead of requests and also struggle with adhering to time-outs during conflict. Conversely, people who feel dependent on their partner may have difficulty asserting themselves and negotiating their needs and wants.

Failure: This schema often results in difficulty taking in feedback and validating a partner's feelings and needs. When a partner wants something, it's interpreted as proof of failure, of having done things wrong, or of not being good enough. And the response is defensive. Negotiating is also difficult because it requires acknowledging the legitimate needs of the other.

Entitlement/grandiosity: Individuals who score high on the entitlement/grandiosity schema tend to struggle with negotiating fairly and validating their partner's needs. They often minimize or belittle a partner's desires and focus on advocating for their own instead. They have difficulty using collaborative strategies when negotiating and don't feel obligated to compromise. They may also have problems hearing limits, accepting no for an answer, and empathizing with a partner's emotions. Individuals with an entitlement schema may benefit from working on reflective listening skills, perspective-taking skills, and negotiation skills. More important, partners of individuals with such schemas are likely to need help with assertion and negotiation skills.

Self-sacrifice/subjugation: Individuals who score high on the subjugation schema may have difficulty identifying their needs and feelings in the moment. They tend to be passive, and they don't recognize when their boundaries have been crossed. They often feel a sense of guilt and obligation to meet their partner's needs, and struggle with making requests, saying no, giving consequences, and setting boundaries and limits. Their compliance may also lead them to build resentments and express anger in ineffective ways.

Unrelenting standards: People who receive a high score on perfectionism tend to have difficulties negotiating, especially in the area of brainstorming, identifying alternative (compromise) solutions, and remaining flexible with their ideals. Their unrelenting standards may also prevent them from expressing appreciation (because nothing is ever good enough), validating a partner's struggles, and positively reinforcing their partner's desirable behaviors.

Listening

Listening is an important skill that helps partners better understand each other's experience and build empathy. When partners are better able to listen to each other with genuine curiosity and openness, they are better equipped to understand each other and potentially meet each other's needs. Helping partners hone their listening skills will increase intimacy and improve relationship satisfaction.

The role of the listening partner is to actively listen to the speaking partner and provide empathy and validation. The therapist coaches the receiver to listen for feelings and underlying needs, and reflect back understanding. The receiver paraphrases what he or she has heard and reflects the speaker's feelings and needs without personalizing or taking responsibility for a partner's experience. The goal is not to intellectually understand but to emotionally connect and empathize.

One of the key challenges is to listen with genuine curiosity. Active listening means understanding the speaker's full experience, including how he or she thinks, what he or she feels, and what he or she needs. When partners are experiencing trouble, it is often because they have become preoccupied with their own defensive responses or have reached conclusions before hearing the entire message. They may attempt to avoid schema pain by using tactical measures that block listening.

Barriers to Empathic Listening

What follows are ten common barriers to empathic listening (also available in appendix D and online at http://www.newharbinger.com/34800). All of these strategies function as barriers to effective listening because they all attempt to minimize, reduce, or influence the experience of the speaker. When these tactics are used, they don't allow the listener to fully understand and validate the speaker's perspective.

Explaining. You can recognize that partners are defending, overexplaining, or justifying their position when they come up with reasons and rationalizations as to why they are not at fault. These defensive tactics may minimize the speaker's feelings and needs. "I couldn't call you because…" "I tried my best to show up on time, but…" "I didn't know that the event was so important to you."

Reassuring. This strategy replaces listening with behavior that functions to console or reassure the other. The purpose is to make it better and lessen the pain. This can be experienced as minimizing or belittling the emotional response. "I do care about you," "It's not your fault," "Your boss is not going to fire you," "There's nothing to worry about," "It will be okay."

Interrogating. Interrogating functions as a barrier when the listening partner is more concerned about getting the facts right and understanding his or her own perspective rather than understanding the speaker's viewpoint. Here partners ask a lot of questions, trying to reason and rationalize out of the emotion. "What time did you expect me to call you?" "Why does your boss's opinion of you matter so much?" "Why do you care if your brother doesn't come to dinner?" "Why is it necessary for us to be on time for everything?"

Problem solving. Problem solving can also be useful. However, this technique is usually effective after individuals feel heard and understood. When partners move on to problem solving prematurely, it often functions to avoid staying with the speaker's emotions. In this barrier, a partner jumps into giving advice or trying to problem solve rather than listening. "You shouldn't let your boss talk to you that way," "You should tell Jenny that it's none of her business," "We can tell your mom that she can babysit next week."

Placating. Partners are placating when they agree with everything without truly listening. They're more preoccupied with pleasing the other person, smoothing things over, or avoiding conflict rather than understanding. They take responsibility, apologize, or comply in order to have the conversation end, which blocks true understanding.

Derailing. Derailing commonly happens in conflict. Partners derail the conversation when they change the subject or steer it in another direction. It functions as a barrier because it moves the conversation in a different direction than the speaker intended. The speaker's agenda gets sidetracked.

Correcting. This behavior refocuses the conversation toward getting the facts "right" and examining minutia rather than understanding the partner's experience. "I called you at 5:15, not 5:25," "That happened on Tuesday night, not Friday." This often feels confusing and distracting for the speaker and invalidates his or her emotional response.

Judging. Partners are judging when they make global evaluations about the speaker and use it as justification for not listening to the whole message. "You're never satisfied with anything," "You're selfish," "You're too sensitive." Partners are also judging when they only respond to parts of the message that confirm their own beliefs.

Identifying. Partners are identifying when they connect what the speaker is saying back to themselves and launch into a story about their own experience. "I felt exactly the same when you abandoned me on my birthday last year," "Well, what about that time when you called me a jerk?" "My mom also intrudes on our relationship." The focus then turns to the listener's concerns rather than what the speaker is attempting to convey.

Mind reading. Partners are engaged in mind reading when they respond to what they believe the speaker's intentions are rather than what the speaker is actually saying. When partners are mind reading, they attend to assumptions about what the speaker "really means" or what his or her hidden motives are.

It will be helpful for the therapist to take a direct approach to these barriers by stopping the behaviors and coaching the listener (who hasn't been listening) to reflect back feelings and needs. You can directly point out the barrier that is being used and ask the listener to reflect instead. For example, "Joe, you are giving Heather advice about what to do with her boss, but would you be willing to reflect back some of the feelings and needs that Heather is expressing right now?"

The therapist may also want to employ defusion and mindfulness techniques with schema-driven thoughts and feelings that block reflective listening. Encourage couples to resist blaming each other and, instead, direct their attention back to the feelings and underlying needs being expressed in the conversation. When partners separate themselves from the responsibility of fixing or changing the other's pain, they have the freedom to accept full responsibility for their own feelings, needs, intentions, and behaviors. This creates the ability to truly understand and empathize with each other's experience.

Key Skills for the Listening Partner

Teaching cornerstone listening skills can help partners overcome the previously discussed listening barriers:

Paraphrasing. Paraphrasing involves reflecting back and summarizing what the speaker communicated, using one's own words. Have the listener summarize what he or she understood. Use the List of Feelings and List of Needs In a Relationship to have the listening partner articulate the speaker's experience and help the speaker feel understood.

Confirming. Confirming means clarifying whether the message was heard correctly. After the listening partner has summarized the message, have him or her ask questions to confirm that the message was correctly understood. "Is that correct?… Is there anything else?" Make certain to have the listener get verification from the speaker before giving any feedback.

Validating. Validating goes a step beyond paraphrasing. The listener confirms that the speaker's reactions are valid and make sense given the speaker's schemas and experiences. The listener makes statements that convey empathy and validation such as, "It makes sense that you feel scared when we're in new situations, given that your mother was so unpredictable," "It makes sense that you feel alone when I go away on work trips because your dad was often preoccupied with work." These statements reflect to the expressing partner that his or her responses make sense and are understandable.

Responding. Once the listener has heard and understood the whole message, he or she can respond and give feedback. The feedback should include his or her thoughts and feelings but be expressed, to the extent possible, without judgment. Once the speaker feels heard and understood, partners can reverse roles.

Asserting

A crucial step toward effective communication is teaching couples about the important skill of asserting themselves. Teaching couples to express themselves effectively will help listening partners hear and validate expressing partners' experience. The following guidelines break down this skill into three steps: observing, stating feelings, and expressing underlying needs. After the expressing partner has gone through the steps, the listening partner uses the skills from the previous section to validate the experience before moving towards problem solving. The guidelines are followed by important handouts that assist couples in identifying feelings and needs, along with a discussion about the difference between needs and wants. We wrap up this skill with formulas for making assertive requests and setting boundaries.

Assertion Guidelines

Explain the following three assertion guidelines to partners:

STEP 1. OBSERVE

The first step is to assist the expresser in describing the triggering event using facts and observations. What did he or she observe? What actually happened in the situation? What did the partner say or do? The key is to articulate this observation without placing judgment. Observations, unlike judgments, are stated facts, free of evaluations. Judgments are statements that inherently impose evaluations and moral assumptions. Observations and descriptions identify facts that can be tested, versus judgments and evaluations, which reflect our own subjective reality.

Distinguishing between judgments and observations is tricky. Our minds fool us into believing that our judgments are actual descriptions of facts. For example, stating that a chair is comfortable is a judgment about that chair. It's not a true description of the chair. Stating that a chair is tall is also a judgment. Describing a chair made out of wood or saying that it is black would be a true observation. It is a fact about the chair. Often our mind comes up with judgments about our partners that masquerade as facts or descriptions. Because judgments may make others defensive and block effective listening and communication, it is important to catch judgments in session and help partners turn them into observations.

Separate the behaviors from the person. Have partners avoid using global labels such as, "You're selfish," "You're lazy," "You're too sensitive," "You're cruel." Suggest they use facts to describe hurtful behaviors. Attacking a partner's character rather than giving feedback about his or her behavior puts the partner on the defensive.

STEP 2. STATE FEELINGS

Next, have the expresser state the feelings that result from the unmet needs. Have partners describe emotions using simple labels of affect (see List of Feelings When Needs Are Unmet in Relationships and List of Feelings When Needs Are Met in Relationships provided in this chapter, in appendix D, and online at http://www.newharbinger.com/34800). Help the asserter use "I" statements of emotion rather than "You" statements. "I" statements are non-blaming and put the responsibility on the speaker. "You" statements blame and suggest that the person receiving the message is the cause for the speaker's problems. And "you" statements pull the listener to feel responsible for fixing the expresser's experience, rather than validating it. For example, "You make me angry" can be restated as "I feel alone."

Beware of judgments disguised as feelings. Some experiences—"I feel rejected," "I feel manipulated," "I feel abandoned," "I feel dismissed"—are not feelings; rather, these are judgments about the partner's intentions and behaviors. Also, whenever the words "I feel" are followed by the words "you," "like," "that," "it," "as if," or "because," they usually do not describe actual feelings. In order to avoid judgments that masquerade as feelings, have partners look at the List of Feelings When Needs Are Unmet in Relationships, the List of Feelings When Needs Are Met in Relationships, and the List of Pseudo-Feelings (in this chapter) while practicing this skill.

STEP 3. EXPRESS NEEDS

Behind all negative feelings lie unmet needs. If partners have difficulty identifying their needs, have them look at the List of Needs in Relationships later in this chapter. When individuals describe negative feelings such as hurt, fear, or shame, it means that there is an underlying need that's causing them pain. When people use aversive strategies to express their feelings, it is a desperate and unskilled attempt at getting needs met.

The therapist helps the expresser turn criticism into descriptions of needs by translating judgments into yearning. For example, if a partner says, "You're so cold," the therapist can translate this into having a need for warmth and empathy. If a partner says, "You're so critical," you might call this a need for acceptance and support. If a partner says, "You're a liar," reframe this as a need for honesty and trust in the relationship. After the expressing partner has described each of these three steps, the listening partner uses the listening skills from the previous section to validate the expressing partner. Once validation has occurred, partners can decide whether they would like to make a request, utilize problem solving, or negotiate. It is critical that validation and understanding occur before partners take steps toward problem solving.

List of Feelings When Needs Are Unmet in Relationships*

Afraid
Aggravated
Agitated
Agonized
Alarmed
Alienated
Aloof
Ambivalent
Angry
Anguish
Animosity
Annoyed
Anxious
Apathetic
Appalled
Apprehensive
Ashamed
Baffled
Beat
Bereaved
Bewildered
Bored
Burned out
Cold
Concerned
Conflicted
Confused
Contempt
Cranky
Dazed
Defeated
Dejected
Depleted
Depressed
Despair
Desperate
Despondent
Detached
Devastated
Disappointed
Disconcerted
Disconnected
Discouraged
Disgruntled
Disgusted
Disheartened
Dismayed
Displeased
Distant
Distracted
Distraught
Distressed
Disturbed
Doubtful
Drained
Dread
Edgy
Embarrassed
Enraged
Envious
Exasperated
Exhausted
Fatigued
Fidgety
Flummoxed
Flustered
Fragile
Frantic
Frazzled
Frightened
Frustrated
Furious
Gloomy
Grieved
Guarded
Guilty
Heartbroken
Heavyhearted
Helpless
Hesitant
Hopeless
Horrified
Hostile
Hurt
Impatient
Indifferent
Indignant
Inhibited
Insecure
Irate
Irritable
Irritated
Isolated
Jealous
Jittery
Leery
Lethargic
Listless
Livid
Lonely
Longing
Lost
Melancholy
Miserable
Mistrustful
Mortified
Mournful
Nervous
Numb
Outraged
Overwhelmed
Panicked
Perplexed
Perturbed
Pessimistic
Petrified
Powerless
Puzzled
Rattled
Regretful
Remorseful
Removed
Repulsed
Resentful
Reserved
Resigned
Restless
Sad
Scared
Self-conscious
Sensitive
Shaky
Shocked
Skeptical
Startled
Stressed-out
Stuck
Surprised
Suspicious
Tense
Terrified
Tired
Torn
Troubled
Turbulent
In turmoil
Uncertain
Uncomfortable
Uneasy
Uninterested
Unnerved
Unsettled
Vulnerable
Wary
Weak
Weary
Withdrawn
Worn out
Worried
Wretched
Yearning

* Adapted from *Nonviolent Communication* (Rosenberg, 2003).

List of Feelings When Needs Are Met in Relationships**

Absorbed
Affectionate
Alert
Amazed
Amused
Appreciative
Aroused
Astonished
Awed
Blissful
Calm
Centered
Cheerful
Clearheaded
Comfortable
Compassionate
Confident
Content
Curious
Delighted
Eager
Ecstatic
Elated
Empowered
Encouraged
Energetic
Engaged
Enthralled
Enthusiastic
Entranced
Equanimous
Excited
Exhilarated
Expectant
Exuberant
Fascinated
Fulfilled
Glad
Grateful
Happy
Hopeful
Inspired
Interested
Intrigued
Invigorated
Involved
Joyful
Lively
Loving
Mellow
Moved
Open
Openhearted
Optimistic
Passionate
Peaceful
Playful
Pleased
Proud
Refreshed
Rejuvenated
Relaxed
Relieved
Rested
Restored
Safe
Satisfied
Secure
Serene
Sexy
Silly
Stimulated
Surprised
Sympathetic
Tender
Thankful
Thrilled
Touched
Tranquil
Trusting
Vibrant
Warm

** Adapted from *Nonviolent Communication* (Rosenberg, 2003).

List of Pseudo-Feelings

These are common judgments that often get confused for feelings (Rosenberg, 2003; Lasater, 2010).

- Abandoned
- Abused
- Attacked
- Belittled
- Betrayed
- Bullied
- Cheated
- Cornered
- Criticized
- Diminished
- Dismissed
- Disregarded
- Ignored
- Inadequate
- Incompetent
- Insulted
- Intimidated
- Invalidated
- Manipulated
- Minimized
- Misunderstood
- Neglected
- Patronized
- Provoked
- Rejected
- Taken for granted
- Threatened
- Tricked
- Unappreciated
- Uncared for
- Unheard
- Unimportant
- Unloved
- Unseen
- Unsupported
- Unwanted
- Used
- Violated
- Wronged

List of Needs in Relationships***

Safety

- Balance
- Compassion
- Consistency
- Predictability
- Presence
- Privacy
- Reliability
- Respect/self-respect
- Rest
- Security
- Stability
- Touch
- Trust

Self-Worth

- Acceptance
- Appreciation
- Challenge
- Effectiveness
- Equality
- Growth
- Hope
- Meaning
- Praise
- Progress
- Purpose
- Reassurance
- To know and be known
- To matter
- To see and be seen
- Validation

Connection

- Affection
- Attention
- Awareness
- Belonging
- Celebration
- Closeness
- Communication
- Community
- Companionship
- Empathy
- Guidance
- Harmony
- Inclusion
- Intimacy
- Love
- Nurturing
- Support
- Tenderness
- Understanding
- Warmth

Autonomy

- Adventure
- Choice
- Discovery
- Freedom
- Independence
- Space
- Spontaneity
- Stimulation

Self-Expression

- Authenticity
- Clarity
- Creativity
- Fun
- Honesty
- Humor
- Inspiration
- Integrity
- Passion
- Sexual expression
- Transparency

Realistic Limits

- Consideration
- Contribution
- Cooperation
- Fairness
- Mutuality
- Participation
- Reciprocity

*** Adapted from *Nonviolent Communication* (Rosenberg, 2003).

Underlying Needs vs. Wants

According to *nonviolent communication*, what drives all of our behaviors are underlying needs that we are seeking to meet (Rosenberg, 2003). These are universal needs that we long for and desire in our relationships. It's important to help couples distinguish between *wants* (requests) and *needs*, because although our wants may clash, our needs can still be met (Rosenberg, 2003).

Wants are the specific behaviors we would like from a partner in order to meet certain needs. For example, an individual who needs support may want her partner to accompany her to a medical appointment or help choose among treatment options. When we want something from our partner, we ask for it by making an assertive request (described in the next section). The need describes the underlying yearning, while each want is a specific opportunity to satisfy the larger need.

Identifying needs helps couples reach win-win negotiations. This is accomplished by helping each partner understand the underlying need of the other. Understanding each other's needs can facilitate the negotiation process because underlying needs rarely conflict; they create a common ground and can be met in many different ways (Rosenberg, 2003). If partners become embroiled in the content of what they are stating they *want* (or are requesting), they can fall into win-lose negotiations in which one partner gets what he or she wants and the other doesn't. But if you help partners clarify their underlying needs, they'll find that they can reach fair agreements most of the time. Although agreements may differ from the original request, they may still satisfy the underlying needs of both partners.

For example, let's imagine partner A *wants* to go to a friend's birthday party, and partner B *wants* to stay at home. Partner A feels that he tends to go to events that B values but that B doesn't go to events that A values. On the other hand, partner B feels that A makes unilateral decisions and doesn't take B's wants into account when making plans. After exploring their underlying needs, you realize that partner A *needs* fairness and partner B's underlying *need* is collaboration. With a clear acknowledgment of their needs, the couple can discuss attending the birthday party in detail and make specific decisions regarding how long they will stay, how much alcohol they will drink, their mode of transportation, and so on.

A key principle in couples therapy is that each partner's needs are equally valid. Even when partners have very different needs, both should be recognized as equally important. For example, if partner A needs space, and partner B needs nurturance, these apparently contradictory needs should be considered as equal. Once the principle of equally valid needs is established, partners can negotiate solutions that address—at least in part—both of their underlying needs.

Needs are not the same as values. As we've discussed in chapter 4, values reflect the kind of actions we want to take as a person, whereas needs are our desires for the way we want our partner to be. Values are about our own behaviors, whereas needs are about what we want to get from others. Values are always under our control. For example, we can behave compassionately whether or not others treat us with compassion. Needs are often met or not met depending on our partner's behavior.

Let's imagine that support is an important value for a partner. Here are some examples of what steps can be taken to move toward the *value* of being a supportive partner:

- Encourage my partner when he feels overwhelmed with work.
- Ask my partner how he's feeling about work.
- Help out more around the house when he has a deadline coming up.
- Remind him of his positive qualities when he's feeling insecure.
- Give compliments and express gratitude when he makes an effort.

Here are some examples of *needs* around getting support:

- I need my partner to support my friendships.
- I need my partner to support my career.
- I need my partner to support me with our daily tasks.
- I need emotional support from my partner.

Here are some examples of what *requests* partners make when needing support:

- Would you be willing to help me with the chores when I have a deadline coming up at work?
- Would you be willing to pick up the kids after school this Friday?
- Would you be willing to help me problem-solve an issue I'm having with a coworker?
- Would you be willing to help me edit a paper?
- Would you be willing to chat with me about a problem I'm having with a friend?

Making Assertive Requests

The *request* describes what a partner would like in order to get his or her underlying need met. An effective request is a very specific and doable behavior. It is stated in positive language, meaning it describes an action partners *want* rather than something they don't want. For example, a negatively stated request would be, "Can you spend less time with your friends?" Whereas a positively stated request might be, "Would you be willing to spend two evenings a week together at home?" Requests that are stated in the negative don't provide a clear description of the actions one really wants; they also tend to provoke resistance (Rosenberg, 2003). The clearer and more specific partners can be about what they want, the more likely they are to get their needs met.

Requests take on the appearance of *demands* when feelings and underlying needs are not expressed. Conversely, when requests are accompanied by a description of feelings, underlying needs, and a clear objective, the receiver is more likely to respond empathically (Rosenberg, 2003).

Use the following formula to help partners make requests of each other using *complete messages*:

When ______________________________

I felt [or feel] ______________________________.

I have a need for ______________________________.

Would you be willing to ______________________________?

Example:

When *we make an agreement to meet up at a certain time and you show up late*

I feel *hurt.*

I have a need for *reliability and respect.*

Would you be willing *to meet tomorrow at 3 p.m. on time as we agreed?*

The requesting partner has the right to make any request he or she would like to make, as long as the other person is free to say no. When the partner making the request doesn't accept no for an answer, it is a demand, not a request. A partner faced with a demand only has two choices: submit or rebel (Rosenberg, 2003). To identify in session whether a partner has made a request or a demand, observe how he or she responds if the request is denied. Responding with blame, guilt, attack, or punishment is evidence of a demand process. You then need to label the demand as such and ask the requesting partner to reformulate what he or she is asking for.

Stress to the couple that they have the freedom to meet any request or not meet it. But also offer these additional options:

- Take time to evaluate your partner's willingness to meet the request.
- Negotiate the terms of the request: "I'm willing to do A, but not B." Or "I'm willing to do C, but under these conditions."

After a receiving partner has agreed or declined to meet a request, help the requesting partner to express appreciation and gratitude if the answer was yes. You can also engage in negotiation if a partner was unwilling to meet a request.

Often individuals with entitlement, self-sacrifice, subjugation, and deprivation schemas have difficulty making requests or negotiating them fairly. Individuals with a self-sacrifice/subjugation schema struggle with identifying what they want or need. They may not know what their ideal outcome would be or what to request. Individuals with an emotional deprivation schema tend to confuse demands for requests, which may lead to a self-fulfilling prophecy of feeling deprived. That is, they often suppress their emotions and needs until they feel an intense yearning. They may then become demanding and urgent about their needs. This can lead the receiving partner to feeling pressured, possibly resulting in resistance.

Individuals with an entitlement/grandiosity schema have difficulty taking their partner's needs into consideration. They resist agreeing to requests and often don't follow through with agreements made. If one partner habitually fails to follow through with agreements, use the skills in the next section to help the requesting partner set boundaries and protect him- or herself in the relationship.

Setting Boundaries

Boundaries are personal guidelines, rules, and limits to protect oneself from intolerable behavior. It should be noted that a number of behaviors are uncomfortable but not necessarily intolerable. It's important to help partners distinguish between these two types of behaviors. It will be useful to distinguish behaviors that they dislike but are tolerable from behaviors that are intolerable and simply unworkable in the long run.

For example, an individual may dislike that his or her partner watches too much television, is messy, or doesn't eat healthy food. But these behaviors may not be deal breakers. When uncomfortable behaviors are tolerable, help partners negotiate what behaviors they are willing and unwilling to change. If a partner isn't willing to change his or her behavior, the requesting partner has the choice to:

1. accept the behavior as tolerable and let go of struggling to change it,
2. decide that the behavior is intolerable and change the response to it in order to protect oneself,
3. decide that the behavior is intolerable and end the relationship, or
4. decide that the behavior is tolerable or intolerable and continue to stay in the relationship and engage in old, ineffective efforts to change the behavior.

If individuals choose the latter, help them assess the cost of these strategies in the long run and whether these strategies are workable in light of that cost.

Behaviors that are intolerable for a partner—such as excessive drinking, negative habits, cheating, lying, or physical violence—and that continue despite promises and failed agreements, require more assertive limit setting. This may also require an exploration of the workability of the relationship itself. Helping partners set these stricter boundaries involves identifying the problem (intolerable behaviors), what precisely will happen if the intolerable behavior recurs (consequences), and supporting consistent follow-through with consequences.

Verbalizing feelings and needs is only a part of creating boundaries. Clarifying consequences and following through consistently is necessary. Often partners get stuck verbalizing their boundaries by overexplaining and convincing—they fuse with the idea that if they can just get the other person to get it, to truly understand the impact of the problem behavior, then they can persuade their partner to change. This is generally not an effective boundary-setting technique and may be viewed by many as nagging.

Explain to couples that boundaries are freely chosen, that they don't have to be explained, justified, validated, or understood. However, partners are responsible for identifying boundaries (what is tolerable and intolerable), clarifying limits, and implementing consequences.

You can use the following formula (an extension of the formula for complete messages) to help partners set boundaries for self-protection/self-care:

When ____

I felt [or feel] ____.

I need ____.

If you ______________________________ [the problem behavior]

I will ______________________________ [your specific self-care action] in order to take care of myself.

If you continue to do this behavior, I will ___________________________.

For example:

When *we make plans to meet at a particular time and you show up late*

I feel *hurt.*

I need *you to respect my time.*

If you *are late again,* I will *wait 15 minutes for you before I leave.* If you continue to *show up late for our plans,* I will *meet you at my house, where I can do other things.*

Another example: When *you lie to me about who you're with,* I feel *scared and helpless.* I need *you to be utterly truthful about what you're doing and who you're with.*

If you *lie again about your activities,* I will *move out.*

Often people mistake consequences and setting limits for retaliation or threats. Setting limits is distinguished from retaliation in that the consequence is expressed clearly and provides the other person the opportunity to avoid it. What differentiates a threat or an ultimatum from a consequence is how it is carried out and what the function is. A consequence is not provided for the purpose of punishing a partner, teaching him or her a lesson, or making him or her feel bad. The function of a constructive consequence is always to protect oneself and to create safety.

The following Consequences vs. Threats handout (also provided in appendix D and online at http://www.newharbinger.com/34800) can help partners understand this distinction.

Consequences vs. Threats

Consequences	Punishments and Threats
Neutral tone of voice	Angry tone of voice
Using leverage to set consistent limits	A consequence that is not followed through with is a threat
Boundary is clearly expressed beforehand	Not stated ahead of time
Compassionate but firm stance	Hostile stance
The function is to protect yourself and create safety	Functions to change or control your partner
Provides choices (e.g., we can have dinner together at the agreed-upon time or you can have dinner alone if you are more than 15 minutes late)	Unwilling to give a choice, unwilling to hear no
Reasons for boundaries are given	Reasons are arbitrarily related to the problem
Are logically connected to the problem behavior	Are not logically connected to or do not follow the problem behavior

Negotiating

You can help couples who have conflicting desires reach a fair agreement by using the negotiation skills described in this section. These skills are crucial, as they can turn any conflict into an opportunity for positive change.

Some people are very good at negotiating. They are able to describe their desired outcomes clearly and can advocate for themselves. Others struggle with articulating their needs and lack clarity about what it is they actually want in a particular situation. Specifically, individuals with self-sacrifice/subjugation schemas tend to struggle with identifying their needs and their ideal outcomes. Individuals with an abandonment schema may also have difficulty articulating and negotiating their needs for fear of being rejected. Conversely, individuals with an entitlement/grandiosity schema are usually very clear about their ideal outcome but have difficulty negotiating fairly and taking their partner's needs into account. Individuals with an emotional deprivation schema fail at times to advocate for their needs, and at other times they fight for their needs with hard negotiation tactics and demands. Both strategies are likely to result in more deprivation.

As you practice negotiating with couples, encourage couples to use these techniques outside of session, especially during times when they have opposing interests or are seeking to reach a collaborative decision. When partners practice negotiating outside of session, they should fill out the Shared Interests Worksheet (provided in this chapter, in appendix D, and online at http://www.newharbinger.com/34800) in order to prepare ahead of time to negotiate effectively.

Ground Rules for Fair Negotiating

Before discussing the topic that is being negotiated, clarify the ground rules for effective negotiation. This step includes identifying both partners' values and clarifying what kind of actions each would like to take in terms of values while facing conflict. Review the following guidelines with partners before starting the negotiation:

- **Be collaborative**: Fair negotiation involves being committed to finding a mutually agreeable outcome. This means letting go of having it be a particular way, staying focused on the needs of each other, and reaching a collaborative solution that takes everyone's needs and feelings into account.
- **Stay flexible**: Remaining flexible means letting go of preconceived solutions and staying open to new ideas and unexpected resolutions. It involves being curious about each other's perspective so that partners can remain open to creative solutions. When couples remain flexible, they are less invested in winning and more concerned with learning a fair process to reach resolutions.
- **No dirty tactics**: Help partners resist labeling, attacking, guilt tripping, or discounting the other person's needs and feelings.

- **Stay empathic**: Have partners put themselves in each other's shoes so that they can try to deeply understand what each of their underlying needs and interests are.
- **Listen**: Use active listening skills, including paraphrasing, reflecting, asking questions, and validating.

The Five Stages of Negotiation

There are five stages to negotiating as a couple: discussion, exploration, identification, proposing solutions, and resolution. Initiate the negotiation process in moments when you recognize that partners (1) have opposing interests and need to problem solve, or (2) need to make a decision. In this section, we'll go through the negotiating process with Amanda and Bob. Amanda wants to spend time with family during Christmas, but her family lives in a different state and, therefore, she and Bob would have to travel to see them. Bob, on the other hand, would rather spend the money to go on vacation for Christmas break.

STAGE 1: DISCUSSION

During the discussion stage, have both partners explore the conflict by stating the facts about the situation and their positions. Each partner takes turns discussing his or her particular view of the situation. For example, Bob (speaking to Amanda) might say, "For the past three years we've spent Christmas with your family, and we have not had the time or the money to take any vacations. I prefer that this year we take a vacation instead of visiting with family."

After Bob says this, the therapist should encourage each to describe their feelings and needs, for example, Bob: "I feel overwhelmed and stressed with work; I need rest." After each partner's views are clear, the couple will move into the discussion stage in earnest using *complete messages*, described earlier in this chapter, to explore the facts of the situation and validate feelings and underlying needs. Include the following four elements in the discussion:

- **The situation**. Begin by describing the situation. This includes all the facts of the matter and each person's opinions: "My family invited us to stay with them during Christmas break, and Bob prefers to take a vacation instead."
- **Feelings**. Next, have partners describe the feelings that this situation brings up for them: "I feel torn because spending time with my family and with Bob for Christmas is important to me… I feel guilty if I don't spend time with my family or with Bob during Christmas… I feel frustrated that Bob prefers to take a vacation… I miss my family."
- **Needs and values**. Have partners express the needs and values that are connected to the situation: "I need collaboration and teamwork… I need to maintain family connection… I need community and cooperation."

- **Ideal outcome (wants).** Finally, have partners describe their interests and wants in the form of an ideal outcome (the solution they most desire): "To see my parents, to spend time with my brother and with friends, and to share time with Bob during Christmas."

STAGE 2: EXPLORATION

In the exploration stage, partners identify mutual interests as well as shared values and needs to aid them in exploring possible solutions. The goal is to identify common interests rather than focusing on competing positions that may create distance. When partners truly understand the values and needs behind each other's interests, they are more able to propose solutions that incorporate both partners' needs. Clarifying underlying needs and values creates flexibility to reach win-win solutions because a need can be met in many different ways.

Partners should fill out the following Shared Interests Worksheet (also provided in appendix D and online at http://www.newharbinger.com/34800) and discuss it with each other in session. Assist individuals in staying curious about their partner's underlying needs and values, validating the importance of each other's interests, and finding areas where interests overlap. Rather than focusing on ways that their needs are opposing, help them notice the underlying commonalities that connect them.

Shared Interests Worksheet

My interests	My values and needs	My partner's interests	My partner's values and needs	Shared interests, values, and needs

In the first column, have each partner list what he or she ideally wants in the situation. Encourage them to list the actions and outcomes that they desire, regardless of whether the other will agree.

In the second column, have each partner list his or her underlying needs and values. This includes what each partner finds important and what's driving their interests. Values might include respect, fairness, closeness with family, autonomy, independence, and so on. They may also include values domains that are of significant importance, such as education, being a responsible parent, health, maintaining friendships, or career.

In the third and fourth columns, have individuals fill out the same information for their partner. They should write down what they think applies to their partner and then talk about it. In the last column, have couples list their shared interests, needs, and values. This column is an important one and will assist partners in proposing solutions to conflicts that are based on areas of agreement.

Example: Amanda's Shared Interests Worksheet

My interests	My values and needs	My partner's interests	My partner's values and needs	Shared interests, values, and needs
To spend Christmas with my family and with Bob	Fairness, Closeness to family, Celebration, Belonging	To take a vacation	Shared experiences with family, Peace, Fairness, Spontaneity	Closeness, Shared experiences with family

After partners have identified shared interests, move on to identifying each partner's ideal, acceptable, and unacceptable solutions.

STAGE 3: IDENTIFICATION

In the identification stage, each partner lists his or her ideal solution to the situation, as well as what are acceptable and unacceptable solutions. You can have partners explore these options by writing down the answers to the following questions:

What is my ideal? Have each partner identify his or her ideal solution. This should be very specific and no longer than a few sentences.

What is acceptable? This describes what each partner could live with. It may not be an ideal solution, but it is tolerable. This section should be the longest. It is important to identify as many acceptable alternatives as possible.

What is unacceptable? This section should include the outcomes that are unacceptable and intolerable to the individual.

The following is an example of this three-step process:

Ideal outcome: "Bob and I spend Christmas with my family."

Acceptable outcomes: "Bob takes a short vacation during Christmas break and makes time to also spend Christmas Eve and Christmas day with me and my family. Or Bob spends Christmas day with me and my family and we take a vacation during Thanksgiving break. Or Bob spends Christmas with my family this year, and we take a vacation next Christmas break."

Unacceptable outcome: "Bob never spends any Christmases with me and my family."

STAGE 4: PROPOSING SOLUTIONS

Using the information gathered, starting with shared interests, and including each partner's ideal, tolerable, and intolerable outcomes, have the couple propose possible solutions. If partners aren't able to generate solutions and are stuck, you can help them brainstorm.

Brainstorming involves making a long list of possible solutions. Encourage an attitude of openness to the idea that there are many agreeable options to resolving any conflict. Guidelines for brainstorming include:

- **No judgments.** Write down every single idea that comes up. Don't evaluate any ideas until later.
- **More is better.** The longer the list and the more ideas partners can write down, the greater the likelihood of reaching a good solution. The more bizarre and wild the ideas are, the better. Encourage partners to think outside the box, even if the idea seems absurd.
- **Satisfy mutual needs.** Encourage partners to propose solutions that either address a mutually shared need or that satisfy various needs from the Shared Interests Worksheet.
- **No repercussions.** Neither partner should be criticized or blamed for any ideas that are suggested.
- **Be collaborative.** Have partners contribute, making suggestions that include changes in behavior on both their parts.

Here are the results from Amanda and Bob's brainstorming session:

- Bob spends this Christmas with Amanda and her family.
- Bob goes on vacation by himself.
- Bob and Amanda go on vacation for Christmas break.
- Bob and Amanda both stay home for Christmas break.
- Bob and Amanda spend all holidays with family except for Christmas.

- Bob and Amanda only spend time with family during Christmas.
- Bob and Amanda take extra time off of work to take a vacation.
- Bob and Amanda switch off every year, one year vacation and the next year with family.
- Bob and Amanda go on vacation every Christmas and spend every Thanksgiving with family.
- Bob and Amanda spend Christmas with Bob's family.
- Bob and Amanda invite Amanda's family to spend Christmas at their house so they can save money for a vacation.

Evaluate and adjust at the end. When partners can't think of any more ideas, have them review the list and discuss it. Cross out all ideas that aren't workable or are intolerable for either partner. Elaborate on ideas that seem workable, and combine ideas to make them better.

To facilitate this process, you can use the following six strategies for compromise:

1. *If you do this for me, I'll do that for you.* If Bob spends Christmas break with Amanda's family, she'll go on vacation with him for Thanksgiving break.
2. *Part of what I want with part of what you want.* Cut Christmas break in half. Spend four days with Amanda's family and four days in Hawaii.
3. *This time my way, next time your way.* This Christmas Bob visits Amanda's family, and the next Christmas Amanda and Bob go on vacation.
4. *My way when I'm doing it; your way when you're doing it.* When I'm driving, we'll go fast; when you're driving, we'll drive slow. When I cook, you'll clean the dishes; and when you cook, I'll clean the dishes. (This strategy can't be applied to this particular example.)
5. *This thing my way; that thing your way.* Christmas every year is Amanda's choice, and New Year's every year is Bob's choice.
6. *Split the difference or reach a middle ground.* Bob goes to Hawaii for Christmas and Amanda visits her family.

STAGE 5: RESOLUTION

Make certain that the decision reached truly feels acceptable and tolerable for *both* partners. Neither partner should compromise underlying needs or values. Although it may be that neither partner gets his or her ideal outcome, the solution shouldn't include either partner's intolerable outcomes. Amanda and Bob decided to use the "part of what I want with part of what you want" strategy and agreed to spend six days in Hawaii together and six days with Amanda's family. This solution felt fair to both of them, and they were able to enjoy their Christmas break together.

The goal is for the therapist to help couples reach a compromise that both find acceptable. But sometimes resolution cannot occur and partners end in disagreement. In that case, have partners continue to explore their own needs and interests, and ask them to agree to return to negotiation at a later time. If partners continue to reach an impasse, each should utilize skills from the "Asserting" section—and each may need to develop his or her own self-care solution.

Pausing with Time-outs

Following through with a time-out during moments of upset is a crucial skill for keeping fights from escalating to abusive levels. When schemas are too activated for partners to be able to communicate effectively or nonaggressively, it's best to disengage from the situation and return to it after partners have taken a pause to cool down. Key to effective use of this strategy is to apply it before a fight gets out of control and before partners engage in hurtful behaviors. The therapist, therefore, helps couples create a time-out contract and assists them in developing strategies for calling time-out in a loving, kind, and collaborative way.

Start by identifying the signal that partners will use when a time-out is necessary. This signal can be a nonverbal gesture, such as the time-out hand signal used in sports. Or it can be a verbal signal, such as the words "Let's stop." It can also be a statement such as, "We're triggered," or "We're not being effective right now," or "I need a time-out." The partner calling the time-out should use non-blaming language that includes "we" or "I" statements. Using "we" language is effective because it suggests that a time-out is being executed for the benefit of both partners and that neither one is at fault. It also serves as a reminder that the time-out contract was a collaborative decision and that both partners had agreed to implement this technique.

After you have identified the signal that partners will use to initiate a time-out, have partners agree on the early warning signs and cues that a time-out is necessary. Discuss with partners what typical behaviors lead to fights. Identify the SCBs that partners engage in that lead to escalating—name calling, attacking, loud voices, or threats are all indicators that a time-out is required.

Finally, have partners agree on a specified time that they will return from the time-out. If a break is too short, partners may still be in a triggered state, and if the break is too long, partners may end up feeling rejected and abandoned. Generally, one hour is a good time frame for a time-out. It provides a long enough period for partners to de-escalate and explore their feelings and needs.

Utilizing Time-outs Effectively

The function of a time-out is to stop ineffective communication during moments of upset and to help couples de-escalate. Time-outs should not be used to avoid uncomfortable subjects but should be initiated when there are actual symptoms of anger and damaging communication (name calling, "you" statements, threats, accusations). Often time-outs fail because they are utilized as avoidance or control strategies. These are ways that partners avoid the discussion to make themselves feel better in the moment, at the expense of solving the problem at hand or dealing with the emotions that conflict brings up. When control strategies occur, they can backfire and become a source of more escalation. Therefore, returning to the topic (after a break) while using problem-solving skills and negotiating fairly is crucial.

A time-out is more effective when partners use the time to explore the conflict from the point of view of values rather than use the time to avoid or distract from the subject. Using a time-out effectively can help partners return to the conversation in a more skillful way: describing their experience, reflecting their experience nonjudgmentally, and taking responsibility for their part of the conflict. This helps soften the tone of the conflict and reduces defensiveness.

The following handout (also provided in appendix D and online at http://www.newharbinger.com/34800) provides couples guidelines for the use of time-outs.

Time-out Guidelines

When a time-out has been called:

1. Stop immediately. When one partner calls a time-out, the discussion should end immediately. The time-out should be respected, and there should be no further explaining, defending, rebuttals, or last words. Everything stops.
2. Leave immediately. The partner who initiated the time-out should leave the location and make actual physical space from the other partner. If partners are physically unable to leave (because they're in an airplane or a car, for example), they should stop all talking and interaction for the agreed-upon period of time.
3. Use the time-out effectively. The break shouldn't be used to escalate anger and ruminate about the issues. Rather, the focus should be self-reflection and taking responsibility for one's experience. A time-out is more effective when partners use the time to identify values, feelings, and needs.
4. Always return at the agreed-upon time. If a partner doesn't return at the agreed-upon time, the time-out will backfire and make things worse. If one partner was left feeling scared and confused, he or she will have difficulty adhering to future time-outs, and the process won't be effective in the long run.
5. Return to the issue. Time-outs don't mean the end of the discussion; a time-out just means postponing the discussion until both partners are able to be more effective.

   During a time-out:

   Defuse from schema-driven thoughts. Observe and let go of these thoughts and return to the present-moment experience.

Use self-compassion. Practice being kind to yourself, and be willing to observe emotional pain. This pain gives you information about what you feel and what you need in the relationship. You shouldn't try to manage or control the pain with blaming thoughts or judgments.

Physicalize the experience. Imagine your feelings have a physical form. Ask yourself where in your body does this pain feel most intense? What color, shape, size is it? How intense is it? Notice any movements or subtle shifts. Practice emotion exposure and/or use the Exposure Worksheet to stay mindfully present with any difficult emotions during a time-out.

Observe action urges. Notice any urges to use old SCBs or try to suppress the pain. Notice any urges to control or change your experience, or to try to change your partner.

Clarify values. What are your most important values in this moment? What do you want to stand for when this pain shows up? What values can help guide your actions and clarify how you would like to proceed?

Utilize problem solving. Use the time-out to gain understanding of the conflict by identifying your feelings and underlying needs and using problem-solving skills. Use the Problem-Solving Worksheet to make your time-out more productive.

Couples can fill out the following worksheets (also provided in appendix D and online at http://www.newharbinger.com/34800) during a time-out in order to make this period more effective.

Exposure Worksheet

To be used during a time-out.

What sensations am I experiencing in my body right now?

Where in my body does this experience feel most intense?

How intense does this experience feel physically in my body on a level from 0 to 10?

Describe the experience:

Color:

Shape:

Size:

Movement:

What are my fears about this time-out?

What are my thoughts or beliefs about this time-out? What is my prediction about this conflict?

What are my values?

Problem-Solving Worksheet

To be used during a time-out.

What schemas got triggered for me?

What is my typical response to this schema? What coping behaviors do I tend to engage in?

What was the specific trigger?

What are my feelings?

What are my needs?

What are my values regarding this conflict?

What would a values-based request look like?

When ____

I felt ____.

I need ____.

Would you be willing to ________________________________?

Appreciating

Given that our minds are self-protection machines that constantly search for threat, gratitude doesn't always come easily to us. It's easier to see the negative qualities about a partner than to see the ways he or she contributes to one's quality of life. In the beginning of a relationship, when partners first fall in love, they often only see the positive qualities and strengths in each other. As time passes, however, partners may start taking the other for granted, focusing attention on a partner's negative qualities and the ways he or she detracts from a desirable life.

Appreciation and gratitude are important skills to hone in order to improve relationship satisfaction. Countless studies have shown that expressing appreciation is the main factor in maintaining a satisfying relationship. The happiest couples report giving each other five times more praise than criticism (Gottman, 1999). Couples who express gratitude report feeling closer to one another, have a sense of greater fulfillment in the relationship, and are more likely to stay together.

Appreciation Reinforces Desired Behaviors

Expressing gratitude for the positive actions of a partner directly influences how the partner behaves in the relationship. Just as children will increase positive behaviors when rewarded by praise, partners increase positive behaviors that have been reinforced by appreciation. When couples want each other to decrease or increase certain behaviors, the most effective way to accomplish that is to consistently reward the desired behavior.

Trying a new behavior in one's relationship is incredibly difficult, and it also involves taking a risk. If a new behavior is not reinforced, it will quickly disappear. It's important to recognize and reward behaviors that partners want more of in order for the frequency to increase. When an old trigger shows up for one partner and he or she engages in new, values-based behaviors, it provides an important opportunity for the other partner to appreciate and reinforce that new behavior. This entails acknowledging how difficult it is to do the new behavior and appreciating the effort.

Helping partners cultivate appreciation involves (1) building mindfulness to notice what they appreciate, and (2) helping partners express appreciation clearly. The next section will provide strategies for helping partners build awareness of positive behaviors in everyday life and identify techniques for expressing appreciation effectively.

Mindful Appreciation

The following techniques can help partners cultivate appreciation and gratitude:

- *Noticing positive qualities about one's partner.* Encourage partners to notice positive qualities that they appreciate about each other every day. These qualities may be personality traits or values, character or behavior, or appearance. Examples might include an act of kindness or generosity, a partner's sense of humor, the way he or she smiles or smells, or the greeting the partner gives when he or she returns home.

- *Noticing the specific ways a partner contributes.* Encourage individuals to notice all the little ways that their partner contributes to their everyday life. What has their partner done today? Did their partner listen to them, help them problem-solve, cook dinner, clean the dishes, provide affection or support?
- *Imagining life without one's partner.* Have individuals imagine that their partner is on his or her deathbed. What would they want to share about things they've appreciated the most? What would they miss the most about their partner? How would their life change? How has their partner contributed to their overall quality of life?
- *Appreciating differences.* Ask partners to think about the positive aspects of certain differences between them. What might they be lacking that their partner has in abundance? Maybe they are messy and their partner is organized. Perhaps they are efficient and their partner is spontaneous, or they are shy and their partner is outgoing. Help partners recognize how these differences have enhanced their lives together.
- *Recalling the honeymoon phase.* Ask partners to think back to those moments when they first met each other. What qualities did they admire about the other? What were they initially attracted to? What were the personality traits and strengths that they saw? Most likely, these strengths are still present; how do these strengths and positive qualities manifest in daily life?
- *Recognizing new behaviors and values-consistent actions.* Encourage individuals to pay close attention to the behaviors that their partner is working on decreasing or increasing, and acknowledge these efforts. Remind partners that changing behaviors is difficult, and it is crucial to notice these moments and express gratitude. Encourage partners to connect each other's behaviors to important values. For example, if a partner has identified being vulnerable as a value and shares an emotion during the week, it's extremely important that this new behavior is responded to with appreciation.

You can have couples fill out the following Appreciation Log (also provided in appendix D and online at http://www.newharbinger.com/34800) to help them track and notice all the ways that a partner contributes to their daily life.

Appreciation Log

Fill out this worksheet throughout the week to build awareness of the ways your partner contributes to your daily life.

	How did my partner contribute to my life today?	**What qualities do I appreciate about my partner today?**	**What about my partner do I find attractive?**	**How did my partner's strengths show up today?**
Monday				
Tuesday				
Wednesday				
Thursday				
Friday				
Saturday				
Sunday				

Expressing Appreciation Directly

Helping couples increase awareness of what they appreciate about each other is a good start, but more is needed. It's important to also help couples express their gratitude for each other in ways that ensure their partner will see and feel it. Direct appreciation can be expressed in actions—a loving hug, kiss, smile, glance, stroke, or rub—and words. When appreciation is expressed verbally, it is important to articulate one's gratitude using *complete messages*.

A complete message incorporates three elements:

- The specific behavior that is being appreciated
- The resulting feelings induced by the behavior
- The reason the behavior is appreciated (the underlying needs that the behavior fulfilled) (Rosenberg, 2003)

Using complete messages is more reinforcing because it helps the receiving partner feel validated and increases the likelihood that the desired behavior will recur. Partial messages, such as "Thank you," or "I appreciate it when you're loving," or "I love it when you're supportive" are too vague. The receiving partner may not know exactly what is being appreciated or why. Effective expressions of appreciation make use of the complete message. For example, "When you told me that you were proud of me for finishing my project…" (the specific behavior that is being appreciated) "…I felt happy and touched…" (the resulting feelings induced by the behavior) "…because it's important to me that you recognize my hard work, and I appreciate your support" (the reason the behavior is appreciated, or the underlying needs that the behavior fulfilled).

In summary, helping partners appreciate each other is paramount for creating a lasting, successful relationship. It's especially important to recognize and acknowledge when partners attempt to engage in new behaviors and values-consistent actions. When partners reinforce new behaviors by responding with appreciation, they are more likely to persist.

Overcoming Communication Skills Deficits

It won't be necessary to teach all five key skills to each partner. However, most couples struggle with one or more skills deficits. Once you have given a couple basic instruction in a specific skill, keep working the skill into each subsequent session. Ask questions such as, "How could you express appreciation at this moment?" or "How could you assert your need right now in a non-blaming way?" or "What are you hearing your partner say? Can you paraphrase it right now?" Constant in-session practice of the key skills, especially when partners are triggered, will make them more accessible for use outside of session.

CHAPTER 9

Values-Based Problem Solving

When partners are in avoidance mode and using SCBs to cope with schema pain, conflict resolution (problem solving) is impossible. As previously noted, the treatment focus now must be on process rather than content (e.g., specific conflict issues). With each partner, the therapist explores schema-driven emotions, avoidance urges, and situation-specific needs. Only when partners have stopped—at least temporarily—using SCBs, and are connecting without avoidance, does problem solving become possible.

Prerequisites for Problem Solving

The prerequisites for beginning problem solving are as follows:

- Partners are emotionally connected, not in avoidance mode.
- Partners have explored emotions related to the conflict.
- Partners have shared specific needs related to the conflict.
- Partners and therapist are vigilant for avoidance urges—SCBs—that may be triggered by addressing the conflict.
- Partners have identified values relevant to the conflict situation.

Example Dialogue

Laura and Amy are struggling with feelings of loneliness. Laura's schema of not belonging leaves her feeling unseen by her partner and alienated from her in social situations. Laura copes by withdrawing and wandering off when the two are spending time with friends and family. Amy struggles with a deprivation schema that triggers feelings of emotional hunger and aloneness. She attempts to overcome the pain by criticizing Laura and making demands. Amy's criticism leaves Laura feeling more unseen and alienated; Laura's withdrawal deepens Amy's aloneness.

The therapist focuses on process rather than the specific conflict (Amy wanting more time with Laura on the weekends).

Therapist: [To Amy] You've been talking about wanting to feel connected to Laura when you're both spending time with friends and family, and I notice your voice is rising and your hands are clenched. What are you feeling right now?

Amy: Sad, angry. Sad and angry.

Therapist: Can you tell Laura about the sadness?

Amy: Like it'll never happen—a real us. I feel alone, left. And that it's not going to get better.

Therapist: Can you stay with the feeling—just watch it for a moment?... What's the need that goes with that emotion?

Amy: I feel this often—when we're at social events, Laura just checks out, disappears. I wish Laura could understand how alone and disconnected I feel.

Therapist: [After a silence] And then, if she understood? Is there anything else you need?

Amy: To be together when we're socializing. To feel like we're a couple, that we're there together? To feel...a softness between us. To feel connected.

Laura: What does that mean? We're always socializing as a couple. [Crossing arms and sitting back in her chair]

Therapist: [To Laura] What's happening right now? I see your posture change. Are you pulling away a bit?

Laura: [Nodding]

Therapist: Can you look at Amy and tell her your feelings right now?

Laura: Scared. That we don't really belong together. That you need someone who isn't me, and I need someone who isn't you. I'm afraid we're going to fall apart, and then I'm afraid we *should* fall apart and won't.

Therapist: You're looking away from Amy. Can you look at her and tell her what you need right now?

Laura: I need you to know how freaked out I am that I don't belong anywhere. How alone I feel. And sometimes, when we're socializing with friends, the feeling's worse.

Amy: Oh.

Addressing ambivalence about facing pain

Therapist: [To Laura] You feel like you don't belong, and when you and Amy are around others, it feels even scarier. And then you have an urge to isolate and withdraw from other people and from Amy. [Pause] As you move toward each other, and act more on values, that pain is going to be there.

For a time, as you say, it might even get worse. Could I ask you this: Would you be willing to work toward strengthening your relationship—even if it means feeling this pain?

Laura: [Silence] That's what I came here for...yes. I still want that.

Therapist: Do you want to move closer to Amy? Even when you feel disconnected from her in social situations; even if it means feeling this pain?

Laura: I do. I just feel so far away from her when we're around her friends and family.

Therapist: Amy, what are you feeling right now?

Amy: Sad. That you feel so alone. Even when we're in these social situations. [Starting to cry] But I guess that's just the truth and I have to...I think I understand better.

Transitioning to problem solving

Therapist: I wonder if you're ready to go back to that issue—spending time with friends and family together and staying connected with each other. What are the values that you'd like to bring to that conversation?

Steps to Values-Based Problem Solving

The foundational element for ACT-informed problem solving is a clear awareness of values. What kind of relationship do partners want to have? How do they want to treat each other as they negotiate their needs? At this point in the treatment process, having spent time identifying core values, partners are usually quick to recognize one or two values that can guide their behavior.

For Amy, the values are being caring and understanding her partner. Laura's values are respecting Amy's feelings and being supportive. The therapist emphasizes that every choice of words and gestures can be drawn from these values, and that the entire problem-solving process is powered by the ways partners commit to treating each other. In essence, the couple will be cocreating new values-based actions.

The second step in problem solving is brainstorming. This component of the classic problem-solving protocol (D'Zurilla & Goldfried, 1971) is adapted for couples by having each partner take turns proposing solutions to a particular conflict that *addresses some of the needs of both*. Brainstorming is covered in detail in chapter 8, but let's review a few key points, such as the brainstorming guidelines:

- No criticism of proposed solutions.
- The more ideas, the better.
- Freewheeling is good—the wilder, the better.

- Look for opportunities to combine and augment proposed solutions.

Ask individuals to avoid saying no to proposed solutions from a partner. Such nay-saying tends to obstruct the process. Encourage them to say, "yes—and..." so the message is, "That's a good idea, and here's something we can add to it." The therapist can make a list of solutions as they are proposed, being sure to appreciate ideas without endorsing them by saying, "Another interesting idea" or "Another possibility," and so on.

In some cases, partners will linger over an idea, work with it, and propose modifications. Support this process. If something appeals to them, wait and see where they go with it. In other cases partners will get off topic. Keep attention on the core conflict, and ask questions such as, "These are very useful ideas, but I wonder what we do about..."

Be careful not to let one partner propose most of the solutions. Facilitate a shared process by sticking to the structure of taking turns. If you notice one partner being relatively passive, ask him or her for a proposed solution and wait for a response. Encourage reluctant or passive partners by reminding them that no idea has to be perfect and that sometimes the strangest ideas turn out to be most helpful.

Throughout the brainstorming process, remind partners that proposed solutions should address *some* of the needs expressed by *each* of them. Entirely self-serving solutions are unlikely to solve the conflict and tend to alienate the other partner. If a partner proposes more than one self-serving solution, ask: "I wonder how this [the solution] includes some of your partner's needs?" Then reiterate each partner's needs and validate their importance.

As always, throughout ACT couples therapy, if avoidance surfaces, stop focusing on content and shift to process (emotions, urges, and needs).

Sometimes partners will seize on and mutually endorse a solution, or, with small modifications, they'll rapidly approach agreement. Other couples will hover around an idea but have very different notions of how to implement it. For these persons, the third step in problem solving—negotiation—will be helpful.

Negotiation has also been covered in detail in the previous chapter, but at this point you can review with partners its main strategies:

- My way this time, your way next time.
- My way when I'm doing it, your way when you're doing it.
- If you do ___________________ for me, I'll do ___________________ for you.
- Part of what I want with part of what you want.
- Try it my way for a week. If you don't like it, we'll go back to the old way.
- Split the difference.
- _________________________________ is important to me. What would I need to do to make it worth your while to go along this time?

Negotiation requires active coaching on the part of the therapist. The core idea, as with brainstorming, is for each partner to get some of what he or she needs. Encourage partners to see each other's needs as valid and important, and to regard negotiation as a tool to include both partners' needs in any solution.

It's not uncommon for individuals to get stuck in the wrong negotiation strategy. If they aren't getting anywhere, encourage partners to review the list of strategies and choose another one. Again, your coaching skills will be critical. Don't let couples flounder—step in and direct them to choose a different negotiation approach.

The fourth step in values-based problem solving is self-care solutions. Not all agreements are going to work out. Partners, for various reasons, may fail to fulfill their new commitments. It's often helpful to have the couple anticipate this possibility and to plan how they will *take care of their own needs* if the agreement falls apart.

Self-care solutions should be addressed without implying blame or failure. Suggest that the new agreement is a good one, yet there's always the possibility that a partner may get overwhelmed by pain or difficulty when carrying it out. What then? Will the partner whose needs are unmet collapse into helplessness or resentment? Will he or she return to old, relationship-damaging SCBs? To avoid this, self-care solutions often include the following elements:

- A clear statement of the partner's primary need
- A plan, should the agreement fail to work, for how the partner will meet his or her need *autonomously*
- Non-blaming language

Self-care solutions are not always needed by *both* partners. You may suggest self-care solutions only for the partner who's in the most pain or whose needs have initiated the conflict.

Some examples of self-care solutions:

- Partner A is concerned about partner B's overspending, and they agree to a monthly cap on discretionary outlays. Partner A includes the following self-care solution: "It's really important to me that we save toward a down payment rather than each month spending more than we make. If our spending cap doesn't work, I'm going to put my paycheck in a separate account."
- Partner C has complained about getting little help from Partner D with housecleaning chores. They've agreed to set two hours aside each Saturday to work together to maintain their home. Partner C includes this self-care solution: "I've every hope our solution will work. But if I'm still doing the lion's share of housework, I'll hire a maid and we can share the cost."

Example Dialogue

Laura and Amy—from the previous example—are struggling with Amy's need to stay connected in social situations, and Laura's need to have her fear and uncertainty in social situations be seen and understood.

Remind the couple of their values

Therapist: As we return to the question of spending more time together with friends and family, there are values that might help you choose the words and ways to talk about this. Amy, you want to be caring and really try to understand Laura. Laura, you want to stay connected and be supportive of Amy's feelings. Can you commit to keeping those in mind as we talk about the issue of being social together?

Laura and Amy: [Nodding]

Brainstorming

Therapist: What I'd like to do is have each of you take turns suggesting possible solutions. But here's the catch: Whatever you propose should provide for at least some of what you *each* need. Here's what I mean: Amy, you need to feel connected to Laura in social situations and to feel that Laura understands your loneliness and how important feeling connected is to you. Laura, you need Amy to see and understand your fear and uncertainty in social situations, and that you sometimes feel more alone, even when you're socializing together.

Laura and Amy: [Silence]

Therapist: I know. Your needs are different, and it's a challenge to see ways to put them together.

Amy: I'd like to have at least one social event a week, and Laura can choose the activity. It can be whatever [looking pointedly at Laura, while Laura says nothing].

Therapist: That's a start. I wonder if we can include Laura's need to have her uncertainty recognized and understood. Any ideas, Laura?

Laura: [Laughs]

Therapist: Is there a way you could shift or modify Amy's idea to make room for some of what you need?

Laura: I guess if I could tell her when I'm getting freaked out.

Therapist: Okay, put that together with her idea.

Laura: We'd spend time socializing together, and I'd tell her if I was feeling weird or freaked out, and then we'd leave.

Amy: How about we don't leave, and if you feel weird or scared, we talk about it?

Laura: How 'bout if I send up a white flag and just give you everything you want? [slumping, looking at the floor]

Deal with avoidance

Therapist: Are you pulling away, disconnecting?

Laura: [Nodding]

Therapist: Can you look at the pain? What's the feeling that came up?

Laura: Just scared. That everything is wrong, and I'll never stop feeling this way.

Therapist: Can you use your value of being supportive and tell Amy? Look at her.

Laura: I'm sorry. I hate myself when I'm like this. I'm scared we'll be doing these social things and I'll feel alone and totally freaked out.

Amy: [Acting on her value of understanding] I want to understand you. If you feel that way, let's stop what we're doing, and tell me about it.

Laura: We both like movies. My idea is that we go to church together on Sundays.

Amy: But you can't socialize in a movie theater.

Therapist: It's an idea. We never know what an idea will turn into [writing it down].

Amy: How about we get dinner with your friend Eric on Saturday and after that we decide whether to do anything further?

Laura: I feel bad. Look, how 'bout if we plan something for Saturday, and if Saturday morning rolls around and I'm freaked, I'll tell you?

Amy: And we don't do it?

Laura: I don't know.

Therapist: You have some good ideas, but it's hard to do brainstorming when every solution hurts and feels triggering. I wonder if we can use some of those negotiation skills we talked about.

Negotiation

Therapist: [Reminding couple of key negotiation strategies] Which one might be useful now?

Laura: What makes sense to me is: "My way this time, your way next time." So one week we could go to dinner with a friend no matter what, and the next weekend, if I get overwhelmed, you go to dinner without me.

Amy: Okay, but I'd like you to tell me how you feel, even if you're freaked out about going to dinner.

Laura: [Long hesitation] I guess so… Okay, I can do that.

The Solution

As every couples therapist knows, the path to a given solution is often full of emotion and difficult truths. And the solution, once reached, may be a rickety platform that collapses under the weight of the next conflict. The object of problem solving is to build both the trust and the skills to face conflicting needs *as partners*.

With Amy and Laura, whether a particular agreement works is less important than the experience of sharing their needs and pain—without running away. For them, the process builds trust that conflicting needs can be faced *as partners*. Each problem-solving session can be a step toward knowing each other better and learning the limits and possibilities of their relationship.

Here are a few special problem-solving techniques that you can teach partners:

Reverse Role-Play

One way to build compassion during problem solving is to use reverse role-play, during which partners respond as each other. This technique can only be used *after* you have thoroughly explored each partner's feelings and needs regarding a particular conflict. You can use this strategy as follows:

1. Ask partners—while playing each other—to talk about their pain related to the conflict.
2. Ask partners—while playing each other—to describe their wishes related to the conflict.
3. Take partners out of role and encourage each to talk about what he or she learned about the other. Do they have more empathy or compassion for a partner's pain? Do they have a stronger appreciation for the needs of the other?

During the negotiation phase, partners can again use reverse role-play as they suggest compromises and reach for a solution.

Modeling

In this technique, also called *doubling*, the therapist role-plays one of the partners, expressing his or her feelings and needs to the other partner. There are several advantages to modeling: partners may gain important communication skills; those who have difficulty articulating their pain get the experience of hearing it expressed clearly; and those who tend to explain themselves with attacking or blaming language get to hear their pain described nonjudgmentally. Partners also experience modeling as validating—someone finally understands what they feel. Finally, modeling the expression of needs can be clarifying and lead to better outcomes during negotiation.

Cocreating solutions

The solutions couples reach for often require one or both to try new behaviors. And the new behavior is far more likely to take root if it is values based. Ask partners these questions regarding the conflict: "What would the *solution* look like if it was shaped by your values? What would your *behavior* (in the conflict situation) look like if it was shaped by your values?"

Have each partner answer, and write the answers down. Give the couple your notes and ask them to work together—as partners—for a few minutes to combine both responses into a single solution.

Clarity about values is essential to problem solving for couples. The skills (see chapter 8) are not enough for effective problem solving. Values and intentions give the skills direction and context for more effectual solutions.

CHAPTER 10

Perspective Taking

When couples are together for a long time, they build stories about each other. These stories can unintentionally place limits on the partners' understanding of each other—each predicting the other's responses and intentions during conflict. When schema pain is activated, it is even more difficult for partners to see each other flexibly and wholly. Once partners are triggered, they may be blinded to what's actually happening, filtering interactions through their images of the other. Maintaining a healthy relationship requires the ability to remain open to each other's present-moment experience without letting the story dictate one's responses.

As Tirch and colleagues (Tirch, Schoendorff, & Silberstein, 2015) have observed, "perspective taking...allows us to step outside of ourselves and psychologically view the world from the perspective of another being, which provides the basis of a compassionate viewpoint." Flexible perspective taking is a skill that can be cultivated to help partners hold more lightly the stories that they have about each other. Letting go of stories that limit one's perspective can build empathy, helping partners step into each other's shoes and see the world as their partners view it. This strategy can also show that the stories they have about each other may not always be true.

Perspective-taking skills have two components: (1) seeing oneself as separate from one's thoughts, feelings, and sensations, and (2) cultivating a compassionate and flexible view of one's partner as a whole, separate from the *other's* thoughts, feelings, and sensations.

As a part of this process, therapists will want to assist the pair in recognizing that couples consist of two individual people. Additionally, acknowledging and accepting both human experiences as valid will be important. This doesn't mean condoning or excusing problem behaviors; it means understanding how each partner perceives life and the relationship.

From an ACT viewpoint, perspective taking is rooted in the (self-as-context) observing self, the self that *experiences* but doesn't *become* content (thoughts, emotions, sensations). This capacity to observe experience and disidentify with content also allows us to take the perspective of another, to observe experience as a partner sees it, and to live for a while in his or her skin.

Strategies for building perspective taking include using reverse role-play, revisiting key childhood events, and awareness exercises to help partners understand each other's worldview and schema pain. The relationship is used as a space to experiment with new behaviors and learn to meet needs that weren't met in the past. Partners learn to relate to each other's primary pain and needs in ways that can heal old wounds and create a restorative emotional experience based on validation.

Revisiting Childhood Events

Because key childhood moments are often the origin of schemas, exploring these through discussions and visualizations can help couples understand each other's schema pain. This is the essence of perspective taking.

There are two ways to assist partners in connecting current triggers to key childhood events. You can do this in the form of a discussion or as a visualization. First, have both partners either discuss or visualize a recent schema-triggering event. Encourage partners to make full contact with emotions, physical sensations, needs, and urges. Then ask them to go back in time to a relevant childhood moment when they had the same feelings. They should fully visualize this event, observing how they felt and how those feelings connect to current schemas and conflicts. Finally, ask partners to share their experiences with each other out loud. Help them use active listening to validate how these early experiences connect to the schema pain each one struggles with today. Helping partners understand the origin of schema pain and how it connects to current triggers builds empathy. Here's an example of the technique. Shelly and Jim have had a recent fight about their children's bedtime.

Example Dialogue

Therapist: Let's go back and look at that argument. I know that it triggered both of you. Please close your eyes and see if you can recall what happened—who said what. Just see if you can watch and hear the scene unfolding... Now pay attention to the emotions that came up then, and that are probably coming up now. See if you can find words for those feelings. How big are they? Are they small and easy to hold, or are they big and overwhelming? Are they pea-size, the size of a bread loaf, the size of a truck? Do they have a texture? Are they smooth, rough, or really jagged? What sensations in your body go with these emotions? Where do they seem to be located in your body? Are there urges that go with the emotion—do they make you want to do something? Notice, if you can, what schema this emotion connects to. Just be aware of the connection without judgment...

Now I'm going to ask you to go back in time, back to the days of your childhood. Let yourself go to a time, early in your life, when you had these similar emotions, this same painful feeling. [Pause] When you remember the scene from your childhood, see if you can recognize where you are and who you are with, if anyone. Watch the scene unfolding from the perspective of your child self. As you watch what happens, notice your feelings. As you imagine yourself as that child, notice what it feels like in your body right now in this moment. Notice how you feel about yourself and the situation, and also how similar the feeling is to that recent upset about the argument you had…about the kids' bedtime. Just let yourself be aware of how old this feeling is and how it connects to your schemas today. Just take a breath, feeling the "you" then and how hard the moment was. And gently turn to the "you" you are today, the "you" now, struggling about bedtimes.

Okay, when you're ready, slowly open your eyes, take your time, and come back to the room. Who'd be willing to share their experience first?

Shelly: I felt really sad. I really wanted Jim to support me and back me up trying to get the girls to bed earlier. I just feel so alone, like I'm doing this whole parenting thing by myself. Yeah, it's big, the sadness. It feels bigger than this room [laughs].

Therapist: What in your childhood did it connect to?

Shelly: The time I asked my father to help me with some stupid essay I was writing. He was an English professor, but he couldn't be bothered. I needed ideas, but he told me to write it and he'd look it over later. But he never did. It was that same feeling…like the things I cared about didn't matter to him. Like I didn't matter to him. [Starts to cry] That's the feeling—that I don't matter. And I'll never get what I need because my needs don't matter.

Therapist: And that's the deprivation schema that got triggered when you were fighting about bedtimes. It's the same feeling—almost a despair—that no one cares, that no one will give you the support you need.

Shelly: [Nodding, crying]

Therapist: Jim, can you put Shelly's experiences in your own words?

Jim: Your father didn't care. He left you to struggle alone with that paper, and a lot of things. You ended up feeling that he didn't care, and that you'd never get the support you need. And that's how you feel now—when I'm pretty laissez-faire about the girls' bedtimes.

Therapist: [Facilitating validation] Does Shelly's sadness—that maybe she'll never get the support she needs—make sense to you, in the light of her memory?

Jim: I'm not your dad, but…yeah, I can see why my not helping you get the girls to bed earlier could feel like I don't care. It makes sense you'd feel that way 'cause growing up, no one cared and no one helped.

The therapist then repeats the entire process, focusing on Jim's emotions during the fight (feeling forced and controlled), his childhood memory (his stepfather calling him a "lazy slouch" and forcing him to march "ramrod straight" back and forth in the living room), and the schema (subjugation). Finally, the therapist helps Shelly use active listening and validation to appreciate Jim's experience.

Notice how the therapist models for Jim how to validate Shelly's schema pain by tying together her childhood experience and their recent conflict. The listening partner is then encouraged to generate his own validation statement, and the therapist uses leading questions and coaching to help him engage the process in a useful way. Specifically, Jim is invited to see how scared Shelly is by imagining a father that wouldn't help when help was needed. Shelly is later asked to imagine what it was like for Jim to witness her marching back and forth in the living room. Each is able to get a sense of what the other experienced through this visualization.

At the end of the exercise, the therapist should also encourage the couple to generalize. Are there other conflicts that can be tied to these same schema feelings and early childhood experiences? Encourage partners to recognize how these painful childhood experiences and the schemas linked to them keep showing up in their here-and-now day-to-day life.

Self-as-Context

Mindfulness training, as Tirch has observed, "helps us humans maintain a sense of the 'I-here-now-ness' of our experience" (Tirch et al., 2015). In ACT, the mindful skill of observing our own experience while disidentifying with schema-driven narratives is referred to as *self-as-context*. Mindfulness training not only builds the capacity to observe the flow of experience (self-as-context) but can allow a partner to take the perspective of the other—recognizing his or her feelings, needs, and experience—which serves as the foundation for building compassion (Tirch et al., 2015).

Perspective-Taking Awareness Exercise

This is an example of a formal mindfulness exercise that builds perspective taking. Begin this exercise by having partners sit across from each other with their eyes closed. Read the following script:

> Bring your attention to the sensation of your breathing. Notice the rising and falling in your chest and in your belly as you exhale and inhale. Notice the sensations in your nostrils as you breathe in and out. Where in your body do you feel your breath most easily? If any of your thoughts capture you, simply notice, and bring your attention back to your breath. Keep noticing the sensation of breathing. [Have partners do this for two to three minutes.]
>
> Now gently open your eyes and raise your gaze to look at your partner. As you focus on your partner's eyes, try to imagine him/her as a little child. Imagine what he/she might have been like. How did he/she look? Imagine him/her interacting with his/her family. Imagine how he/she went through all the similar phases in life that you have faced: going to school, getting through puberty, romantic heartaches, becoming an adult, and moving away from home. Notice that your partner has had many experiences, thoughts, memories, and feelings. He/she has experienced many changing emotions, including loss, love,

rejection, joy, longing, excitement, deprivation, fear, hope, and many others. Notice that your partner is a separate person with his/her unique stories and experiences. Your partner is a human being, trying his/her best—just like you.

Gently shifting away from this recognition of your partner as a full human being, I now invite you to bring to mind an early memory of meeting your partner. [Pause] What was he/she like when you first met? What were your experiences together? Now bring to mind a moment when you felt your partner was at his/her best—and you felt extreme love and certainty about your partner. Now bring to mind a memory of when your partner was at his/her worst. [Ask partners to raise their fingers when they have the image in mind.] Notice that your partner is still the same person. Sometimes, you view him/her at his/her best, sometimes at his/her worst, but he/she remains the same. Sometimes you are more connected, other times you feel more distant, and yet he/she is still the person in front of you with all these different qualities.

Now I invite you to begin to imagine what your partner will look like as he/she gets older. Look into his/her eyes and try to picture this face as it is aging. Be aware that, just like you, your partner will continue to age into the next stages of life. Imagine what this will be like for him/her—the experience of his/her body growing older and changing over time. Yet, your partner will still be the same human being. Your partner's body will have changed. He/she will have experienced many emotions, thoughts, and sensations, but your partner will still be there, the same human being who was there as a child, was there when you met, was there for the good and the bad, and is here now.

Notice all the different stages of life that you and your partner have been through, and others that are on the way. Now gently bring your attention back to the moment and the experience of gazing into your partner's eyes.

When we can see ourselves and others as larger than any momentary experience, it helps us to be more flexible in our understanding of each other. Given that perspective taking is the foundation of fostering compassion, helping partners cultivate the observer self and a flexible perspective will build greater empathy and attunement.

Movie Screen Metaphor

Metaphors are a useful way to help couples connect to perspective taking. They can provide an easy-to-understand sense of what experience is like from an observing perspective. This can also assist partners in taking a step back, seeing each other as larger than any single event and the content of their minds.

To use the movie screen metaphor, you can ask the following:

The next time one of your schemas gets triggered during a conflict, try to step outside of the situation and observe it as if you're watching a movie screen. See if you can notice all of the different characters in the movie. What are they saying to each other? How are they feeling? What do they need? What do their facial gestures look like? What do their nonverbal behaviors tell you about their experience?

Try to really step outside of the scene and just observe it as if you're watching a very interesting movie, as if you're narrating the movie and describing the thoughts, feelings, behaviors, needs, and values of the characters in the scene.

As you are observing, notice that you don't have to respond, and you don't have to react in any way; just pay close attention to all the parts of the scene and all the different characters without being reactive or acting on any urges. What schemas are triggered for you? What are your thoughts pulling you to do? Notice any strong urges and emotions. What role are you playing in this moment in the scene? Is this a common role you fall into? Does this role reflect your values? Notice and label your partner's behaviors. Notice and label the behaviors that are triggering you. Nothing has to be changed, fixed, or resolved—see if you can just observe the scene unfold and stay mindful of all the different aspects of the scene.

The movie screen metaphor exercise helps couples step outside of their emotional and cognitive reactions to conflict and become witnesses to the process. By watching the scene, they can distance from content and observe the here-and-now flow of events. This builds awareness to notice moments of choice to respond differently. Observing the conflict can give partners the freedom and behavioral flexibility to act on values.

Using Reverse Role-Play to Build Empathy

Using reverse role-play is a key technique in couples therapy. It helps partners build a flexible perspective and deepens compassion.

When doing a reverse role-play, it's essential to clarify ground rules. Explain to partners that the purpose of the role-play is not to mock the other person, to prove oneself right, or to make partners feel each other's pain. The purpose of reverse role-play is for partners to fully put themselves in each other's shoes.

When conducting a reverse role-play, it's important that partners already have an understanding of each other's schema pain, the origin of each other's schemas, and a sympathetic framework for the other's experience. There are four basic steps to conducting reverse role-plays to help couples cultivate empathy:

1. **Identify the conflict to role-play.** Have partners identify a recent conflict that they would like to discuss. The conflict should be a recent situation that clearly connects to core schemas and themes in the relationship. It should be a conflict that they have some insight into and that they have discussed in the past.

2. **Conduct reverse role-play.** Next, have partners enact this conflict using a reverse role-play, with each partner playing the role of the other in the scene. Ask couples to act out the scene exactly as they remember it. Encourage partners to portray each other genuinely (regardless of whether there is anger) and to connect to each other's experience in the present moment while role-playing the other. Have them connect to what the other may be feeling and needing in that moment.

3. **Discuss role-play.** Discuss the role-play and each partner's experience. Have both partners discuss and identify how they understand their partner's experience at the time. What schemas were triggered? What difficult emotions showed up for the other person? Have them empathize with the pain and connect it to specific values and needs in the relationship. Guide the discussion in such a manner as to build empathy and understanding for the other's perspective. This will help them redo the reverse role-play more effectively. Assisting them to understand the other's perspective involves clarifying each partner's triggers, feelings, and needs in the situation. It may help to have partners connect the trigger of the current conflict to an early childhood experience when they felt similarly, one that illustrates the origin of their schema. This latter work can assist in building empathy. During the discussion, have partners identify their needs and validate each other's experience.

4. **Redo role-play.** Last, have partners redo the role-play while practicing more-effective behaviors. This is the most important part of the process because partners can learn how they could behave differently the next time a similar conflict arises. Here, the therapist can either (1) redo the role-play by conducting a regular role-play and have partners play themselves, while practicing new behaviors, or (2) redo the reverse role-play by having partners playing each other again, modeling how the other can respond more effectively. During the reverse role-play, have individuals (playing the other) role-model to their partner how they would've liked their partner to respond differently in advocating for their needs.

Conducting Reverse Role-Play with Couples

Let's look at an example of the four steps of role-play. To initiate the reverse role-play, identify a specific trigger that occurred during the previous week, and have each partner play the role of the other. In the scene, have them get in touch with their partner's underlying needs, values, and schemas, and the thoughts, feelings, and urges that might come up. Have partners role-play each other in the scene exactly as they remember it. The goal is to pay attention to how the other perceived them during the conflict.

Example Dialogue

Below is an example dialogue between Charles, who has a failure schema, and Annabel, who has a self-sacrifice schema. Charles and Annabel are in the process of planning a wedding, and Annabel is very anxious about meeting everyone's needs and making sure that everyone gets the seating that they requested.

Charles (as Annabel): [Speaking urgently and quickly] Charles, there is some issue with the seating arrangements, and now my sister is going to be sitting next to Mark. I'm trying to figure out what to do about it because she's going to be upset about having to sit next to him. The other option is moving Molly to that seat, but she won't be sitting next to Dave, and then she'll be unhappy.

Annabel (as Charles): [Sounding impatient and on edge] So Molly won't sit next to Dave. That's fine.

Charles (as Annabel): Then Molly is going to be upset. I'm very anxious about it. The whole thing is a mess.

Annabel (as Charles): We have the seating map right here—it's all figured out. If you want to move Molly we can move her, but even if we don't move Molly, the seating is going to work out fine. It's not such a big deal.

Charles (as Annabel): Yes, it is a big deal. You don't understand how my sister gets. She's going to get really upset, and it's going to be all about her and it's going to ruin the whole day.

Annabel (as Charles): Your sister will realize that it's your wedding day and it will be okay. She's not going to make a scene. She's the maid of honor. She's not going to act like she usually does.

Charles (as Annabel): You don't get it, Charles. If she's not going to get to sit where she wants, she'll be frustrated. And she's not going to care about whether she's the maid of honor. She's just going to flip out and ruin the day. Why don't you understand that?

Annabel (as Charles): [In a frustrated tone] What do you want from me, Annabel? Do you want me to call Mark and see if he would be willing to sit next to Molly?

Charles (as Annabel): No. That's not what I want right now. I want you to understand what the issue is.

Annabel (as Charles): You're really blowing this out of proportion. It's going to be fine. It's already settled; the seating is already done.

Charles (as Annabel): [Angry] You're so selfish. You don't give a shit about this wedding or about me or about helping out.

Annabel (as Charles): I can't deal with this right now. You're overreacting. It's always about the wedding.

Charles (as Annabel): Don't tell me I'm overreacting.

Annabel (as Charles): What do you want from me, Annabel? I can't do this all the time.

At this point the therapist stops the reverse role-play to process the experience. The partners then discuss the experience and what they learned. The discussion can involve asking a number of questions. For instance: How did it feel to be in the other's shoes? What were they needing when in the other's role? What was the experience like? What were moments when they felt defensive or triggered? Have partners explore and identify each other's feelings and needs. When you are doing the exercise, you will want to encourage individuals to fully discuss how it felt both in the role as their partner and observing the other portraying him- or herself. More specific, have partners explore these key questions with each other:

What do you imagine your partner was feeling and needing during the conflict? What were you feeling and needing during the conflict?

Did you notice anything about your partner's portrayal of you that came across in a way that was hurtful or defensive? How would you like to express yourself differently?

Do you have relationship values that could be used to improve how the role-playing partner expressed your feelings?

Here is how Annabel and Charles discussed the role-playing process:

Therapist: Charles, as you watched Annabel role-play her portrayal of you during your argument about the seating arrangements for the wedding, what did you notice?

Charles: She played me really harsh, really sharp edged. Which is probably how I sound to her. I think she was feeling dismissed by me, as if I was frustrated with her or I wasn't hearing her.

Therapist: [To Annabel] Were you feeling that way during the conflict?

Annabel: Yes. It seemed like he wasn't hearing my feelings. He just wanted to give me suggestions and try to fix the issue. What I really needed was to share my feelings about how conflicted and anxious I felt. He seemed to just want a solution and to stop talking about it.

Therapist: What was that like for you as you were role-playing Charles?

Annabel: I felt stuck. Like I was in a lose-lose situation. I felt very frustrated. I think he was feeling like he had no options at the time. Like anything he said was wrong, and he felt helpless and stuck.

Therapist: Charles, is that how you were feeling during the conflict?

Charles: Yeah. I felt like everything I suggested made it worse. I was trying to help her figure out a solution and nothing made her happy. Nothing was good enough.

Therapist: [To Charles] What do you think Annabel needed at that moment?

Charles: I realized that Annabel was feeling a lot of guilt and despair about her sister. I think she just needed me to hear how painful that is and how stuck she feels.

As the discussion progresses, Annabel realizes that Charles is feeling pressure and urgency to fix the situation. He had received an important e-mail from work and was feeling torn between his needs and hers. Charles realizes that Annabel needs to be heard and have her feelings validated. The more Charles tries to offer her suggestions, the more frustrated and alone she feels. During the reverse role-play, both are able to recognize that Annabel needs understanding from Charles and is worried that he won't make the time to discuss the seating arrangements with her. Charles becomes frustrated because the more he tries to problem solve, the more frustrated Annabel becomes, and the more helpless he ends up feeling.

Following this discussion, the therapist coaches partners to use each other's feedback to retool their requests. The goal is to replay the original conflict using knowledge gained from the first role-play and discussion. This form of perspective taking allows partners to choose their words while (1) simultaneously seeing the conflict from both perspectives, and (2) honoring important relationship values.

At this point, you can choose whether to redo the role-play with partners playing themselves, or have them redo the reverse role-play while playing each other. This time, partners use each other's feedback about more-effective values-based communication strategies. When couples are redoing the scene, have them keep a key value in mind as they express each other's emotions and needs.

The example below involves a reverse role-play redo of Annabel and Charles (playing each other). In this reverse role-play, they model for each other what they most want to hear and show the other how they could have responded differently.

Charles (as Annabel): Hey, Charles, do you have a couple of minutes to talk about the seating for the wedding? I am feeling kind of frazzled about it and I need some reassurance. Can you help put me at ease?

Annabel (as Charles): I actually just got this e-mail from work two minutes ago and I'm very anxious about it. Do you think that I could return the e-mail first and then talk about this in 15 minutes?

Charles (as Annabel): I understand that this e-mail is important, and I'm okay with you returning it first, but I want you to know that it's very important to me that we come back to this and make the time to talk about it.

Annabel (as Charles): I promise that we'll talk about this. I know this is important to you. It's important to me, too. I feel like I'll be more able to support you once I get this e-mail out of the way.

Charles (as Annabel): Let's come back to this in 15 minutes.

Both: Okay.

Annabel (as Charles): [Pretending it's 15 minutes later] Hey, Annabel, I finished the e-mail. What's going on?

Charles (as Annabel): I'm feeling really overwhelmed about the wedding. I'm really concerned about my sister overshadowing the day, and I really need your reassurance.

Annabel (as Charles): It makes sense that you're feeling overwhelmed. How can I support you?

Charles (as Annabel): It would help me if you listened to my concerns about my sister and also remind me that this is our day and that you are going to support me if she gets upset or disappointed.

Annabel (as Charles): I know you're nervous about it. We know that your sister is probably going to have some demands or most likely feel disappointed with something. She can be quite difficult at times.

Charles (as Annabel): I guess I'm wondering if you can make some time to look over the seating chart and see if you have any suggestions? I would feel relieved if I knew that you took some time to look over all of it and then we could discuss it together.

Annabel (as Charles): Yeah, I can do that. I understand that you're feeling anxious. It's our day and, regardless of how she reacts, I want to support you.

Charles (as Annabel): Thank you, sweetheart. I really appreciate that.

Reverse role-play allows couples to experience conflicts as their partner did. When individuals are able to take and understand the other's perspective, they can finally model for their partner how to express feelings and needs more effectively.

Perspective Taking in Session

The exercises in this chapter, in addition to fostering flexible perspective, can be resources for responding to one form of therapeutic impasse: when partners are locked in their own point of view and seem incapable of recognizing the very different needs and experiences of the other. This moment comes inevitably in every therapy for couples. Partners lock down into an egocentric view of the relationship, defending themselves through blaming, with a determination to prove that they are right. They are like soldiers in the trenches, protecting their psychological ground.

Using any of these three perspective-taking exercises can break couples out of their self-focused rigidity and narrow stories about each other. Perspective taking can assist partners in seeing each other's pain, in recognizing important needs, and in knowing more fully each other as whole human beings, with their own struggles, desires, hopes, and joys.

CHAPTER 11

Session Structure: The Eight-Step Protocol

Once the ACT processes, plus nonviolent communication skills, have been introduced to the couple, each session will integrate the skills and processes using a consistent protocol. From now on, one session will resemble another in terms of format and key therapy interventions. The sequence will typically include the following steps:

Step 1

Review specific conflicts and triggers that occurred during the week. Start by checking in to see what issues and struggles have shown up for the couple. Just get a brief overview without exploring much of the content or triggering affect. Covertly decide which of the issues will present the best learning opportunity (i.e., taps into schema pain and problematic coping behaviors).

Step 2

Predict that schemas and SCBs will get triggered during the session. Before looking deeply at a particular conflict, explicitly suggest that both partners are likely to experience schema pain and will want to escape that pain with schema coping behaviors. Mention a key schema for each partner, and encourage vigilance for the moment it gets activated. Also predict which schema coping behaviors are likely to be used by the couple.

Encourage the couple to see that the work now is recognizing (1) the schema pain and (2) the SCBs (experiential avoidance).

Step 3

Remind the couple of the moment of choice: to act on values or the old avoidance strategies. Explain that all three of you will need to be mindful of when schema pain shows up, of the urge to avoid, and the possibility of choosing a different response (values-based action).

Example Dialogue

Michael and Fatima arrive in couples therapy with painfully complementary schemas. Michael's primary schemas, including unrelenting standards schema and an entitlement schema (given a more benign name: "things have to be right"), frequently collide with Fatima's self-sacrifice and failure schemas. The schema affect for Michael is profound disappointment and loss, and his schema coping behaviors include attack, blame, and withdrawal. Fatima experiences deep shame when faced with any kind of failure, and guilt and confusion when connecting to her own needs. SCBs begin with denial and excuse making, followed by surrender and (if all else fails) verbal aggression.

At this point in the dialogue, the couple is entering their sixth week of treatment. They are aware of their schemas and SCBs. They've identified values and intentions, particularly in situations when schema pain has been triggered. Finally, they've been introduced to key processes for overcoming barriers to values-based behavior:

- Mindfulness and exposure for schema affect
- Defusion and self-as-context for schema-driven thinking
- Nonviolent communication for interpersonal skills deficits

Reviewing specific conflicts and triggers

Therapist: Let me check in to see how you are, and if any issues have come up this week.

Michael: We had a fight about getting a nonpayment notice on our credit card bill. And there was something—I can't remember...oh, about Fatima being late.

Fatima: There was the vacation thing—not getting to go to Sedona.

Michael: I felt very let down by that.

Fatima: He makes me feel totally wrong.

Therapist: Would it be okay to explore that issue in here?

Michael and Fatima: [Nodding]

Predict that schemas and SCBs will be triggered

Therapist: Before we look at what happened—

Michael: Fatima set up the trip, so there's no time to visit the place I most wanted to visit—Sedona.

Therapist: Yes, before we get into what happened, there are some things I'd like all three of us to watch for and be aware of. At some point, as we talk about these vacation plans, I think we can expect that schemas will get triggered. For you, Michael, let's watch for the moment when "things need to be right" and the deep feeling of disappointment that goes with it. Can we do that?

Michael: Yes. That's what made leaving Sedona out of our plans so upsetting.

Therapist: Right. And, Fatima, this conflict may trigger the failure schema we've talked about. Let's try to notice if that happens. And watch for the schema pain—the shame feeling.

Fatima: [Nodding]

Therapist: If the schema pain shows up, we'll need to be alert for something else that often happens in response. [Pauses]

Fatima: Coping behavior.

Therapist: Exactly. When the schema pain shows up, we try to avoid it. Everybody wants to do that, me included. Fatima, let's be mindful of those old avoidance strategies—that urge to defend yourself, or then surrender or get angry.

Fatima: Okay.

Therapist: Michael, when that deep disappointment shows up and things aren't the way you want them to be, you have ways of your own to cope and avoid, right?

Michael: [Nodding]

Therapist: Sometimes you blame or try to show Fatima how messed up something is. Or you might withdraw. So let's be aware, if possible, when that happens.

Michael: I'll try to notice.

Remind the couple of the moment of choice and key values

Therapist: Michael, there's going to be a moment of choice when you're triggered: You'll either choose to avoid with the old coping strategies or act on your values. What's your value? How do you want to be with Fatima if you get triggered talking about the vacation plans?

Michael: I want to be compassionate and to listen.

Therapist: Okay, that's how you want to be, even if you're in the middle of schema pain. Fatima, when you are triggered by pain, you'll also have a moment of choice: Do the old schema avoidance behaviors or act on values.

What's your value? Who do you want to be with Michael if you get triggered talking about the vacation?

Fatima: I want to be understanding of him and to tell my own truth—not shut down.

Therapist: So let's try to watch for the moment when that choice shows up.

Step 4

Begin discussion of the chosen conflict. The focus, for the moment, is content, but only until it ignites process. As soon as the content has triggered schema affect and coping behaviors, the therapy shifts to mindful observation of the emotional pain and avoidance urges. Don't stay with content after affect shows up for either partner. The presence of schema pain requires a shift toward observing rather than solving.

Step 5

Therapist and partners mindfully observe process and name moments of activation, triggers, and signs of avoidance behavior as they arise during session. This is the point when the therapist's mindfulness skills are most tested. You'll be watching for any sign of schema affect or avoidance, including nonverbal indications, such as:

- Change in tone of voice (louder, softer, harsher)
- Sighing and/or deep breaths
- Change in facial expression (tightened eyes, jaw, lips; mouth widening in contempt; brows up or down; eye rolling; etc.)
- Change in posture (slumping, arms crossed, pulling back, leaning forward, head tilting or shaking)
- Animated hand gestures (finger pointing, hands in fists)
- Looking down or away

In addition to these more subtle cues of avoidance, you'll also need to watch for overt verbalizations of schema beliefs or coping behaviors. When these signs of affect or avoidance show up, they should immediately be identified and an inquiry begun about the individual's emotions and urges.

Example Dialogue

Begin discussion of the chosen conflict

The vacation issue for Michael and Fatima revolves around Fatima's arrangements for a trip to the Southwest. She had reservations at Bryce Canyon, Grand Canyon, Zion, and Arches National Parks—but has no lodging or time allotted for a visit to Sedona, Arizona. Michael claims that the area he most desires to visit has been ignored by Fatima.

Fatima: [Leaning back in her chair and looking away] You gave me the list of places you wanted to go; there wasn't time for everything.

Michael: [Shaking head, then crossing his arms] You knew that was the place I most wanted to go. [Voice rising] You knew.

Mindfully observe process

Therapist: What do you notice right now?

Fatima: I notice I'm in trouble, as usual. [Soft voice] That's the last thing I plan for us, Michael. [Sighing, slumping a little in the chair]

Therapist: Let's observe what's happening. Michael, you crossed your arms and your voice got a little loud. What are you feeling?

Michael: Disgusted?

Therapist: What's the pain, the schema pain?

Michael: Like I really wanted something and it was taken away from me.

Therapist: You feel loss. Things need to be right, but they're not right.

Michael: [Nodding]

Therapist: And notice what you're starting to do now. How you're trying to avoid the feeling. [Silence] Michael, what are you doing to cope?

Michael: Getting angry. Making a case that she's screwed up.

Therapist: Good, you're noticing what's happening. Fatima, something was going on for you, too. I noticed you sighing and slumping back. What's the feeling?

Fatima: [Shrugs]

Therapist: Is it the failure schema? Being told you didn't plan well?

Fatima: Yeah, like I screwed up.

Therapist: Notice you're having the *thought* that you screwed up.

Fatima: But it's a feeling, too. Of being bad.

Therapist: And then did you try to get away from that feeling, to somehow protect yourself from it?

Fatima: Like we talked about before—I wanted to give up. Let him deal with the vacation shit. [Makes a fist]

Therapist: Notice the anger, too. Another way to avoid the pain.

Fatima: [Disgusted look, nodding]

Therapist: As soon as we got into this, the pain started, didn't it? And then you tried to protect yourselves from it, and pulled away from each other.

Michael: I see what happens. We both crawl into our foxholes as soon as the emotions start.

Therapist: As sure as the sun's going to come up tomorrow, the shame and the feelings of loss are going to show up when you talk about this issue. But whenever the pain starts, and the temptation to take refuge in the SCBs surfaces, you have a choice. We're going to work on that now.

Step 6

As avoidance behaviors show up, partners are encouraged to turn toward their experience. They stay in direct contact while describing out loud feelings, pain, and needs in the present moment. After you have observed and discussed present-moment schema pain and avoidance, it's time to get the couple back into emotional contact. Have the partners engage with each other: make direct eye contact, hold hands, or touch in some other way. The purpose is to turn toward the pain that each triggers for the other.

Now remind the partners of their relational values. Encourage them to choose words and a tone of voice consistent with their values-based intentions, even when the schema pain surges up.

At this point, the therapist facilitates a new conversation. Not about the problem or content issues. Rather, the focus is on each partner's core experience—his or her present-moment pain, emotions, and needs. Right now this is all that matters. The original problem is minor, merely a gateway to each partner's needs and affect.

Inevitably, as partners share core material, avoidance will resurface. They'll drop hands, or eye contact will be broken. You'll see subtle or blatant SCBs. This is not a therapeutic problem—it's a normal part of the process. Gently point out evidence of avoidance, and encourage partners—despite the pain—to reestablish direct, authentic contact.

Example Dialogue

Therapist: Right now, even though there's pain and you may want to pull away from each other, I'd like you to make contact in some way. Hold hands or look at each other. Would you be willing to do that?

Michael and Fatima: [Reach to hold hands]

Therapist: Part of you may still want to withdraw and avoid. That's okay, but see if you can hold contact in the face of whatever pain you may feel.

Recall key values

Therapist: Michael, you want to be compassionate and really listen to Fatima in your choice of words and tone of voice. Can you commit to acting on those values in this next conversation?

Michael: [Nodding] Yes.

Therapist: Fatima, the person you want to be with Michael is understanding and truth telling. Can you commit to bring those values into this next conversation?

Fatima: I'll do my best.

Explore feelings and needs

Therapist: You've been talking about the vacation plans. Fatima, can you say what you're feeling right now? What the pain is? Would you tell Michael?

Fatima: I feel that I'm wrong and bad. Like when I was little and my mother slapped me for not doing things right… I feel shrunken down, not a good person.

Therapist: What's happening for you, Michael, as you listen to Fatima?

Michael: I feel sad…that she hurts like this.

Therapist: [To Fatima] What do you need right now?

Fatima: [To Michael] I want you to hear me: that I did my best, that I didn't disappoint you for lack of trying. [Starting to cry]

Michael: [Looking away] I guess I don't know how it happened, then. You forgot all the times I talked about Sedona?

Avoidance has resurfaced

Therapist: What's happening right now, Michael? Can you step back and observe it while staying connected to Fatima? Just look and notice what you feel.

Michael: I feel almost…despair. Like I'll never get what I want from Fatima.

Therapist: Stay with that. See if you can observe it a bit longer. Tell Fatima what you feel.

Michael: [Looking deeply at Fatima] Hopelessness. That the things I really need I'll never have. And anger, too. That it hurts so much.

Therapist: Can you say what you need? Remember your value of compassion. See if you can use that to find the words.

Michael: I don't know… I think for you to see me. See when I really need or want something.

Fatima's pain triggers more avoidance and the SCB of surrender

Fatima: [Mouth widening in irritation] Fine.

Therapist: You're starting to pull back. Remember your values of understanding and truth telling. How could they help you tell Michael what you feel and need?

Fatima: [Long pause] I know when you don't get things you want, how painful it is. I see it in your face. And then I feel like I do right now—like there's something really wrong with me. [Beginning to cry again] You know? Like I'm the one who is supposed to give you these things, and I'm a failure at it.

Therapist: What do you need?

Fatima: [To Michael] I need you to know that I love you. I want you to have what you need, and if I don't give it to you, it's 'cause I don't know how. Or maybe that I don't understand… I need you to believe and accept that.

Step 7

Cultivate values-based problem solving. Begin by validating how much pain each partner is struggling with. Point out how pain can be a barrier to staying connected and acting on values. Now shift to a problem-solving process using the following rubrics:

- Partners are encouraged to use values-based, nonviolent communication.
- Partners take turns proposing solutions that address at least some of the needs of both.
- If avoidance or SCBs resurface, problem solving should be suspended. Focus instead on schema affect and needs.

Values-based problem solving involves a certain amount of cheerleading by the therapist. Express appreciation—without endorsement—for every solution partners suggest. Keep focused on the core problem or conflict, and encourage partners to combine and modify good ideas (see "The Five Stages of Negotiation" in chapter 8). Structure the process so partners keep taking turns and refrain from criticizing each other's ideas.

Step 8

Teach partners to notice and take responsibility for moments when they shift into avoidance and SCBs. Once again, you are encouraging partners to recognize the moment of choice. But now you are shifting responsibility for mindfulness and values-based behavioral choices to them. This is accomplished by asking questions such as:

What's happening right now?

What's the choice here?

Are you moving toward or away from your partner right now?

If you choose to act on your values right now, what would that look like?

Who do you want to be right now?

Example Dialogue

Validation

Therapist: The issue of your vacation has brought up a lot of pain for both of you. [Looking at Michael] Deep disappointment and loss. [Nodding toward Fatima] A sense of being wrong and bad. This pain, and the effort to avoid it, can form a barrier to being the partners you want to be to each other—compassionate and listening, understanding and truth telling.

Introduce problem solving

Therapist: I want to go back to the vacation issue. Having had a chance to share some of your pain and your needs, we might be more successful seeking solutions now. Here's what I'd like for us to do. Bearing in mind your values, and the needs you expressed to each other—Michael's need to be seen, Fatima's need to feel accepted—I'd like you to take turns suggesting possible solutions to the vacation problem.

Don't criticize ideas you hear. If you like the idea, say so. If you want to propose an alternative, say, "Yes, and..." In other words, "That idea's okay, but here's something else we might add to it. Who's willing to go first?"

Fatima: [After a long pause] I suggest we each say what's important to us and then plan things together.

Michael: [Rolling eyes] You only work part-time. I don't have the hours in the day...

Encourage partners to recognize and take responsibility for the moment of choice

Therapist: What's happening right now?

Michael: [Long pause] It's disappointment.

Therapist: Who do you want to be right now—as you respond?

Michael: [To Fatima] I understand why you wouldn't want to do the whole thing. 'Cause I might blame you if it isn't right.

Therapist: Do you have a possible solution to add to Fatima's?

Michael: Maybe to write down the things that are important to us, and talk about them so I feel Fatima understands me.

Fatima: And when we make a plan, to check with each other before it's finalized.

Michael: [Leaning back] So you don't make a mistake.

Fatima: So I don't get a bunch of criticism.

Respond to each episode of avoidance

Therapist: Take a minute and observe what's happening. Fatima, you had a *thought* about being criticized.

Fatima: I felt put down. Yes, I don't want to make a mistake—because I don't want to disappoint you or feel like a failure. Both things.

Therapist: [To Michael] You have choices now.

Michael: I know. [Pauses] I'm listening, Fatima. You want to plan together so neither of us gets hurt by the process.

The Core Processes

The eight steps documented in this chapter get repeated, issue after issue, in the remaining sessions of therapy. Over time, partners will more readily identify avoidance and the moment of choice. Your work is to gradually discontinue prompts and questions, encouraging the couple to take over the responsibility of watching and choosing.

In the end, the therapy gets refined and simplified to four core processes by which partners learn to:

- Recognize triggers and the presence of schema affect.
- Observe schema pain and thoughts.
- Choose values-based responses to schema pain rather than avoidance and SCBs.
- Solve conflicts based on values and awareness of each partner's needs.

You'll notice that defusion isn't emphasized at this point in therapy. You will use it when individuals get attached to a schema thought or when thoughts are clearly driving affect. The focus now is on schema-driven pain and the behavioral choice to avoid or act on values. Therapy, as you can see in the dialogues, circles back constantly to noticing and seizing the moment of choice.

Example Dialogue

Therapist: How has the week been?

Michael: We had a little dust-up on Tuesday but really didn't talk about it. We kind of ignored it.

Fatima: My mother's visiting from Miami. Michael doesn't want her to stay with us.

Michael: Wow, I didn't say that. I just said there won't be much privacy.

Fatima: [Leaning back] Same thing.

Therapist: What are you noticing right now?

Fatima: I feel guilty for wanting her to stay with us.

Therapist: Okay, there's a schema thought—you're doing something wrong. What else?

Fatima: Just the "I'm wrong" feeling [long pause] and loss. I want her to be with me.

Therapist: Can you talk to each other?

Fatima: [Takes Michael's hand] I'm sad. I want her with us, and I feel like I'm messing up. Disappointing you.

Michael: [Breaks eye contact, sighs]

Therapist: Is there a choice here, Michael?

Michael: [Shrugs] Maybe. It's hard when your mother's here.

Fatima: It's just a week, and you'll be at work most of the time.

Michael: [Sighing, staying silent]

Therapist: Are you moving toward or away from Fatima right now?

Michael: Away. I'm feeling controlled. It's really hard to feel this without reacting.

Therapist: You still have a choice. Can you have the feeling and stay in contact with Fatima? And your values?

Michael: [Nodding, silence] I want you to have a good visit with your mother. I know you miss her. [Michael's value of compassion]

Fatima: How is it for you when she's here in our house?

Michael: Thank you for asking.

Fatima: I want to understand. [One of Fatima's core values]

Michael: I'm tense. I feel like I have to be careful all the time.

Fatima: [Nodding]

Therapist: What are you feeling right now, Michael?

Michael: Lighter.

Therapist: Shall we do some problem solving? Take turns suggesting solutions?

Michael: No. [Hesitating] Let's have her with us.

Fatima: Are you really okay with that?

Michael: [Nodding] Something changed when you asked how I felt.

Therapist: You felt seen?

Michael: Uh-huh.

Therapist: [To Fatima] What happened when Michael acknowledged how much you miss your mother?

Fatima: I felt relieved. Now I feel more comfortable about her staying with us.

As the therapist does less prompting, the couple gradually takes over the work of observing process and bringing values to the moment of choice. Over time, these skills migrate from the counseling room into the couple's daily life.

In the end, ACT therapy for couples comes down to one thing: learning to love in the face of pain. There is no promise of happy ever after. There is just the moment—seeing the eternal choice to act on love or avoidance.

APPENDIX A

Research Outcomes

This appendix outlines results from a study that tested the effects of a six-week ACT-based protocol for couples. The randomized, controlled study, conducted by Avigail Lev, used the protocol with twenty-two couples at a private-practice clinic in San Francisco. Participants were randomly assigned to one of two groups: (1) the experimental group (fourteen couples) received the six-week ACT for couples protocol, and (2) the control group (eight couples) were put on a waiting list (and later treated).

The results suggest that the ACT treatment for couples improved relationship satisfaction (as measured by the Relationship Assessment Scale, RAS) and communication skills (as measured by the Experiences Questionnaire), and decreased maladaptive interpersonal behaviors (as measured by the Inventory for Interpersonal Problems, IIP-64).

The RAS was the instrument used to measure relationship satisfaction and resulted in large effect sizes ($d = .94$).

The Experiences Questionnaire was the instrument that measured partner's self-reports of communication skills. This measure also resulted in a large effect size ($d = 1.05$), suggesting that the treatment improved couples' communication skills.

Last, the IIP-64 was used to measure maladaptive interpersonal behaviors. The IIP-64 is a self-report instrument that measures interpersonal difficulties. The results showed a medium-to-large effect size ($d = 0.716$).

As hypothesized, the Young Schema Questionnaire had no significant effect size, which suggests that schemas and core beliefs did not change during the course of treatment and did not mediate change in the other measures.

The Acceptance and Action Questionnaire (AAQ) and the Values Ratings Scale were the two instruments used to examine mediating variables. These were used to determine whether values or experiential avoidance may have mediated the changes that occurred on the RAS, Experiences Questionnaire, and IIP-64. Neither of these measures showed significant effect sizes, suggesting that neither values nor experiential avoidance effected the changes that occurred in the RAS, Experiences Questionnaire, and the IIP-64. Future research should look at the possible mediating effect of defusion. Given that the focus of this treatment is on changing our relationship to schemas (beliefs) and creating distance from schema-driven thoughts, it may be that defusion will turn out to be a mediating variable.

APPENDIX B

Couples Schema Questionnaire

Couples Schema Questionnaire

The following questionnaire will help you determine which schemas are most relevant for you in your relationship. After reading each statement, rate each statement according to how well it describes you, using the scale provided.

Place your answer in the box next to the question. At the end, a brief guide will help you assess your responses.

0—Disagree

1—Neither agree nor disagree

2—Slightly agree

3—Agree

4—Strongly agree

1. Ab/In

_____ 1. I don't feel like I can rely and depend on my partner.

_____ 2. I'm often attracted to partners who are unable to commit to me.

_____ 3. I feel insecure and unstable in my relationship.

_____ 4. My relationship feels fragile, like it can end at any minute.

_____ 5. I can't count on my partner to always be there for me.

_____ 6. I'm constantly afraid that my partner will leave me.

_____ 7. I often worry that my partner will find someone else they prefer to be with.

_____ 8. I get scared spending time away from my partner or when my partner needs space.

_____ 9. When my partner is not around I worry about his/her commitment to me.

_____ 10. I'm often afraid of being abandoned by or losing my partner.

2. M/A

_____ 1. I often worry that my partner is taking advantage of me or using me.

_____ 2. I worry that my partner will hurt or betray me.

_____ 3. It's difficult for me to trust my partner and give him/her the benefit of the doubt.

_____ 4. Most people cannot be trusted.

_____ 5. I need to protect myself and stay on guard in order to feel safe in my relationship.

_____ 6. I am often suspicious of my partner's intentions and motives.

_____ 7. I can't count on my partner to follow through on his/her word.

_____ 8. I have to be on the lookout for my partner lying or breaking promises.

_____ 9. I feel afraid that my partner will mistreat me or become abusive.

_____ 10. I often wonder whether my partner is deceiving me or fooling me in some way.

3. ED

_____ 1. I don't get the love and care that I truly need from my partner.

_____ 2. My partner doesn't understand me or provide me with the nurturing that I need.

_____ 3. I feel unsatisfied in my romantic relationship.

_____ 4. I wish my partner was more emotionally present and available to meet my needs.

_____ 5. It's been difficult for me to feel taken care of by my partners.

_____ 6. My partners have often responded to my emotional needs in a cold and distant way.

_____ 7. I've always needed more attention and affection than my partners have been able to provide.

_____ 8. I often feel deprived by my partner and left wanting more.

_____ 9. It's difficult for me to depend on my partner for emotional support.

_____ 10. I often feel alone or lonely even when I'm with my partner.

4. D/S

_____ 1. If my partner really knew me, he/she would be disappointed by me.

_____ 2. I worry that if my partner saw all my flaws and defects he/she wouldn't accept me.

_____ 3. I worry that if I reveal too much about myself my partner won't love me.

_____ 4. I feel fundamentally bad or broken.

_____ 5. I try to figure out what's wrong with me so I can fix myself.

_____ 6. I worry that if I expose myself fully with my partner he/she will reject me.

_____ 7. I often think my partner is too good for me and that he/she could find somebody better.

_____ 8. My partner wouldn't want to be with me if he/she knew the real me.

_____ 9. I have often been a disappointment to most of my partners.

_____ 10. I can't share my deepest insecurities with my partner.

5. SI/A

_____ 1. I don't feel a sense of belonging with my partner or my community.

_____ 2. I frequently feel left out of groups and like an outsider.

_____ 3. My partner and I struggle with fitting in well with our group of friends.

_____ 4. I feel awkward and different when I try to connect with my partner's friends and/or family.

_____ 5. I worry that my partner and I are too different or we live in separate worlds.

_____ 6. I worry that my partner doesn't want to include me in social situations.

_____ 7. I feel excluded when I'm in social situations with my partner.

_____ 8. I worry that my partner feels embarrassed or ashamed of me in social situations.

_____ 9. I worry that I don't fit in well with my partner's friends and/or family.

_____ 10. I feel embarrassed or self-conscious when I'm in social situations with my partner.

6. De

______ 1. It's difficult for me to get things done without my partner's help.

______ 2. I prefer for my partner to make most of the decisions.

______ 3. It's difficult for me to be alone for long periods of time.

______ 4. I need my partner's help with many issues that I can't handle on my own.

______ 5. It's difficult for me to make my own decisions without my partner's feedback.

______ 6. I depend heavily on my partner for help and/or advice.

______ 7. I can't handle most problems without my partner's support.

______ 8. I often feel helpless or at a loss concerning what to do.

______ 9. I need assistance and reassurance from my partner to solve everyday problems.

______ 10. I fear that I will make mistakes and reach the wrong decisions without my partner's advice.

7. Fa

______ 1. I worry that I will not meet my partner's expectations.

______ 2. I've been a disappointment to most of my partners.

______ 3. I've failed at most of my relationships.

______ 4. I don't trust myself to make good decisions.

______ 5. When my partner asks me to do something, I usually end up messing it up.

______ 6. I'm afraid I won't measure up to my potential.

______ 7. I always fall short in my accomplishments.

______ 8. I'm constantly failing and disappointing my partner.

______ 9. I don't live up to my partner's standards.

______ 10. I mess up everything I attempt.

8. En

______ 1. I get angry when I don't get what I want from my partner.

______ 2. I often feel that my partner needs too much from me.

______ 3. I usually get what I want in my relationship.

______ 4. I don't accept my partner telling me what to do.

______ 5. I often feel frustrated by my partner constraining me.

______ 6. I shouldn't have to put my partner's needs before my own.

______ 7. My partner shouldn't stop me from doing what I want.

______ 8. I feel that I shouldn't have to accept some of the limitations placed on me by my partner.

______ 9. When it comes to the good things in life, I mostly get what I deserve.

______ 10. I am good at convincing my partner to do things my way.

9. Su/SS

______ 1. It's difficult for me to get my needs met in relationships.

______ 2. I feel guilty if I put my own needs before my partner's.

______ 3. I feel afraid to disagree with or say no to my partner.

______ 4. I find myself usually going along with my partner's plans.

______ 5. I often agree to do things for my partner that I realize I didn't want to do.

______ 6. I feel afraid that if I don't meet my partner's needs he/she will retaliate against me or punish me.

______ 7. It's difficult for me to identify what I want in the moment.

______ 8. I try hard to please my partner, and put his/her needs before my own.

______ 9. It's difficult for me to stand up for myself or advocate for my own needs in my relationship.

______ 10. I have trouble making my own wants and needs known.

10. US

_____ 1. I set very high standards for my partner and myself.

_____ 2. Very little of what I do satisfies me; I usually think I could do better.

_____ 3. It's easier for me to see my partner's shortcomings than the way he/she contributes to my life.

_____ 4. I easily feel like I'm stagnating if I don't accomplish enough.

_____ 5. I get critical when my partner or I make a mistake.

_____ 6. Failure is very upsetting to me.

_____ 7. I often feel disappointed that my partner isn't meeting my expectations.

_____ 8. I notice the ways my partner could be better or could have done something better.

_____ 9. I set high expectations of my partner and myself.

_____ 10. I never get enough done.

Scores

_____ 1. Abandonment/instability

_____ 2. Mistrust/abuse

_____ 3. Emotional deprivation

_____ 4. Defectiveness/shame

_____ 5. Social isolation/alienation

_____ 6. Dependence

_____ 7. Failure

_____ 8. Entitlement/grandiosity

_____ 9. Self-sacrifice/subjugation

_____ 10. Unrelenting standards

Interpreting a Couple's Schemas

0–10: Not applicable. This schema probably doesn't apply to the individual.

11–19: Fairly low. This schema may have a marginal impact on the individual.

20–29: Moderate. This schema has a moderate impact on the individual.

30–40: High. This is an important schema for the individual.

APPENDIX C

ACT for Couples Session Dialogue

The following dialogue depicts a session of the ACT for Couples protocol that incorporates all of the processes described in the book. As you read, observe how the therapist hones in on the schema pain and coping behaviors playing out between Henry and Ann and leads them to realize moments of choice where they might act differently.

Therapist: All right, Henry and Ann. Do you want to tell me a little bit about what's bringing you in today?

Ann: Well, I feel like he's been really withdrawn and resistant to share what's going on with him.

Therapist: Mm-hmm.

Henry: I share plenty.

Ann: No, he doesn't. I feel like he gives me one-word answers and doesn't always look at me when I'm asking him questions. He turns away and—

Henry: You always do this. Like, with what happened at work the other day, you kept asking me, "What were you doing, what happened at the meeting, what's going on with you?" You know, I can't download to you every single moment of my day about everything that happened to me all day long.

Ann: But that's what marriage is.

Henry: It's not! I come home, I wanna relax. I don't want to be put through the interrogation all night long.

Therapist: So can you give me a specific moment this week when you felt this had happened? When you felt interrogated?

Henry: Well, yeah. The Billing account. A big meeting happened on Wednesday, and I hadn't even taken my coat off when I got in the door before she was demanding to know how it went. You know, I work hard, all week long, and I try, and sometimes things just don't work out the way I want them to work, and I don't really feel like I need to explain that all night long at home, where I'm trying to get away from the office. And then the nagging starts. You know, like [imitating his wife] "Oh, what about the dishes? Oh, what about the laundry? Oh, who picked up the kids from soccer?" I mean, I try my best, and it's just never good enough.

Therapist: And so let's see if we can start with Wednesday, when you had the meeting. What had happened?

Ann: I approached him and said, "How did it go?" He'd been working late the night before, organizing his materials and his spreadsheets, and so I just wanted to know if it went well for him.

Therapist: So you went up to him and said…

Ann: So I went up to him and said, "Can you share with me how the meeting went? I'm really curious and—"

Henry: [Overlaps] And I said it was fine.

Therapist: Uh-huh. And when he said it was fine, what happened for you, Ann?

Ann: I felt like it was just a…a wall. Like there was no reaching him.

Henry: [Sighs]

Ann: It was a big meeting that he'd been prepping for…and it was just, "It was fine," and then he turned his back and he went to go look at his phone. And so I didn't think he really wanted to talk about it with me, and I felt really cut off from something that was important to him.

Therapist: You felt alone and cut off. And when he did that, when he cut off from you, what did you do in that moment? How did you respond to him?

Ann: Well, I said, "You know, how am I supposed to understand how you're feeling or what's going on in your life if you're gonna turn your back on me and not get into any detail about what actually happened at this meeting? It just doesn't seem like we're gonna get anywhere with supporting each other."

Therapist: So you're telling him, "We're not gonna get anywhere…"

Ann: Yeah.

Therapist: "…We're not supporting each other"?

Ann: Yeah. "And if you keep doing this our marriage is going to deteriorate. We're just gonna become more and more distant. And if you keep withdrawing, how am I supposed to continue caring about—"

Henry: [Interrupts, angry] This is how it always is. [Stammering] It's always like this.

Therapist: So what's happening for you right now, Henry?

Henry: Nothing I ever do is good enough. I go to work. I try to help out, and it's…it's always the same. It's always, "Oh, it's not enough. My needs aren't being met."

Therapist: So you're feeling really stuck. You're feeling like you're in a lose-lose situation? Helpless? Is that correct?

Henry: I'm sure it's my fault. I'm sure that I'm not holding up my end of the marital bargain.

Therapist: Mmm. So it also feels like it's your fault. You feel guilty?

Ann: Well, it's not enough. It's not enough, what he's sharing. I don't think it's enough. I think it's…it's not something that's workable.

Therapist: [Overlaps] So let's notice what seems to be happening right now. [To Ann] You're saying it's not enough, and [to Henry] you're distancing a little bit. Do you notice that? Is that correct?

Henry: Whatever.

Ann: It feels very familiar.

Therapist: And that day when Ann was asking you about the meeting and saying that the support is not there—what did you do after Ann said that? How did you respond?

Henry: I try to go away. You know, I just leave the house, walk around the block.

Ann: See… That's what happens.

Therapist: You start shutting down. You start distancing, and when he does that, what happens for you?

Ann: I feel alone and frustrated.

Therapist: How do you respond? What do you do when he starts walking away?

Ann: I open and close cabinets really loudly to try to get his attention. I sort of stomp around, I guess you could say. To show him that I'm angry.

Therapist: And then what happens? When you show him that you're angry, what happens in this relationship?

Henry: This!

Ann: Typically we just end up not talking for the rest of the night. We go to bed really tense. He'll end up sleeping in the den with his computer. I watch my cheesy reality shows in bed with my laptop, and that's what has become of our relationship.

Therapist: So [to Ann], you've been trying to get away from this aloneness and this very, very painful sense of aching and yearning, and [to Henry] you have been trying to get away from this feeling of not being good enough—not meeting Ann's needs and failing in some way. These are very painful experiences.

[To Ann] You've been trying to get away from being alone. Trying to shake him and get him to see, and sometimes getting angry and attacking, pursuing. And [to Henry] you've been trying to cope with this very painful feeling of not being good enough by just trying to get away, backing off, and getting to a safe emotional distance. And you've both been trying to get out of this pain. For a long time. And, what I'm wondering is, has the pain gotten any better? Has your sense of loneliness and deprivation gone away? Do you feel more connected?

Ann: I feel as alone.

Therapist: Okay, and what about you, Henry? Have you been able to protect yourself from that sense of being somehow not good enough, not meeting her needs, or is that feeling pretty strong still?

Henry: No! It's getting worse!

Therapist: So in spite of everything you've done to try to fix this pain—and it's very understandable—trying to get away from it in your case [to Henry], and in your case [to Ann] trying to shake him and get him to pay attention and connect, the pain is still there. Both these behaviors are very reasonable ways of trying to cope with this. But you're telling me that the pain is still there—and if anything, it's worse.

Ann: [Nods]

Henry: Yeah.

Therapist: So this is the question, and it's a funny question because I don't know the answer—we'll have to see what the answer is for you. But if trying to get away from the pain—all the things you've done, very reasonable things—to get away from the pain, to fix the aloneness, fix the sense of not being good enough—if all those things have actually made it worse, is there something else we can do with this pain? 'Cause the pain doesn't seem to be going away. What's going away is your relationship. That's getting worse.

Henry: Right.

Therapist: And hurting more.

Ann: Yeah.

Therapist: So if the pain isn't going to go away…

Ann: Mm-hmm.

Therapist: …What else might we do with this pain? Is there another direction we can take? Getting away, trying to stop it, block it, fix it? I'm just curious if you have any thoughts about what else we might do with this pain. Other than try to get away from it.

Ann: Well, what if we tried to share it with each other?

Therapist: To talk about it?

Ann: Mm-hmm.

Therapist: So to allow the pain to be there, together?

Ann: Right. Like what if in those moments I was able to say, you know, "I'm feeling alone, and I'm hurt," and then maybe he could say something about how he's feeling not good enough?

Henry: So I'm gonna be interrogated again. What if I didn't want to talk about this in the first place? I don't see how talking about it solves the problem.

Therapist: Yeah. I can completely understand that. But the thing is that not talking about it hasn't solved the problem either, so that's what I'm a little worried about…

Ann: Right.

Therapist: …Because I think that trying to get away from the pain by not talking about it—at least this is what you're telling me—hasn't allowed you to actually feel less of that not-good-enough feeling.

Henry: Mm-hmm.

Therapist: So, I'm not suggesting we ought to do exactly that, but what is intriguing is the idea of somehow allowing the pain to be there and not trying to fix it right away: to do something else with it. Not necessarily explain every detail of the pain, but if we let it be there and we're able to do something else while it is there, without trying to get rid of it, without trying to push it aside, but to let it…be there and do something else—

Henry: What?

Therapist: What? That's a good question.

Ann: Well, right. I could go write in my journal about how I'm feeling.

Therapist: Well, that's true. But as you're sitting here together right now, and this pain comes up, as it is right now—I can feel it as you're looking at me.

It's this sense of [turning to Henry] "Here we go again. I'm being cast to the wolves, the guy who doesn't do it right, doesn't do this marriage right." I can feel it even as we're talking; the pain is here. And the old way of coping is to pull back, try to get a safe distance from it, or [turning to Ann] go after him and try to get him to see how much pain you're in.

Ann: Right.

Therapist: But…I'm just curious. What if we were willing to allow the pain, and try something else? Not get rid of it but do something else while the pain is there? Would that be something you'd be willing to consider?

Ann: Like a different tactic?

Therapist: Like a different way. Instead of trying to get away from pain and using these coping strategies we talked about, when the pain shows up, do something different.

Ann: Mm-hmm. Like change the tone of my voice or change how distant I am?

Therapist: For example, how do you want to be in this relationship? Who do you want to stand for in this relationship?

Ann: I want to be compassionate. I want to be supportive.

Therapist: Okay. And you, Henry?

Henry: I want to be honest.

Therapist: Okay.

Henry: I want to speak my mind. I want to express how I really feel.

Therapist: Okay. I hear you. So, honest about your experience and what's happening for you?

Henry: Yes.

Therapist: Okay. Well, then let's just tack that onto that question I asked you a minute ago. Would you be willing to have the pain, that need to connect and that aloneness, or that feeling that you're not good enough, and act on those values in this relationship? At that moment the pain shows up?

Ann: Right.

Therapist: Not try to get away from it, but say, "Okay, here it is, and I'm just going to be truthful about my experience, about what's happening to me at this moment. I'm not going to disengage and run away. I'm going to stay here and be truthful, and I'm going to stay here…with compassion"?

Henry: Mm-hmm.

Therapist: Because that would be another way.

Ann: That sounds possible.

Henry: Yeah.

Therapist: Okay.

[Time has elapsed.]

Therapist: Last week we talked a little bit about what to do at those moments when you get so triggered and in so much pain that you just can't seem to act on your values. And we also talked about taking a brief time-out, waiting just a little while until you come back and finish the conversation, to return from the time-out and talk to each other from your values, your experience, and your feelings. And I'm wondering how that worked for you?

Henry: Poorly.

Therapist: Really?

Henry: Yes, really. I don't understand how you could have a time-out that lasts for four seconds before she's storming in after me to demand to know what I'm thinking.

Therapist: Uh-huh. [Turning to Ann] And what was the experience for you?

Ann: Just the same old withdrawal and resistance.

Therapist: So you felt alone and disconnected?

Ann: Mm-hmm.

Therapist: [Turning to Henry] And you felt ashamed and engulfed?

Henry: Ashamed and belittled, yes.

Therapist: [Nods] What's happening right now as we're talking about this? I'm curious because I can feel something, some kind of energy with you… What's happening right now?

Henry: I'm…I'm angry.

Therapist: Okay.

Henry: I'm angry because this, this scenario keeps playing itself out over and over again. And it needs to stop! [Yelling] It needs to stop!

Therapist: And is part of that anger disconnecting you from Ann, right now? It seems as if you're kind of pulling back from her. Trying to get a safe distance.

Henry: Yes!

Therapist: And what's happening for you [turning to Ann] right now?

Ann: Well, I don't feel like we're close. I feel like we're farther away.

Therapist: Yeah. So you're feeling very disconnected and alone right now? At this moment? Is that correct?

Ann: Yes. And in those moments when we tried the time-outs.

Henry: [Deep sigh of disgust, leans back in chair and folds arms across his chest]

Therapist: I understand. You're pulling away a little bit. But now, let's think back to those values again. And what I want to do is see if we can do something very different. I'd like to see if we could continue this conversation about how it felt to do the time-out, and this time stay in contact with each other and your experience.

Ann: Right. Like I'm just alone in this marriage.

Therapist: And now you're starting to express some of your pain by blaming a little bit.

Ann: Right. Well, I do think it's kind of his fault.

Therapist: And that's a thought, and the experience you're having is feeling alone. Wanting and yearning for something different in this relationship.

Ann: [Sighs] Right.

Therapist: So now the pain has showed up, and let's think back to those values that you had. What do you want? What do you want to do when this pain shows up? What was it that you wanted to do, Henry?

Henry: I wanted to express honestly what I was actually feeling.

Therapist: Yeah. Okay. So that's gonna be a challenge because all you want to do is just kinda get angry and pull back and get a safe distance. But to be able to talk about what you're feeling, which includes feelings of not being good enough and feeling like there's something wrong with you, that's hard. Being honest might include some of that, as well as how hard it is to feel that and express it. And for you, Ann?

Ann: Well, what I want is to be supportive and compassionate and intimate.

Therapist: And so our work now would be having this conversation again about the time-out and seeing if you can stay in contact with those values, even though a big part of you wants to go after him and shake him and say, "You're not—"

Ann: [Overlaps] Right.

Therapist: And staying in contact with that value is going to be a real challenge. And what I'd like you to do, if you're willing, is to just hold hands. It might sound hokey, but holding hands is just part of that commitment that we're going to stay in contact, we're going to stay together in this relationship instead of pulling back into those avoidant strategies. We're going to stay and see if we can take steps toward these values.

Ann: It's hard when I feel angry toward him. To reach out…

Therapist: Both of you are in that pulling-back place. You're both trying to avoid the pain. This is the pain avoidance that we talked about.

Ann: Right.

Henry: I'll do it [sticks out his hand to Ann].

Therapist: [To Ann] Would you be willing?

Ann: Okay. All right. [She takes his hand.]

Therapist: So why don't you take a look at each other and see if you can hold hands. And now, this is going to be hard, and pain and fear will come up. You might find yourself getting nervous and laughing, or you might find yourself getting pulled to do old behaviors.

Ann: Mm-hmm.

Therapist: And you might want to start getting away by shifting into this safe distance. So that can come up. But let's go back and start talking about the experience of the time-out and seeing if you can stay in contact and notice. We're all trying to be aware and mindful of those moments when you start avoiding, start pulling away from the pain.

Ann: Okay.

Therapist: Okay. Then we keep watching for that?

Ann: Yeah.

Therapist: Okay. [Turning to Henry] So could we start with you? What was your experience of the time-out? What did it feel like for you?

Henry: [Sighs] Well, it began when I got home on Thursday, and you asked me how my day was, and honestly it was pretty shitty, and talking about it just made it worse.

Ann: Mmm. I understand that.

Henry: And what I really needed was for you to laugh or joke or change the subject or anything else other than ask about the day.

Ann: Mmm. Your day was really hard. You couldn't handle talking about it at that moment.

Henry: It was—it was more than I could bear, and then when I tried to change the subject, you came back to it again, and you were asking me in a different way, and I really started feeling overwhelmed. That's why I asked for the time-out. And you did do it for a short while, but I mean ten seconds later you asked again, and it was just more than I could handle.

Therapist: So you didn't get to recover enough? Huh?

Henry: Yeah.

Therapist: You needed…more time or…what did you need? Can you tell her?

Henry: I feel like what I actually needed was some space to have distance from it and process it before talking about it. I just did not want to think about it anymore.

Ann: Mm-hmm. Okay.

Henry: I mean, it was a bad meeting. I was already gonna lose the account and, I don't know, it was hard.

Therapist: So would it be—I'm just checking—would you, in fairness, say that you wanted to stay together and talk, but just about something else? Is that correct?

Henry: Well, I mean I could stay together and talk if we were talking about something else. Just not about the many ways in which I've failed.

Therapist: [To Ann] Can you talk a little bit about your experience with the time-out? What's happening right now as you're listening?

Ann: Well, I guess I…I hear that. You know, I hear that he would feel better not talking about it, but I do wonder how we're going to connect over what's really going on with us…

Henry: [Breaks from grasp, throws hands in the air, utters a little pshaw in disgust] This is the same—it's the same shit.

Therapist: This is really good. Now, this is one of those moments. I'm so glad actually that this happened. I know it's not any fun to feel this, but what I mean is I'm glad it happened because this is a chance for us to work on this. You can feel the pain coming up, right? Is that the I'm-not-good-enough pain? Did you notice that? You could feel it?

Henry: [Nods]

Therapist: And then you feel like you just have to get rid of this pain. And at that moment you threw up your hands and broke connection. That's fine. I understand. But let's just notice that. The pain came up and you just had to get away from Ann for a minute. And for you, what happened just then?

Ann: Well, I guess I'm still holding onto that need.

Therapist: Well, there was pain for you because you were starting to say that you're worried about disconnection. Maybe you started feeling deprived and alone?

Ann: Right.

Therapist: And then of course, for you, Henry, that immediately triggered this feeling of not being good enough: "I'll never get it right, no matter what I do." So let's just notice that. And let's see if we can go back to the value.

Ann: Okay.

Therapist: This is hard, but let's see if we can get back in contact and continue the conversation, noticing that the pain just came up and you both did some of the things that you do sometimes to cope—

Ann: Right.

Therapist: Let's go back to the values and start connecting again and continuing the conversation a little bit. Is that okay? Are you willing to do that?

Henry: Mm-hmm.

Therapist: Are you willing to do that?

Ann: Yes.

Therapist: And so when the pain shows up and we start talking about it—whatever your reaction is—see if you can talk about it in a way that reflects your values, which is to be compassionate, supportive, and aware of what is happening for Henry.

Ann: Okay.

Therapist: Okay? So that's the work we're going to do right now. So can you hold hands again and tell a little bit about your experience with the time-out? And just keep noticing that the pain may come up and see if we can, in the face of that, just stay connected and keep talking about what you feel, what you need, using your values? Use your most honest self, and your compassion and awareness of what Henry may be feeling.

Ann: All right.

Therapist: So what's the experience for you with the time-out?

Ann: I feel bad that he went through something difficult. I feel sad to know that he went through something difficult and tried so hard at work. And I'd like to be supportive in some way.

Therapist: So you feel sympathy about what a hard day it was.

Ann: Yes.

Therapist: Anything else that's going on for you right now in terms of the time-out or…is there something you want from Henry? He said something about what he wanted, of his experience of that day. Is there something that you needed?

Ann: [Deep breath] I think that I do need him to be honest about what's coming up for him when I ask him, because I think I can respond to that need.

Therapist: So if Henry said what? What would have helped you?

Ann: If he was honest about the fact that it was a painful situation and that he just didn't feel like revisiting it at that moment. I can understand that.

Therapist: That would be helpful to you?

Ann: Yes, that would be helpful to me in understanding where he's coming from and why he was having that reaction.

Therapist: [To Henry] I'm just curious about what it feels like to hear that from Ann, that she'd actually like to know if something has been hard for you, without necessarily having to know all the details of the content.

Henry: Well, it's actually pretty encouraging. You know, it's really hard for me to relive these defeats. It's like I have to go through it all over again, and I really do try, and just...it hasn't been happening lately. And that's really hard.

Therapist: What Ann wants more of is to understand this experience and for you to tell her more about it. You don't have to get into every detail. Just help her understand that it's hard for you to revisit it at that moment.

Henry: [To Ann] Well, it's like I always feel like you're trying to catch me or find some way that I'm to blame for what's happened.

Therapist: Ann, when you know he's been through something, but you don't know what it is and you can't seem to find out, what happens to you?

Ann: Um, I just feel like there's a wall going up between us.

Therapist: And when that wall goes up, what happens inside you?

Ann: I feel shut out.

Therapist: What kind of pain is that, shut out?

Ann: I just feel sort of deprived in some way. I feel like I'm not there, I'm not needed. I'm alone.

Therapist: Can you tell him that? Tell him that sometimes, when you don't know what's going on for him, you feel alone and deprived? Can you tell him about that feeling of not being needed?

Ann: It just makes me feel like I'm not needed, like I'm not the person in your life that you come to for solace, and all I want to be able to offer is love and support when you go through whatever experience it might be. I want to share that with you.

Henry: Well, I hear that, but what it makes me feel when you do that is that I'm failing you somehow, like I need to be some other way than how I am.

Ann: Mm-hmm. I don't want to make you feel that way.

Henry: And that makes me feel like I'm not doing right by you.

Therapist: You feel guilty and stuck. So one thing that's happening is that you now have another choice. When that pain comes up of not feeling good enough and failing Ann, you could actually act on your value of being honest and say, "Boy, I'm really in a lot of pain right now. I had a bad day, and it's really hard to talk about, and I need support in some other way." So that might be a choice that you can make instead of trying to get rid of this pain by withdrawing and being angry. That value of honesty might be another choice.

Henry: Yeah. I can try that. It will be difficult.

Therapist: And for you, Ann, when you're having that moment of feeling that deep aloneness and that despair that you'll never get that connection and the kind of closeness that you need—how could you act on your value at that moment? What could you do in that moment?

Ann: I could just allow him to be and get curious about what he needs.

Therapist: So acting on your compassion—would you find out what he needs at that moment? Would you get some information about him? Is that a part of that value, or would it not be?

Ann: I suppose. I'm concerned that that would make him feel like I'm pursuing him still.

Therapist: [To Henry] How would it feel if she asked you for what you need?

Henry: It might feel okay. It would feel better than being asked specific interrogative questions. Give me more space.

Therapist: So let's see how that goes. What's really important is that you've been able to stay in contact, connected in the face of the pain today.

Henry: Okay.

Therapist: You kind of broke off once, but you've been able to stay in contact, and act on your values, and have a conversation that's very different from how it started.

Ann: That's true.

Therapist: And that's what our work is. To have a very different conversation while acting on values instead of the old behaviors to get away from the pain.

Henry: Hmm. Okay.

Therapist: Okay.

APPENDIX D

Handouts

Understanding Couples' Schemas Handout

A schema is a core belief about yourself and your relationship. It creates a feeling that something is wrong with you and/or your intimate connection. Schemas are formed in childhood and develop as a result of ongoing dysfunctional experiences with caregivers, siblings, and peers.

Schemas come from repeated messages that we have gotten about ourselves (for example, "You're bad" or "You can't do anything right") or from specific traumatic events. Once a schema is formed, it's extremely stable and becomes an enduring way to see and understand yourself and your relationships.

Schemas are like sunglasses that distort all of your experiences. They color the way you see things, and they influence assumptions and predictions that tell you the schema is true or will turn out to be true. Schemas formed during childhood are triggered throughout your life. Common triggers include conflict, strong needs, and difficult thoughts and feelings. Once a schema gets triggered, it brings up extremely painful feelings (shame, loss, sadness, fear, anger, etc.). Schemas interfere with your ability to feel safe in a relationship, your ability to get your needs met, and your ability to meet the needs of others.

Characteristics of Couples Schemas*

They are experienced as self-evident truths.

They are self-perpetuating and resistant to change.

They seem to predict the future, particularly what will happen in your relationship, because they create the illusion that you can see what's coming and prepare accordingly.

They're usually triggered by stressful events, typically something painful in your relationship, that activate old beliefs about yourself.

They are always accompanied by high levels of emotion.

---

* Adapted from *Acceptance and Commitment Therapy for Interpersonal Problems* (McKay, Lev, & Skeen, 2012).

Thoughts Journal

Event with Partner	Feelings	Thoughts

10 Schemas for Couples

1. Abandonment/instability: the belief that your partner is unreliable and that he or she will disconnect or leave.

2. Mistrust/abuse: the expectation that your partner will harm, abuse, or neglect you.

3. Emotional deprivation: the expectation that your need for emotional support will not be met.

    a. Deprivation of nurturance—the absence of attention

    b. Deprivation of empathy—the absence of understanding

    c. Deprivation of protection—the absence of help

4. Defectiveness/shame: the belief that you are somehow defective, inferior, or unlovable.

5. Social isolation/alienation: the belief that you don't fit, that you don't belong with anyone. The sense of being alone while together, being unseen and not understood.

6. Dependence: the belief that it would be hard to survive emotionally without your partner, and that you would not be able to take care of yourself outside the relationship.

7. Failure: the belief that you will fail in your relationship (and key aspects of life).

8. Entitlement/grandiosity: the belief that your partner should provide for your needs, and that you have a right to expect his or her constant support.

9. Self-sacrifice/subjugation: the belief that you must always place your partner's needs over your own—either because your partner's needs are more important or because you fear rejection.

10. Unrelenting standards: the belief that you, and your partner, must meet high standards of performance—in life and in the relationship. And if these standards aren't met, you or your partner are wrong and deserve criticism.

Schema Affect

Schema	Affect
Social isolation/alienation	Loneliness, shame, dejection, embarrassment, isolation, desolate yearning, fear, anxiety
Self-sacrifice/subjugation	Guilt, fear, helplessness, obligation, anger
Entitlement/grandiosity	Anger, disappointment, deprivation, engulfment
Abandonment/instability	Fear, loneliness, jealousy, insecurity, longing, grief
Failure	Fear, sadness, disappointment, helplessness, anger, shame
Emotional deprivation	Loneliness, urgency, deprivation, hunger, helplessness, yearning, sadness, anger
Defectiveness/shame	Shame, sadness, fear, helplessness, anger
Unrelenting standards	Disappointment, discontent, emptiness, fear, dissatisfaction, frustration, shame
Mistrust/abuse	Fear, suspicion, loneliness, caution, doubt, anger, yearning
Dependence	Fear, uncertainty, loneliness, vulnerability, inferiority, doubt, confusion, anxiety

Schema Triggers for Couples

Schemas tend to distort our view of relationships, particularly in situations when each partner's needs are different. When our schemas get triggered, we react in ways designed to protect ourselves from the emotional pain that results. Triggers are unavoidable in our relationships. However, if you can identify the triggers for your main schemas, you'll be one step closer to changing the reactions that fuel fights and conflicts. Here are some of the typical triggers for each schema:

Abandonment/instability: This schema is likely to be triggered for you when your partner is withdrawn, shut down, or unavailable. It can also be activated when your partner is critical, seems dissatisfied with the relationship, or has directly or indirectly threatened to leave.

Mistrust/abuse: This schema is often triggered when your partner says or does something that hurts you, when you perceive your partner as not caring, or when your partner pushes for things that don't seem good for you.

Emotional deprivation: This schema can get triggered if you feel lonely, if your partner seems detached, or if you don't feel understood, protected, or loved.

Defectiveness/shame: Activation of this schema can follow being criticized, or when you feel that you aren't living up to your partner's expectations. Messages that you aren't worthy, or aren't good enough, are also highly triggering.

Social isolation/alienation: This schema can be triggered when you feel different from your partner or your partner's friends or family (in values, interests, tastes, etc.), or don't feel seen and understood. Sometimes it can be activated by feeling alone while sharing the same space as your partner.

Dependence: This can be triggered when facing difficulties or challenges and your partner seems withdrawn and unavailable. Any situation when you need your partner and he or she isn't there—emotionally or physically—can be triggering. Any threat to the relationship can also activate this schema.

Failure: This schema is likely to be triggered by mistakes, criticism, or the message that you aren't living up to your partner's expectations. The suggestion that something is lacking about your accomplishments, talents, competence, or intelligence will also activate this core belief.

Entitlement/grandiosity: This can be triggered when your partner doesn't do what you want or need, or when a partner chooses his or her own needs or desires over yours.

Self-sacrifice/subjugation: This schema can be triggered whenever your partner needs something from you and you feel compelled to give it. It can also be activated by the sense that your partner's needs control you, forcing you to go along whether you want to or not.

Unrelenting standards: This can be triggered when either you or your partner doesn't live up to standards you hold for how to behave in an intimate relationship. This schema can also be activated by criticism, conflict, or feelings of dissatisfaction.

Schema Triggers Log

Triggering Situation	Schema	Emotion	Behavior (What You Did)

10 Common Schema Coping Behaviors in Relationships

The following is a list of 10 common maladaptive coping behaviors that couples engage in when triggered:

1. Attacking: blaming, criticizing, aggressive speech, belittling, accusing, imposing intentions
2. Demanding: controlling, insisting, making excessive requests, and requiring attention, support, or caretaking
3. Surrendering: giving up, giving in, complying, self-sacrifice, being passive or submissive
4. Clinging: dependence, seeking attention and help with problems, seeking reassurance
5. Withdrawal: silence, disconnection, stonewalling, or retreating emotionally, physically, and sexually
6. Stimulation seeking: avoiding by seeking excitement and distraction through compulsive shopping, sex, gambling, risk taking, overworking, and so on
7. Addictive self-soothing: avoiding by numbing with alcohol, drugs, food, TV, Internet, and so on
8. Manipulating: threats to do or not do something, derailing, seduction, dishonesty, guilt-tripping
9. Punishing: taking away, passive-aggressive procrastination, lateness, complaining
10. Discounting: suggesting or asserting that the other person's needs are unimportant, minimizing, defending, explaining, justifying

Values in Relationships

These are examples of values in relationships to help couples clarify key values.

Accepting
Adventurous
Altruistic
Appreciative
Assertive
Attentive
Attuned
Available
Committed
Compassionate
Composed
Considerate
Consistent
Contributing
Curious
Decisive
Deliberate
Dependable
Determined
Empathic
Encouraging
Engaged
Expressive
Fair
Firm
Flexible
Forgiving
Forthright
Fun
Generous
Gentle
Genuine
Grateful
Honest
Humorous
Independent
Inquisitive
Kind
Loving
Loyal
Mindful
Patient
Persistent
Present
Productive
Punctual
Reliable
Respectful
Romantic
Self-advocating
Self-aware
Self-compassionate
Self-disciplined
Sensitive
Sensual
Sexual
Spontaneous
Supportive
Tactful
Trustworthy
Understanding
Validating
Vulnerable

Values Domains Worksheet

Relationship Domains	Importance (0–10)	Values	Values-Based Action
Communication			
Sex			
Parenting			
Money			
Affection			
Work			
Conflict			
Decision Making/ Negotiation			
Friendship/ Extended Family			
Shared Activities			

Values-Based Actions Worksheet

Value	Importance (1–10)	Values-Based Behavior	Thoughts That Act as Barriers (stories, expectations, predictions)	Feelings That Act as Barriers (shame, guilt, fear, helplessness)	When will I practice this new behavior?	Am I willing to have these barriers and still take steps toward my value?

Weekly Triggers Log

Trigger	Thoughts (thoughts, stories, expectations, predictions, etc., that acted as barriers)	Feelings (feelings that acted as barriers: shame, fear, guilt, etc.)	Behavior (What did you do?)	Values (What values is this behavior connected to? Was your behavior consistent with those values?)	Values-Based Action (How would you have liked to behave differently?)	Moment of Choice (When did you have a choice to behave differently?)

Monitoring Values Throughout the Week

Thinking about the past week, how consistent have your behaviors been with your values? How consistent have your partner's behaviors been? First, begin by entering each of your values, then rate the importance of each value. For each value, rate yourself on how consistent you have been between 0 and 100 percent, 100 being that all your behaviors have been consistent with this value, and 0 being that none of your behaviors were consistent with this value. Then rate your partner.

Relationship Values	Importance (1–10)	My Consistent Behaviors (0–100%)	My Partner's Consistent Behaviors (0–100%)

Alignment with Values Worksheet

Thinking about the past week, how consistent were *your behaviors* with your values? First, begin by entering each of your values. Then write down actions you've taken during the week that were *consistent* with those values. Include how your partner responded to your behaviors. Next, write down the actions you've taken that were *inconsistent* with those values, as well as how your partner responded. Finally, give *yourself* an overall rating (0–100%) for values-consistent actions for the week.

Relationship Values	Values-Consistent Actions	Outcome (How did your partner respond?)	Values-Inconsistent Actions	Outcome (How did your partner respond?)	Rating for Values-Based Actions This Week (0–100%)

Alignment with Values Worksheet for Partner

Thinking about the past week, how consistent were *your partner's behaviors* with your values? First, begin by entering each of your values, then write down actions your partner has taken this week that were *consistent* with those values. How did you respond to your partner's behaviors? Next, write down behaviors your partner did that were *inconsistent* with those values. How did you respond? Finally, give *your partner* an overall rating (0–100%) for values-consistent actions for the week.

Relationship Values	Partner's Values-Consistent Actions	Outcome (How did you respond?)	Partner's Values-Inconsistent Actions	Outcome (How did you respond?)	Rating for Your Partner's Values-Based Actions This Week (0–100%)

Interpersonal Experiences Log

Event	Schema Emotions	Schema-Driven Thoughts	Sensations	Urges	Did you act on the urge?

List of Needs in Relationships

Safety

- Balance
- Compassion
- Consistency
- Predictability
- Presence
- Privacy
- Reliability
- Respect/self-respect
- Rest
- Security
- Stability
- Touch
- Trust

Self-Worth

- Acceptance
- Appreciation
- Challenge
- Effectiveness
- Equality
- Growth
- Hope
- Meaning
- Praise
- Progress
- Purpose
- Reassurance
- To know and be known
- To matter
- To see and be seen
- Validation

Connection

- Affection
- Attention
- Awareness
- Belonging
- Celebration
- Closeness
- Communication
- Community
- Companionship
- Empathy
- Guidance
- Harmony
- Inclusion
- Intimacy
- Love
- Nurturing
- Support
- Tenderness
- Understanding
- Warmth

Autonomy

- Adventure
- Choice
- Discovery
- Freedom
- Independence
- Space
- Spontaneity
- Stimulation

Self-Expression

- Authenticity
- Clarity
- Creativity
- Fun
- Honesty
- Humor
- Inspiration
- Integrity
- Passion
- Sexual expression
- Transparency

Realistic Limits

- Consideration
- Contribution
- Cooperation
- Fairness
- Mutuality
- Participation
- Reciprocity

List of Feelings When Needs Are Unmet in Relationships

Afraid
Aggravated
Agitated
Agonized
Alarmed
Alienated
Aloof
Ambivalent
Angry
Anguish
Animosity
Annoyed
Anxious
Apathetic
Appalled
Apprehensive
Ashamed
Baffled
Beat
Bereaved
Bewildered
Bored
Burned out
Cold
Concerned
Conflicted
Confused
Contempt
Cranky
Dazed
Defeated
Dejected
Depleted
Depressed
Despair
Desperate
Despondent
Detached
Devastated
Disappointed
Disconcerted
Disconnected
Discouraged
Disgruntled
Disgusted
Disheartened
Dismayed
Displeased
Distant
Distracted
Distraught
Distressed
Disturbed
Doubtful
Drained
Dread
Edgy
Embarrassed
Enraged
Envious
Exasperated
Exhausted
Fatigued
Fidgety
Flummoxed
Flustered
Fragile
Frantic
Frazzled
Frightened
Frustrated
Furious
Gloomy
Grieved
Guarded
Guilty
Heartbroken
Heavyhearted
Helpless
Hesitant
Hopeless
Horrified
Hostile
Hurt
Impatient
Indifferent
Indignant
Inhibited
Insecure
Irate
Irritable
Irritated
Isolated
Jealous
Jittery
Leery
Lethargic
Listless
Livid
Lonely
Longing
Lost
Melancholy
Miserable
Mistrustful
Mortified
Mournful
Nervous
Numb
Outraged
Overwhelmed
Panicked
Perplexed
Perturbed
Pessimistic
Petrified
Powerless
Puzzled
Rattled
Regretful
Remorseful
Removed
Repulsed
Resentful
Reserved
Resigned
Restless
Sad
Scared
Self-conscious
Sensitive
Shaky
Shocked
Skeptical
Startled
Stressed-out
Stuck
Surprised
Suspicious
Tense
Terrified
Tired
Torn
Troubled
Turbulent
In turmoil
Uncertain
Uncomfortable
Uneasy
Uninterested
Unnerved
Unsettled
Vulnerable
Wary
Weak
Weary
Withdrawn
Worn out
Worried
Wretched
Yearning

List of Feelings When Needs Are Met in Relationships

Absorbed
Affectionate
Alert
Amazed
Amused
Appreciative
Aroused
Astonished
Awed
Blissful
Calm
Centered
Cheerful
Clearheaded
Comfortable
Compassionate
Confident
Content
Curious
Delighted
Eager
Ecstatic
Elated
Empowered
Encouraged
Energetic
Engaged
Enthralled
Enthusiastic
Entranced
Equanimous
Excited
Exhilarated
Expectant
Exuberant
Fascinated
Fulfilled
Glad
Grateful
Happy
Hopeful
Inspired
Interested
Intrigued
Invigorated
Involved
Joyful
Lively
Loving
Mellow
Moved
Open
Openhearted
Optimistic
Passionate
Peaceful
Playful
Pleased
Proud
Refreshed
Rejuvenated
Relaxed
Relieved
Rested
Restored
Safe
Satisfied
Secure
Serene
Sexy
Silly
Stimulated
Surprised
Sympathetic
Tender
Thankful
Thrilled
Touched
Tranquil
Trusting
Vibrant
Warm

List of Pseudo-Feelings

Abandoned
Abused
Attacked
Belittled
Betrayed
Bullied
Cheated
Cornered
Criticized
Diminished
Dismissed
Disregarded
Ignored
Inadequate
Incompetent
Insulted
Intimidated
Invalidated
Manipulated
Minimized
Misunderstood
Neglected
Patronized
Provoked
Rejected
Taken for granted
Threatened
Tricked
Unappreciated
Uncared for
Unheard
Unimportant
Unloved
Unseen
Unsupported
Unwanted
Used
Violated
Wronged

Consequences vs. Threats

Consequences	Punishments and Threats
Neutral tone of voice	Angry tone of voice
Using leverage to set consistent limits	A consequence that is not followed through with is a threat
Boundary is clearly expressed beforehand	Not stated ahead of time
Compassionate but firm stance	Hostile stance
The function is to protect yourself and create safety	Functions to change or control your partner
Provides choices (e.g., we can have dinner together at the agreed-upon time or you can have dinner alone if you are more than 15 minutes late)	Unwilling to give a choice, unwilling to hear no
Reasons for boundaries are given	Reasons are arbitrarily related to the problem
Are logically connected to the problem behavior	Are not logically connected to or do not follow the problem behavior

Barriers to Empathic Listening

All of these strategies function as barriers to effective listening because they all attempt to minimize, reduce, or influence the experience of the speaker. When these tactics are used, they don't allow the listener to fully understand and validate the speaker's perspective.

Explaining. You can recognize that partners are defending, overexplaining, or justifying their position when they come up with reasons and rationalizations as to why they are not at fault. These defensive tactics may minimize the speaker's feelings and needs. "I couldn't call you because..." "I tried my best to show up on time, but..." "I didn't know that the event was so important to you."

Reassuring. This strategy replaces listening with behavior that functions to console or reassure the other. The purpose is to make it better and lessen the pain. This can be experienced as minimizing or belittling the emotional response. "I do care about you," "It's not your fault," "Your boss is not going to fire you," "There's nothing to worry about," "It will be okay."

Interrogating. Interrogating functions as a barrier when the listening partner is more concerned about getting the facts right and understanding his or her own perspective rather than understanding the speaker's viewpoint. Here partners ask a lot of questions, trying to reason and rationalize out of the emotion. "What time did you expect me to call you?" "Why does your boss's opinion of you matter so much?" "Why do you care if your brother doesn't come to dinner?" "Why is it necessary for us to be on time for everything?"

Problem solving. Problem solving can also be useful. However, this technique is usually effective after individuals feel heard and understood. When partners move on to problem solving prematurely, it often functions to avoid staying with the speaker's emotions. In this barrier, a partner jumps into giving advice or trying to problem solve rather than listening. "You shouldn't let your boss talk to you that way," "You should tell Jenny that it's none of her business," "We can tell your mom that she can babysit next week."

Placating. Partners are placating when they agree with everything without truly listening. They're more preoccupied with pleasing the other person, smoothing things over, or avoiding conflict rather than understanding. They take responsibility, apologize, or comply in order to have the conversation end, which blocks true understanding.

Derailing. Derailing commonly happens in conflict. Partners derail the conversation when they change the subject or steer it in another direction. It functions as a barrier because it moves the conversation in a different direction than the speaker intended. The speaker's agenda gets sidetracked.

Correcting. This behavior refocuses the conversation toward getting the facts "right" and examining minutia rather than understanding the partner's experience. "I called you at 5:15, not 5:25," "That happened on Tuesday night, not Friday." This often feels confusing and distracting for the speaker and invalidates his or her emotional response.

Judging. Partners are judging when they make global evaluations about the speaker and use it as justification for not listening to the whole message. "You're never satisfied with anything," "You're selfish," "You're too sensitive." Partners are also judging when they only respond to parts of the message that confirm their own beliefs.

Identifying. Partners are identifying when they connect what the speaker is saying back to themselves and launch into a story about their own experience. "I felt exactly the same when you abandoned me on my birthday last year," "Well, what about that time when you called me a jerk?" "My mom also intrudes on our relationship." The focus then turns to the listener's concerns rather than what the speaker is attempting to convey.

Mind reading. Partners are engaged in mind reading when they respond to what they believe the speaker's intentions are rather than what the speaker is actually saying. When partners are mind reading, they attend to assumptions about what the speaker "really means" or what his or her hidden motives are.

Shared Interests Worksheet

My interests	My values and needs	My partner's interests	My partner's values and needs	Shared interests, values, and needs

Time-out Guidelines

When a time-out has been called:

1. Stop immediately. When one partner calls a time-out, the discussion should end immediately. The time-out should be respected, and there should be no further explaining, defending, rebuttals, or last words. Everything stops.
2. Leave immediately. The partner who initiated the time-out should leave the location and make actual physical space from the other partner. If partners are physically unable to leave (because they're in an airplane or a car, for example), they should stop all talking and interaction for the agreed-upon period of time.
3. Use the time-out effectively. The break shouldn't be used to escalate anger and ruminate about the issues. Rather, the focus should be self-reflection and taking responsibility for one's experience. A time-out is more effective when partners use the time to identify values, feelings, and needs.
4. Always return at the agreed-upon time. If a partner doesn't return at the agreed-upon time, the time-out will backfire and make things worse. If one partner was left feeling scared and confused, he or she will have difficulty adhering to future time-outs, and the process won't be effective in the long run.
5. Return to the issue. Time-outs don't mean the end of the discussion; a time-out just means postponing the discussion until both partners are able to be more effective.

During a time-out:

Defuse from schema-driven thoughts. Observe and let go of these thoughts and return to the present-moment experience.

Use self-compassion. Practice being kind to yourself, and be willing to observe emotional pain. This pain gives you information about what you feel and what you need in the relationship. You shouldn't try to manage or control the pain with blaming thoughts or judgments.

Physicalize the experience. Imagine your feelings have a physical form. Ask yourself where in your body does this pain feel most intense? What color, shape, size is it? How intense is it? Notice any movements or subtle shifts. Practice emotion exposure and/or use the Exposure Worksheet to stay mindfully present with any difficult emotions during a time-out.

Observe action urges. Notice any urges to use old SCBs or try to suppress the pain. Notice any urges to control or change your experience, or to try to change your partner.

Clarify values. What are your most important values in this moment? What do you want to stand for when this pain shows up? What values can help guide your actions and clarify how you would like to proceed?

Utilize problem solving. Use the time-out to gain understanding of the conflict by identifying your feelings and underlying needs and using problem-solving skills. Use the Problem-Solving Worksheet to make your time-out more productive.

Exposure Worksheet

To be used during a time-out.

What sensations am I experiencing in my body right now?

Where in my body does this experience feel most intense?

How intense does this experience feel physically in my body on a level from 0 to 10?

Describe the experience:

Color:

Shape:

Size:

Movement:

What are my fears about this time-out?

What are my thoughts or beliefs about this time-out? What is my prediction about this conflict?

What are my values?

Problem-Solving Worksheet

To be used during a time-out.

What schemas got triggered for me?

What is my typical response to this schema? What coping behaviors do I tend to engage in?

What was the specific trigger?

What are my feelings?

What are my needs?

What are my values regarding this conflict?

What would a values-based request look like?

When ____

I felt ____.

I need ____.

Would you be willing to ____________________________?

References

Coughlin Della Selva, P. (2004). *Intensive short-term dynamic psychotherapy*. New York and London: Karnac Books.

D'Zurilla, T. J., & Goldfried, M. R. (1971) Problem solving and behavior modification. *Journal of Abnormal Psychology*, *78*(1): 107–126.

Gottman, J. (1999). *The marriage clinic: A scientifically based marital therapy*. New York and London: W.W. Norton & Company.

Gottman, J., & DeClaire, J. (2001). *The relationship cure: A 5-step guide to strengthening your marriage, family, and friendships*. New York: Random House.

Gurman, A. (2008). *Clinical handbook of couple therapy* (4th ed.). New York: Guilford Press.

Harris, R. (2009). *ACT with love: Stop struggling, reconcile differences, and strengthen your relationship with acceptance and commitment therapy*. Oakland, CA: New Harbinger Publications.

Hayes, S. C., Strosahl, K. D., & Wilson, K. G. (1999). *Acceptance and commitment therapy: An experiential approach to behavior change*. New York: Guilford Press.

Hayes, S. C., Strosahl, K. D., & Wilson, K. G. (1999). *Acceptance and commitment therapy: The process and practice of mindful change* (2nd ed.). New York: Guilford Press.

Hoopes, J. (2009). *Acceptance and interpersonal functioning: Testing mindfulness models of empathy*. Ph.D. dissertation. The University of Texas at Austin.

Johnson, S. (2004). *The practice of emotionally focused couple therapy: creating connection* (2nd ed.). Basic Principles Into Practice Series. New York: Routledge.

Lasater, I. 2010. *Words that work in business: A practical guide to effective communication in the workplace*. Encinitas, CA: PuddleDancer Press.

Lev, A. (2011). *A new group therapy protocol come binding acceptance and commitment therapy (ACT) and schema therapy in the treatment of interpersonal disorders: A randomized controlled trial*. PsyD dissertation. Wright Institute, Berkeley, CA.

Luoma, J., & Hayes, S. C. (in press). Cognitive defusion. In W. T. O'Donohue, J. E. Fisher, & S. C. Hayes (Eds.) *Empirically supported techniques of cognitive behavior therapy*. New York: Wiley.

Luoma, J., Hayes, S. C., & Walser, R. (2007). *Learning ACT: An acceptance and commitment therapy skills-training manual for therapists*. Oakland, CA: New Harbinger Publications.

Luquet, W. (2006). *Short-term couples therapy: The imago model in action*. New York: Routledge.

McKay, M., & Fanning, P. (1991). *Prisoners of beliefs: Exposing and changing beliefs that control your life*. Oakland, CA: New Harbinger Publications.

McKay, M., Lev, A., & Skeen, M. (2012). *Acceptance and commitment therapy for interpersonal problems: Using mindfulness, acceptance, and schema awareness to change interpersonal behaviors*. Oakland, CA: New Harbinger Publications.

McKay, M., Fanning, P., Lev, A., & Skeen, M. (2013). *The interpersonal problems workbook: ACT to end painful relationship patterns*. Oakland, CA: New Harbinger Publications.

Palmer, A., & Rodger, S. (2009). Mindfulness, stress, and coping among university students. *Canadian Journal of Counseling, 43*(3), 198.

Rosenberg, M. B. (2003). *Nonviolent communication: A language of life*. Encinitas, CA: PuddleDancer Press.

Titchener, E. B. (1916). *A text-book of psychology*. New York: Macmillan.

Tirch, D., Schoendorff, B., & Silberstein, L. (2015). *The ACT practitioner's guide to the science of compassion tools for fostering psychological flexibility*. Oakland, CA: New Harbinger Publications.

Twohig, M. (2007). *A randomized clinical trial of acceptance and commitment therapy versus progressive relaxation training in the treatment of obsessive compulsive disorder*. Ph.D. dissertation. University of Nevada, Reno.

Vuille, P. (n.d.). Thoughts as sales representatives. Association for Contextual Behavioral Science. Retrieved November 22, 2015. https://contextualscience.org/thoughts_as_sales_representatives

Walser, R. & Westrup, D. (2009). *The Mindful Couple: How Acceptance and Mindfulness Can Lead You to the Love You Want*. Oakland, CA: New Harbinger Publications.

Young, J. (1999). *Cognitive therapy for personality disorders: A schema focused approach*. Sarasota, FL: Professional Resource Press.

Young, J. (2004). Schema therapy for couples. Workshop, November 5 and 6, New York.

Young, J. (2012). Schema therapy: Beyond the basics. Workshop with Wendy Behery, January 27 and 28, Springfield, New Jersey.

Young, J., & Lindemann, M. (2002). An integrative schema-focused model for personality disorders. In R. Leahy & T. Dowd (Eds.) *Clinical advances in cognitive psychotherapy: Theory and application*. New York, NY: Springer.

Young, Klosko, & Weishaar (2003). *Schema Therapy: A Practitioner's Guide*. New York London: The Guilford Press.

Avigail Lev, PsyD, is a psychotherapist and executive coach in San Francisco, CA. She works with couples and individuals who struggle with interpersonal problems, anxiety, trauma, and mood disorders. Lev specializes in integrating acceptance and commitment therapy (ACT) and schema therapy to strengthen relationships. She is coauthor of *Acceptance and Commitment Therapy for Interpersonal Problems* and *The Interpersonal Problems Workbook*. Lev presents her research at regional and international conferences, and provides consultation, trainings, and workshops on utilizing evidence-based treatments. For more information, visit www.bayareacbtcenter.com.

Matthew McKay, PhD, is a professor at the Wright Institute in Berkeley, CA. He has authored and coauthored numerous books, including *The Relaxation and Stress Reduction Workbook*, *Self-Esteem*, *Thoughts and Feelings*, *When Anger Hurts*, and *ACT on Life Not on Anger*. He has also penned two novels: *Us* and *Wawona Hotel*. McKay received his PhD in clinical psychology from the California School of Professional Psychology, and specializes in the cognitive behavioral treatment of anxiety and depression. He lives and works in the greater San Francisco Bay Area.

Foreword writer **Robyn D. Walser, PhD**, is associate director of the National Center for PTSD Dissemination and Training Division, and associate clinical professor in the department of psychology at the University of California, Berkeley. As a licensed clinical psychologist, she maintains an international training, consulting, and therapy practice. Walser is developing innovative ways to translate science into practice, and is responsible for the dissemination of state-of-the-art knowledge and treatment interventions. Walser has coauthored three books, including *Learning ACT*, *The Mindful Couple*, and *Acceptance and Commitment Therapy for the Treatment of Post-Traumatic Stress Disorder and Trauma-Related Problems*.

Index

D

E

F

G

H

I

J

L

M

N

O

T

U

V

W

Y

Register your **new harbinger** titles for additional benefits!

When you register your **new harbinger** title—purchased in any format, from any source—you get access to benefits like the following:

- Downloadable accessories like printable worksheets and extra content
- Instructional videos and audio files
- Information about updates, corrections, and new editions

Not every title has accessories, but we're adding new material all the time.

Access free accessories in 3 easy steps:

1. Sign in at NewHarbinger.com (or **register** to create an account).
2. Click on **register a book**. Search for your title and click the **register** button when it appears.
3. Click on the **book cover or title** to go to its details page. Click on **accessories** to view and access files.

That's all there is to it!

If you need help, visit:

NewHarbinger.com/accessories